Using Evidence for Advocacy and Resistance in Early Years Services

Insightful and relevant, *Using Evidence for Advocacy and Resistance in Early Years Services* supports practitioners working in early years settings to develop the knowledge and skills required to carry out research into their own practice. Based on the renowned Pen Green approach, which advocates that co-constructed practitioner- and parent-led research leads to more effective practice and improved outcomes for all, contributors to this fascinating book explore a variety of research methodologies and techniques that have been used and developed over thirty years of provision at the Pen Green Centre for Children and Families.

The Pen Green Centre are leaders in the area of participatory research, and for many readers this book will be a primer in this new and developing approach. This practical text, which uses highly inclusive research methods, shows how providing opportunities for workers, researchers, parents, practitioners and children to co-construct the research gives it an authenticity and validity that would otherwise be lacking.

Using Evidence for Advocacy and Resistance in Early Years Services will be of use to practitioners working in early years settings, researchers in early childhood education and policy-makers at all levels of local and national government.

Eddie McKinnon is a researcher and workforce development advisor at the Pen Green Research Base, UK.

Using Evidence for Advocacy and Resistance in Early Years Services

Exploring the Pen Green research approach

Edited by Eddie McKinnon

Routledge
Taylor & Francis Group

LONDON AND NEW YORK

First published 2014
by Routledge
2 Park Square, Milton Park, Abingdon, Oxon OX14 4RN

and by Routledge
711 Third Avenue, New York, NY 10017

Routledge is an imprint of the Taylor & Francis Group, an informa business

British Library Cataloguing-in-Publication Data

A catalogue record for this book is available from the British Library

Library of Congress Cataloging-in-Publication Data

A catalog record for this book has been requested

ISBN: 978-0-415-81643-4 (hbk)
ISBN: 978-0-415-81644-1 (pbk)
ISBN: 978-1-315-88471-4 (ebk)

Typeset in Galliard
by Apex CoVantage, LLC

Printed and bound in Great Britain by
TJ International Ltd, Padstow, Cornwall

Contents

Contributors

Joanne Armstrong was formerly employed in the private sector as an underwriter for three of the world's leading insurance companies. After dedicating herself to her profession, her focus changed when she had three children in the space of 25 months with no multiple births. Having moved to Corby, Joanne's first connection with the Pen Green Centre for Children and Families was as a user of the breastfeeding support group. Her children have all attended the Nursery at Pen Green, and Joanne is now Vice-Chair of the Centre's governing body. One of Joanne's daughters has achondroplasia, and she is active in a support group she initiated that advocates for full involvement and choices for children with disabilities and their families. Joanne is also an active member of the One Corby Parents Coalition, which is working to change the practice of the professionals and practitioners in the town so that the expressed needs of Corby families are more effectively met.

Cath Arnold worked with children and families in Germany before running a private nursery in England in the mid-1980s. She came to work as a Family Worker at the Pen Green Nursery in 1988 and became its Head Teacher in 1994. In 2001 she was appointed as Deputy Director of Research at the Pen Green Research, Training and Development Base until her retirement in 2006. Cath remains active as an Early Childhood Consultant and continued to work as Director of the MA in Integrated Provision for Children and Families at Pen Green until 2013. Cath has published two books about her grandchildren's early development and a third about the links between cognition, schemas and emotions. Drawing on more than 30 years of experience in the field, Cath remains very committed to working alongside parents to understand young children's development and learning.

Carmel Brennan is Head of Practice with Early Childhood Ireland, a member-based organisation that works to support provision and practice in early childhood services. She also lectures on their BA degree in Early Childhood Education. Her PhD on children's participation in sociodramatic play was funded by the Centre for Early Childhood Development and Education (CECDE) and is a study of how children interpret and reconstruct the world of relationships, identities, practices and meaning through their play. She is a member of the Pen Green Research Advisory Board.

Natasha Charlwood undertook the study that led to the chapter in this book as a project for her Intercalated BSc Psychology during her medical training at University College London. She was supervised by Professor Howard Steele and worked alongside the Pen Green Research team. Natasha is a Senior Registrar completing her surgical training in Manchester, where she lives with her partner and their two children.

Colin Fletcher's deep interest in learning, and in the joys of learning, drew him to become deeply involved in community education and community research. He first visited Pen Green in 1987 when he was a Reader in Social Policy at Cranfield University. Over time he became a tutor and advisor for Master Degrees, Corby's Sure Start Local Programme, the training and development of Parent Researchers and the development of the National Professional Qualification in Integrated Centre Leadership. During this time he progressed from being a father to also being a grandfather. Colin retired as Professor of Educational Research from the University of Wolverhampton in 1994 and formed Catalyst Research to develop forms of Peer-Led Research. Since then, and to keep his feet very literally on the ground, Colin has become a smallholder, shepherd and poet living in the Shropshire Hills.

Kirsty Forster currently works as a children's centre coordinator in a small phase two children's centre in Rushden, Northamptonshire. Kirsty previously worked in a private day nursery for just under five years. She completed a Foundation Degree in Early Years in December 2012 at the Pen Green Research Base. Kirsty found that doing the course enabled her to evaluate her past practice and, as a result of the fundamental change in perspective she experienced in relation to how children learn, to think about how to develop her current practice within the childcare field.

Kate Hayward trained to be a teacher after being involved in the early education of her three children, Tom, Hannah and Emily. She has worked in community development projects and health programmes in Britain, Kenya and Papua New Guinea. She is currently Deputy Head at the Pen Green Centre, where she leads on pedagogical support and the professional development programme on parental involvement.

Penny Lawrence has been recording children's lives for more than 20 years, producing programmes for the BBC and C4 and also non-broadcast video to be used in training by parents and professionals. Penny has a particular interest in, and commitment to, representing and understanding the child's perspective within learning relationships. This is reinforced with theoretical understanding from her current doctoral study into 'knowing minds' through the use of video material.

Eddie McKinnon has worked at the Pen Green Research Base since 2002 as a researcher and workforce development advisor. Before that he had spent more than 20 years teaching in schools and the further education sector. Eddie's work at Pen Green includes service evaluation, carrying out research projects into the work of children's centres and supporting practitioners and parents in developing their research skills. He is deeply interested in the connections between politics, economics and social policy, especially as they affect the most disadvantaged families. His PhD study focuses on the ways in which practitioner-led action research learning sets can be sites of emancipatory praxis for practitioners and families.

Julie Medhurst worked in the early years field for 18 years, including time as an early years advisor in Northamptonshire before becoming a senior research fellow at the Pen Green Research Base in 2006. In 2008 she went to Qatar for two years to work on the government's Educational Reform Project for their kindergarten and primary schools sectors. This involved Julie co-constructing a new early years curriculum and a teacher-training programme to support its rollout. Julie returned to the UK in 2010 and is currently teaching in a local primary school and children's centre where she co-leads the provision in the nursery, during which time she has completed her Integrated Provision for Children and Families at the Pen Green Research, Development and Training Centre.

Sally Peerless worked as a research assistant at the Pen Green Research Centre from 2009 until 2012. Alongside her project administrative skills she was very involved in the Pen Green Tracer Study. Sally contacted young people who had been at the Pen Green Nursery more than 10 years ago and used her breadth of technical knowledge to support them to return and carry out their own video-based research focusing on their memories of their time in the Nursery. She also conducted video-interviews of the teenagers and the practitioners who worked with them when they were in the Nursery. Sally left Pen Green to pursue her first love, which is performing arts and musical theatre.

Howard Steele, PhD, is Professor and Director of Graduate Studies in Psychology at the New School for Social Research in New York City. He earned his PhD in Psychology at University College London (1991) and worked there through 2004 when he moved from London to New York. In New York at The New School, Howard co-directs (with Professor Miriam Steele) the Center for Attachment Research (www.attachmentresearch.com). Dr Steele is also senior and founding editor of the international scientific journal *Attachment* *and Human Development*, and he publishes widely on the topics of parenting, attachment, loss, trauma and emotion understanding across the lifespan and across generations.

Colette Tait's daughter and son both came to the Pen Green Nursery in the early 1990s, and she quickly became involved in running groups for other parents at the Centre, initially as a volunteer and then as a paid worker. Alongside this, Colette did administrative work at Pen Green, and, when the Pen Green Research Base was set up in 1996, she became its first administrator. In 2000 she became a researcher at the Research Base and worked on a variety of projects involving children and parents. Colette completed her MA in Integrated Provision for Children and Families in 2007 and managed a children's centre from 2008 until 2013 when she returned to Pen Green to run services in the area of adult and infant mental health.

Margy Whalley is an experienced teacher and community development worker. She was appointed as the first Head of the Pen Green Centre for Children and Families in Corby, Northamptonshire, in 1983. Margy has advised government on early years education and care, the development of Early Excellence Centres and Education Action Zones, Sure Start Local Programmes and the development of children's centres. She is passionate about the need for professionals and practitioners to authentically engage with parents and families in developing the services they need, using co-constructed research methodologies. From 1996 until 2012 Margy was Director of Research at the Pen Green Research, Development and Training Base and Leadership Centre. In January 2013 Margy was appointed as Director of the Pen Green Centre.

Preface

A review of the Pen Green research paradigm

Colin Fletcher

I am using the word *paradigm* to mean a model for expressing truths, a way of doing so that is whole, distinct and different. The history of ideas is one of long struggles between paradigms (Kuhn, 1968). First there were religious explanations, then they were challenged by scientific enquiry. Now they both, in turn, are being challenged by truths that come from democratic engagements. Pen Green's research paradigm is democratic.

The founding vision was clear and explicit about this paradigm. In the next 30 years there were adventures and achievements guided by that vision.

This review opens with a reminder of the founding vision, then looks at how the model is working in 2013 and then discusses some criticisms that have been made so far.

The vision was an invitation to imagine an Early Years Centre that is full of democratic characteristics.

Imagine early years centres where all staff are beginning to be assertive; self critical and supportively critical of others, where the staff are deeply attached to each other, work cooperatively, respect each other's strengths, and celebrate each other's successes and failures. Centres in which the adults, parents and staff are rigorous thinkers, focused and analytical, and yet aware of the rhythms of the organisation and their personal lives; where the work is rooted in the local community but staff also reach out, make their views known and challenge local and central Government over important issues. These would be centres in which children's rich emotional lives were acknowledged and supported, where children were encouraged and cognitively challenged and their learning was promoted. In such centres children could truly become the managers of their own possibilities. (Whalley & the Pen Green Centre Team, 2007: xi–xii).

This vision looks beyond lots of obstacles.

Often these obstacles seem to have been obstinately placed, implying that the vision is idealism, optimism, a pipe dream. So here are some of the obstacles.

'Early Years' is a 'site of contest'; there are serious quarrels over to whom it belongs and what it is for. 'Pre-school' means it is a preparation – not a period of life within its own rights. 'Paediatrics' refers to the medical issues of child development. 'Child Welfare' picks up on the risks and issues of social care.

So unless the different professions of Education, Medicine and Social Work pool their perspectives and extend each other's understanding, children's possibilities are secondary to mutual disdain and border disputes. After all, most professional training carries strong hints of hostility and mistrust. In principle, only professionals who are confident can get round to any sharing with other professionals – never mind with parents.

Involvement in the interests of the child is one of the four essentials in the Pen Green Paradigm. Involvement draws threads between professionals, between them and carers, between all these primary adults and the person that is the child. There are so many kinds of involvement. Three important kinds are

- Turn taking (that is alternating the leadership)
- Visiting each others' domains (staff to the child's home and parents/carers in the Centre)
- Volunteering (staff having a career of further training and qualifications, parents leading and joining parents' groups).

Involvement is a process; one thing leads to another and seems obvious and natural once underway. The big snag is getting started. Access is overcoming obstacles of attitudes ('it's not for the likes of me'), availability of time (and awkward timing) and there being a welcome. There is a move of feelings from 'being allowed' towards 'claiming rights', to just 'getting on with it'.

The Pen Green Paradigm is so stimulating that *insights* abound. Parents and staff looking together at a video of a child's play keep finding out something else. Learning from the child what is important to them, in naming what they are doing, the choices they make, the expected and the unexpected. The more we observe the more we see, the more minute and major changes can be recognised. The more we use the terms for insights, the more we value those terms as we invest some of ourselves in them.

There are also insights about each other. Friendship, kindness, fascination, curiosity are threads in the fabric of involvement, too. Insights that are developed for understanding children are vital to adults understanding each other as well. Their play schemas, their 'chuffedness' (Tait, 2004), their resilience are all bound up in their well-being.

Those who learn to name their insights, who teach each other the contents of each term, are the *carers*. A parent is the primary carer; the paradigm acknowledges that. But the acknowledgement is not taken for granted.

Instead it is an opening into the patterns of care. Be it with a single parent, reconstructed family, grandparent/s for part of the week, the child's care pattern is 'normal' for them. So it has to be 'normal' for staff, too, in the first instance.

Pen Green's paradigm does not presume or patronise material poverty. Yet its location in Corby guarantees that many carers will struggle to make ends meet.

Employment patterns are often those of part-time shift work with carers juggling their responsibilities as a substantial stress.

The paradigm asks for insights with respect to cultures and gender relationships, for amenities and services to be developed and shared. Censuses have to be combed, just as stories have to be heard, fragments pieced together of neighbourhood and community, and the dynamics of deprivation. All the time there is a struggle against taking community characteristics for granted. Carers can be thought of as 'mother' when the single parent is a father. They can be deeply unsettled 'migrant' workers who have been living locally for decades.

Essentially, the Centre is so many things for carers: sanctuary and resource base, career ladder, let-out for loneliness and second chance education and space to find and show their own strengths. In the Pen Green Paradigm it all matters because a stronger person is potentially a gain for all.

So the suffering of the locality is another shared struggle; community development is a purpose, practice and politics in the Pen Green Paradigm. Uncomfortable as it is, and always can be, the Centre puts its head above the parapet. Local leaders are nurtured by being researchers, doing the research and wanting to use the significant results.

And there is another aspect for carers to consider. All too often 'cuts' are proposed and energy has to go into the conflicts of organised resistance. Pen Green is in the public sector and is regularly under threat. Not once have such threats been taken lying down. The leaders of resistance have always been carers, the parents – some of whom were children at the Centre a generation ago.

Local leadership does not end with defending the Centre. The Pen Green Paradigm is not parochial. Carers and staff go together to argue nationally for a rich environment for children. Policy is not the preserve of the professionals.

In the Pen Green Paradigm, involvement begins and ends with an aspiration to equality. There is no pretence here, nor any passing the buck. Staff are the experts on children in general; carers are the experts on the particular child. Their pooling of knowledge makes the chance of engendering progress for the child so much more likely. The attitude is 'we can help each other'. Carers' perspectives are respected and *needed*.

Figure P.1 is a diagram for seeing the paradigm. It is a simplification. I find it useful to see how the paradigm is a whole, and then I am able to go into one part in greater detail. There are so many more details still to come, too, particularly the *ethical code*, the significance of the staff being *part-time researchers* and the *spread of the paradigm's use* so far.

Connections

There is an extensive essay to be written on the ideas and innovators that have been influential. To begin with, there is an honourable history of positive approaches to play. From McMillan in 1939 to Malaguzzi in 1994, these approaches have been tried and found to work. Lev Vygotsky's 'Zone of Proximal Development'

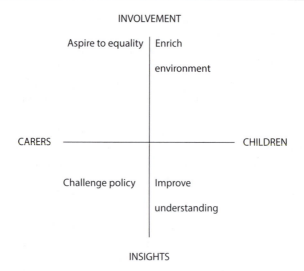

INVOLVEMENT

Aspire to equality | Enrich

environment

CARERS ——————————|————————— CHILDREN

Challenge policy | Improve

understanding

INSIGHTS

Figure P.1 The Pen Green Paradigm's Four Principles.

(Vygotsky, 1978) gave the vital opportunity of developing Possible Lines of Development (PLODs), that is, of putting possibilities in front of children that are consistent with their schemas (Whalley & Dennison, 2007). There are some undeniable ways of learning with and from children, ways that anchor early years professionals in doing what they believe in.

It is of great significance that nursery staff visit each other's nurseries, see for themselves and take back good ideas. Pen Green has had waves of visitors since it opened and sent out groups of staff in return – particularly to Denmark, Reggio Emilia in Italy and New Zealand. The significance is that the paradigm has within it such good ideas. The paradigm is an enquiry into how the 'key concepts' of schema, involvement and well-being can work together. There are realisations for staff and carers in the fine details. Once a first-time parent has expressed their relief, joy and resolve, there is no looking back.

The key concepts are part of the same historical period. The paradigm incorporates them in a way that a 'research methods' style never would. It is not possible to get to grips with the paradigm without appreciating the values and strengths of the parallel lifetimes work of Chris Athey, Loris Malaguzzi and Ferre Laevers. They are mentors to improving understanding. There are more 'insight guides', too, for 'understanding' very young children thanks especially to Trevarthen (2002) and Stern (1985).

No other research paradigm in early years has key concepts for a democratic understanding as one corner of its structure.

There are a range of research methods whose purposes are improvements that have also been coming on stream as the Pen Green Paradigm developed. The methods that matter most are *case studies, action research* and *practitioner research.*

The great value of doing a case study is that the setting can be accepted as unique and described in its significant details. Clearly, early years professionals do think of their own setting as special, with its own fabric and history. In the Pen Green Paradigm this perspective is a strength. Every centre has had its struggles. Through sexism, working with the vulnerable is women's work, poorly resourced, low paid and of low policy priority. Now and then there is a tsunami of national government interest – like Sure Start – a tidal wave of upheaval and welcome investment followed by being beached and marooned before the benefits can be proved. There are always times when each centre faces a lonely destiny. A case study shows what's worth fighting for and where there are weaknesses that have to be addressed. I guess every nursery has done at least one Strengths, Weaknesses, Opportunities and Threats (SWOT) analysis.

Action research does a case study with the personal question of "how can I improve"? Pen Green staff have done action research projects, taught action research in short courses and made it the foundation for those dissertations of degree courses taught at Pen Green. The title of the essential text by John Elliott carries the message *Action Research for Educational Change* (1991). Such small scale projects make 'process information' manageable when 'This sort of information [is] of particular interest to organisations seeking to replicate good practice' (Whalley & the Pen Green Centre Team, 2007: 31).

There is great interest at conferences that report on the case studies with an action research approach. Employers are reassured that they will get something out of it. Those who attend renew and reinforce their enthusiasms.

Action research draws together the community of learners in a centre. They experience confidence in their own capabilities, an informal status as an authority, and passion for improvement. Once the energies released by action research have been felt, there is a shrinking away from surveys and tick boxes.

Practitioner research has a broader palette, though also with the same purpose of improvement. Again the base is that of a constructive dissatisfaction about what is known and done. Donald Schon (1983) wants professionals to get behind that which is taken for granted and more deeply into what actually happens. The approach asks the practitioners to start articulating their own concerns. It offers ways that these concerns can be thought about with questions such as the following:

- What's going on about . . . ? (often the impact of legislation)
- What do we know very little about . . . ? (often parents)
- How can the methods used be improved? (often a new method)
- How can a change be accomplished? (often against unenlightened self-interest!)

(Fletcher, 1993: 7)

Participatory research could be closest to the heartland of the Pen Green Paradigm (Holman, 1987; Hall, 1984; Fletcher, 1988; Gaventa, 1988). The questions that participatory research puts are truly searching:

- Who owns the research?
- Who benefits from the research?

Holman (1987) has proposed a checklist that leads to criticisms of virtually all studies of the poor:

> I suggest that effectiveness is about whether
>
> i   they (the poor) define the issues to be researched
> ii they contribute to deciding how the topic should be researched
> iii they participate in collecting the research material
> iv they interpret the findings
> v   the research enables both researchers and respondents to be more fully aware of the issues being investigated
> vi the poor use the research findings for their own purposes.
>
> In short, the question is, do they own the research? (Holman, 1987: 672)

The heartland has a pathway from carer involvement to community education and onwards to community action to community development, climbing up a

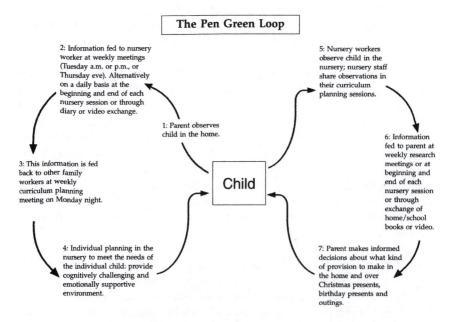

Figure P.2 The Pen Green Loop.

'ladder of citizen participation' (Arnstein, 1969) by way of 'opening up for parents a language of possibilities' (Freire, 1970: 68, quoted in Whalley op. cit.: 35).

There is nothing soft or soggy in the paradigm's views of carers and parents; they are regarded as 'equal and active partners' (Whalley, 1997) and participants in the Pen Green Loop (Figure P.2).

For more than 25 years the 'model' has had democracy in every corner of the diagram:

- democratic intent,
- democratic processes and
- democratic implications.

The paradigm opposes the injustices of inequalities.

And the criticisms?

From some higher education professional researchers can come the question

"Who do they think they are?"

The Pen Green Paradigm is both outside and inside higher education. As outsiders, all researchers are also trainers and are in daily involvement with parents. They are grounded at an Early Years Centre, next to the Nursery – children are in and out of the research base. All researchers, too, have been successful in degree-level studies – or are doing those studies now. Through franchises and partnerships with colleges and universities, the Centre has drawn hundreds of enthusiastic professionals to its courses. As 'insiders' staff are teachers and tutors on the higher education accredited courses taught at Pen Green.

But staff express themselves more as learners than as experts. Their value base is that their work should make a difference. Maybe both aspects of that attitude irk some academics. However, Pen Green does not offer a challenge for the 'big funding'. It does so much with so little, attracts fellow professionals in their droves, and won't use scientific tests. Interesting and important things could be happening in a struggling ex-steelworks town rather than in a large city and its universities.

Not all academics are wary of the Pen Green Paradigm. Chris Pascal, Teresa Smith and Colwyn Trevarthen, for example, see the advantages of insider research. The insights of involvement, enrichment and children's skills have held their interest for years. They recognise the paradigm as complementary to their own of a humanistic science. They know that Pen Green is liminal; it's on the edge.

It could be inevitable that terms like *clique* and *cult* are used. Some are unnerved by the tribe that has built up with such a passionate loyalty. Once one staff member has been to Pen Green, they do tend to bring another, to recruit a like-minded colleague. Two or three working together for their own Centre's improvement can be a formidable force, a force that brings issues to the surface and pushes for something to be done about them.

The dissertation titles of Master's and Bachelor's dissertations, the hundreds of them, show these issues being surfaced and addressed over time. There are issues in historically specific layers. The dissertations are on the edge, too, with the clearest possible identification of the issue in 'their Centre'. Co-constructing accounts with their colleagues can give rise to suspicions that they are working as a clique. They may be. Their Centre's hierarchy could be toxic, using its power to maintain inequalities.

A close look, though, reveals the self-criticism that suffuses dissertations. Humility and integrity are leitmotifs of these dissertations. Tutors can have a job reducing the sheer weight of modesty overpowering candidates' achievements.

Another criticism is that Pen Green's Paradigm depends upon its place and its own people. To be sure, Pen Green staff have been busy making connections across countries and cultures. They go on lecture tours and give papers together at national and international conferences. This way they sharpen the points of their case studies. The claims are to have found possibilities, not to have proofs. Those possibilities come from fastidious attention paid to the details in what Clifford Geertz calls 'thick descriptions' (1973). Enough detail is always given for the reader to be able to reach their own interpretation and so to challenge the sense that has been made in the report.

The proliferation of like-minded and able candidates goes a long way to rebuff the criticism that the paradigm is personnel dependent.

A tentative conclusion

I have put forward Pen Green's 'research methods' to be acknowledged as a paradigm.

The paradigm suits the times and the tasks for Early Years Centres to be defensible and to be able to develop their effectiveness. The genius is out of the bottle in two respects.

First, many Early Years Centres are getting on with using the Paradigm quite independently of the Pen Green Centre.

Second, in a few years' time it will be possible to have *studies of cases*. The wealth of case studies offers a real chance of being analysed, by practitioners, for the common themes. Those themes include the pressures that centres struggle with and the commitments that they nevertheless manage to make. Above all, a 'study of cases' could show what has been making a difference for children, their carers and their communities.

The paradigm has the critical mass of practitioners to survive. More and more parents were once themselves children at centres like Pen Green. The evidence is piling up that a democratic paradigm is established in Early Years Centres.

References

Arnstein, S. (1969) 'A Ladder of Citizen Participation'. *Journal of the American Institute of Planners*, Vol. 35, No. 4, July, 216–224.

Elliott, J. (1991) *Action Research for Educational Change*. Buckingham: Open University Press.

Fletcher, C. (1988) 'Issues of Participatory Research'. *European Community Development Journal*, Vol. 23, No. 1, 40–46.

Fletcher, C. (1993) 'An Analysis of Practitioner Research'. In Broad, B. & Fletcher, C. (Eds), *Practical Social Work Research in Action*. London: Whiting Birch.

Freire, P. (1970) *Pedagogy of the Oppressed*. London: Penguin Books.

Gaventa, J. (1988) 'Participatory Research in North America'. *Convergence*, Vol. 21, No. 2/3, 19–28.

Geertz, C. J. (1973) *The Interpretation of Cultures*. New York: Basic Books.

Hall, B.L. (1984) 'Research, Commitment and Action: The Role of Participatory Research'. *International Review of Education*, Vol. 30, 289–299.

Holman, B. (1987) 'Research From the Underside'. *British Journal of Social Work*, Vol. 17, 669–683.

Kuhn, T. (1968) *The Structure of Scientific Revolutions* (3rd Edition). London: Chicago University Press.

Malaguzzi, L. (1994) 'Your Image of the Child: Where Teaching Begins'. *Early Childhood Educational Exchange*, Vol. 3, No. 96, 52–61.

McMillan, M. (1919) *The Nursery School*. London: Dent.

Shon, D.A. (1983) *The Reflective Practitioner: How Professionals Think in Action*. London: Temple Smith.

Stern, D. (1985) *The Interpersonal World of the Infant*. London: Basic Books.

Tait, C. (2004) *Chuffedness*. Paper presented at the European Early Childhood Education Research Association Annual Conference, *Quality in Early Education*, Malta, September.

Trevarthen, C. (2002) 'Learning in Companionship'. *Education in the North: The Journal of Scottish Education*, No. 10, pp. 16–25.

Vygotsky, Z. (1978) *Mind in Society: the Development of Higher Psychological Processes*. Cambridge, MA: Harvard University Press.

Whalley, M. (1997) *Working with Parents*. London: Hodder and Stoughton.

Whalley, M. & Dennison, M. (2007) 'Dialogue and Documentation: Sharing Information and Developing a Rich Curriculum'. In Whalley, M. & the Pen Green Centre Team, *Involving Parents in Their Children's Learning* (2nd Edition). London: Sage Publications.

Whalley, M. & the Pen Green Centre Team (2007) *Involving Parents in Their Children's Learning* (2nd Edition). London: Sage Publications.

Introduction

The Pen Green Research, Training and Development Base

Margy Whalley

The Pen Green Children's Centre for Children and Their Families was established in 1983 by Northamptonshire County Council and jointly funded through Education and Social Services Departments and the Local Health Authority. Pen Green has become a vital agent for social change in Corby, and a whole raft of services for children and families have been co-produced by staff and parents to serve the whole town. Indeed Pen Green has played an important part in Corby Town's regeneration; it is a centre for the whole community, a centre that has engaged three generations of families. In 2013 we work with more than 40 per cent of the children under 5 in Corby and offer a comprehensive range of services for parents with babies, toddlers, nursery children and children aged 4–11 years in After School Clubs and Play Schemes. The Centre is open 7 days a week, 48 weeks a year and has become a responsive community-based resource where parents determine how services will be used and are very much part of delivering the services.

The Research, Training and Development Base was set up in 1995. We now provide an extensive adult community education programme for parents and have become a 'University of the Workplace' for those in Corby who are interested in Early Years Education and Care or family support. Many subsequently take up careers in early years education or social work. We offer everything from basic literacy and numeracy to family learning: CACHE Diplomas, Foundation Degrees, BA (Hons) Degrees, the Early Years Professional qualifications route, and Masters Degrees and PhDs. Some of those studying on our Honours Degree programme and Masters Programme first came to the Centre as parents who had left school at 16 or earlier. We are proud that we have built capacity in our community, and more than 56 per cent of our 120 staff first used the Centre as parents and trained in the Research, Training and Development Base here at Pen Green.

Building on a long tradition of practitioner research, we decided to formalise our relationship with the research community and the Leadership Centre, Research, Training and Development Base was built with its own library, seminar room and lecture hall. Building on the rich and sustained dialogue that has developed between parents and early childhood educators, parents became involved in the advisory group for the Research Base, working alongside academic experts from several Universities. Parents and staff at Pen Green had developed a commitment to research and evaluation processes from day one. Because the services we were offering were radically different, there had been a great deal of interest in our practice from social scientists and educationalists in universities and research institutions. We grew accustomed to being 'the objects' of other people's research programmes. Involvement and participation in such programmes helped us to become more effective practitioners. However, we were interested in being participants in the research process and were increasingly concerned with developing small-scale action research projects to address our own questions and our own central concerns.

Over the last 16 years, the Research Base has developed exponentially, and we have begun to take ourselves more seriously as practitioner researchers with something to offer to both colleagues and policy-makers and the academic world.

We are collectively committed to undertaking research where the forms of investigation are highly participative. We have been influenced by the work of Bob Holman in developing our practice, and we are excited by his notion of 'research from the underside' (Holman, 1987), where parents and users of the services are engaged as equal and active partners in the research process.

All of the chapters in this book have been written by researching practitioners working in powerful relationships with parents wanting to achieve better outcomes for children and families. Our shared code of ethics was developed with our research partners from academic institutions and the parents, children and community users. We believe that research at Pen Green should always

- be positive for all the participants;
- provide data that is open, accountable to and interpreted by all the participants;
- focus on questions that the participants themselves – parents, children and staff – are asking;
- be based on a relationship of trust where people's answers are believed; and
- produce results that are about improving practice at home and in the Centre for children and families, or at least sustaining it.

Initially much of our research work focused on developing our understanding of an appropriate pedagogy for the early years. Increasingly we have developed research methodologies for exploring parents' involvement in their children's learning (Whalley & the Pen Green Centre Team, 2007), engagement with families and community and researching the impact of our services over time.

As we have developed our practitioner research base at Pen Green, we have come to understand that all children's centres and early childhood settings will need support in becoming effective practitioner researchers skilled in community consultation and able to evaluate the impact and value of their services. Our objective originally was to support all of the staff at Pen Green to become practitioner researchers working alongside parent researchers with appropriate non-contact time so that they could undertake systematic reviews of their practice.

Staff working as co-researchers with parent champions currently carry out local needs assessment, making sure that all our interventions are highly focused. Parent-to-parent interviews are carried out in the family home or in other parts of the community to identify the strengths and weaknesses of our services. We use mass observation approaches so that parents can keep written and audio diaries about their use of the Centre and all the other public sector services they engage with over a week. This has generated critical data on the importance of children's centre services to family life and the potential barriers to access that parents experience in engaging with centres like our own. Now we are working with children's centres and local authorities and supporting their engagement in practitioner research.

Paolo Freire, a hero for many of us at Pen Green, described in 1970 the kind of collective enquiry that this book represents as the 'exegesis of causes' where the enquiring researcher has two principle objectives:

- to know, by asking individuals for their accounts
- to change through collective endeavour.

The chapters that follow represent our collective endeavour to sustain and improve our practice by engaging effectively as practitioner researchers with those who have co-conceptualised, co-designed, co-developed and used the Pen Green Centre for children and families.

References

Freire, P. (1970) *Pedagogy of the Oppressed*. London. Penguin Books.
Holman, B. (1987) 'Research from the Underside'. *British Journal of Social Work*, Vol. 17, 669–683.

Chapter 1

Supporting children's transitions within a nursery school

Julie Medhurst

Introduction

Using observations and video footage during their settling-in period, and again four weeks later, Julie Medhurst examined the relatively under-researched area of young children's transitions within a setting. Employing a case study approach, she followed twin boys aged 2 years and 6 months as they made the transition from the Baby and Toddler Nest to the Den Nursery at the Pen Green Centre for Children and Families. Using narrative observations, video material and interviews carried out with the children's parents and Family Workers, Julie Medhurst examines the effects of the twins' transitions from the Nest to the Den. The critical nature of the relationships between all of these key people was analysed. Julie's research was influenced by the notion that during transitions 'familiar people, places and routines become even more important than usual . . . children need continuity in order to manage change' (Roberts, 2007). Findings highlighted the need to ensure that the emotions of all concerned are contained and supported during transitions – children, parents and workers. This was achieved in this study by the twins' mother and Family Workers closely liaising as the transition approached and then the mother and Family Worker in the Den having opportunities to observe each other's approaches during the twins' two-week settling-in period. Julie Medhurst also comments on the emotional sense of 'loss' experienced by practitioners as children 'move on' and how this can be dealt with, especially for those going through this process for the first time.

My research questions and the ethics of choosing a family

My research in the Pen Green Baby and Toddler Nest focused on how the process of transition was managed from the Nest into the Nursery focusing on the following two questions:

- How effectively were the children in the Baby and Toddler Nest supported emotionally?
- How can we best support infants' transition?

As a researcher undertaking my first research project, it was important for me to develop my understanding of what it means to behave 'ethically'. I was influenced by the thinking of Martin Denscombe, who says that the ethical problem is 'no longer one of what it is possible or logical to do, . . . but one of what ought to be done taking into consideration the rules of conduct that indicate what it is right and proper to do' (Denscombe, 2002: 175).

I drew upon the Pen Green code of ethics throughout my study. I was very taken with the idea that at Pen Green it is important that all research is 'enabling and participative' (Whalley and the Pen Green Centre Team, 2001: 12), the emphasis being on co-construction with the workers, families and children; our belief is that research should not involve 'doing things *to* people' (ibid., emphasis added). Adhering to the Pen Green ethical code

- I spoke to all parties involved, giving them a brief outline of my proposed study before starting it, and liaised closely throughout the project to ensure that meeting times and places were convenient and comfortable for everyone.
- I provided opportunities for all data to be shared and discussed with the parent and Family Workers, clearly informing them that I was writing up my research as a conference paper. Once the interview tapes had been transcribed, I provided a copy for each participant on the understanding that if there was any part that they were unhappy with or did not want to be shared publicly, it would be removed and not used. The parent and Family Workers each received a copy of the finished paper so that they could make amendments as they felt appropriate. At the end of the project all video-taped footage was given to the parent, and the tape-recorded interviews were deleted from recording devices and computers.
- I spoke to the practitioners in the Baby and Toddler Nest team about my interest in transitions and ascertained that this was something that was pertinent to the team. As transitions occur throughout the year within the Baby and Toddler Nest, staff had already given careful consideration to how transitions were managed. In addition to this, during my initial conversations with the parent, it became clear that she had some anxieties about the boys leaving and moving into the Nursery and was interested in becoming involved with this project.
- I endeavoured to earn people's trust. For me, this meant that I made sure that I did exactly what I said I would do and shared the information as I said I would. As a new member of staff to the Centre and to research, it was critical that I was successful in achieving this aspect of the code of ethics. I was asking people to put their trust into an unknown quantity (me), and the success of this study, and the potential to undertake future projects with parents and workers at Pen Green, depended upon me fulfilling my promises.
- I examined the process of transition from multiple perspectives to identify whether or not the process is managed effectively for all of those involved and whether any changes could be made to improve the process of transition

for the Family Workers and the children and families attending the Baby and Toddler Nest.

In addition to the Pen Green code of ethics, I wanted to ensure that I had obtained 'informed consent' as defined by Homan (1991: 71) in that

- "all pertinent aspects of what is to occur and what might occur are disclosed to the subject
- the subject should be able to comprehend this information
- the subject is competent to make a rational and mature judgement
- the agreement to participate should be voluntary, and free from coercion and undue influence".

For the adults involved in my study I was able to draw up an ethical contract that outlined my proposal and how the resulting paper was to be used. I asked each person to read this and sign if they were happy with the content. At each meeting we could revisit the contract and discuss the subsequent procedures, offering opportunities for questions and amendments as appropriate. We discussed the issue of confidentiality and anonymity and the right to withdraw from the project at any time.

However, obtaining 'informed consent' from the two boys involved in my study was less straightforward due to their age (2 years 6 months). As a compromise under these circumstances I relied upon my professionalism, and my developing relationship with the boys, which enabled me to tune in to their body language. If their non-verbal signals indicated that they were uncomfortable or unhappy with either my presence or being video recorded, the process was stopped and either resumed at a more appropriate time or alternative methods were found.

Choosing a family and multiple perspectives

During a discussion with Linda, the manager of the Baby and Toddler Nest, we identified five children who were currently experiencing the process of transition from the Nest into the Nursery. Subsequently, Linda spoke to all of the Family Workers involved, explaining my interest in transitions, and asked if anyone would be prepared to record their thoughts on the process. One Family Worker, Christine, wrote a candid reflection that included not only details of the practical aspects of the process but also alluded to how the process 'felt' emotionally for herself and the parent. While initially my interest had been focussed on the experience of the process of transition for the child, Christine's account made me consider how transitions were experienced by the adults, too. Drawing on Richardson's idea of *crystallization*, exploring the thoughts and feelings of all of the adults involved in this process would give me a much deeper understanding of transitions: 'Crystallization, without losing structure, deconstructs the traditional idea of "validity" (we feel how there is no single truth . . .) . . . crystallization provides us with a deepened, complex, thoroughly partial, understanding of the topic' (Richardson, 2000: 934). As I had already been working alongside Christine for one morning a week in the Baby and Toddler Nest for several weeks, I felt able to approach her myself to discuss my proposal. Mindful of Freire's notion of 'subjects not objects' (1996: 18), I spoke to Christine and asked her if she would be interested in becoming involved in a small study, looking closely at the process of transition for Michael and Martin, twin boys about which she had written her reflective account. She indicated that she would like to be involved, and we discussed what would be the most appropriate way to proceed.

As Michael and Martin's Family Worker, Christine already had an established relationship with the boys' mother, Valerie. We felt therefore that it would be better for Christine to speak with Valerie initially to establish whether or not she would like to be involved in this project. To support this initial discussion, I wrote a letter to Valerie explaining a little about myself, my background and my interest in transitions. Once Valerie had agreed in principle, I arranged a convenient time to meet with her. This was an opportunity to introduce myself and to discuss the project with Valerie in more detail. During this meeting I explained my focus for this study. I asked her if she would consider being interviewed as part of the project, and I explained that the data collected from this study would be used to produce a paper that would be part of a presentation at the European Early Childhood Research Association Annual Conference. Valerie indicated that she was happy for herself, Michael and Martin to be involved with this project. I gave Valerie my telephone number so that she could contact me at any point during the process as she felt necessary, whether to ask further questions, arrange to meet or to talk generally about the project.

Recognising 'that there are far more than "three sides" from which to approach the world' (Richardson, 2000: 934), there was another perspective that was very important during this transition. Margaret would be the Family Worker whose group Michael and Martin would belong to once they had transitioned into the Nursery, and I felt that this project would be incomplete without her perspective. Although I knew Margaret as one of the Family Workers in the Nursery, I had had little contact with her at this point. I therefore arranged a very informal meeting that enabled us to get to know one another a little better. During the meeting we were able to discuss my project and whether or not Margaret would consider being involved. She agreed and I began to consider the methods and techniques that would most effectively capture the essence of the process of transition for all of the participants.

Methodology and methods

Positivist or Interpretive?

As a new researcher it was important for me to understand the main differences between the two main research paradigms that researchers use as frameworks –

Positivist (also referred to as Normative) and Interpretive – and to identify which would best serve the style of research that I was to undertake (Middlewood et al., 1999).

As my research question focused on how transitions were managed from the Baby and Toddler Nest into the Nursery, I was trying to understand the process, how it impacted on the individuals involved and whether or not any improvements could be made. My dataset included my own observations of Michael and Martin along with the perspectives of a range of others involved, so multiple perspectives on the process of transition were gained. My study was small in terms of its scale, concentrating on the experience of the process for one family and two key workers; my research began 'with individuals and set out to understand their interpretations of the world around them' (Cohen et al., 2000: 23). This clearly placed my research into an Interpretive approach.

Methods and techniques

> The fundamental aim of action research is to improve practice rather than to produce knowledge.
>
> (Elliot, 1991: 49)

As the focus for my research question was how to improve transitions from the Baby and Toddler Nest into the Nursery, I had to consider which methods and techniques of data collection would most effectively represent the perspectives of all of the parties involved. The suggestion that 'The involvement of teachers is seen as one way of making research more relevant' (Middlewood et al., 1999: 5) supports the belief at Pen Green that research should be co-constructed with workers, families and children, and this influenced my choice of research methods.

The methods I felt would be most appropriate to use during this study were

- observation
- video recordings and
- semi-structured interviews that were sound recorded and then transcribed.

I devised a timeline plan to organise my data collection, and this proved to be a vital part of my process as it supported me in observing Michael and Martin over the course of a month and ensuring that the interviews with the key people in the research project took place at the end of this process.

Use of observation

The opportunity of a placement in the Baby and Toddler Nest at a set time each week provided me with the opportunity to deepen my understanding of the organisational aspects of the Centre, and also to develop relationships with the workers and the children. Through this, my role became one of participant observer, as described by Cohen, engaging 'in the very activities they set out to observe . . . as far as the other participants are concerned, they are simply one of the group' (Cohen et al., 2000: 186). One of the advantages of this approach is the opportunity to 'develop more intimate and informal relationships with those they are observing, generally in more natural environments than those in which experiments and surveys are conducted' (Bailey, 1978, cited in Cohen et al., 2000: 188).

As a participant observer I was able to observe Michael and Martin in the Baby and Toddler Nest prior to their transition into the Nursery. This opportunity to get to know Michael and Martin in an environment where they felt safe and secure enabled me to tune into similarities and differences in their behaviour during the process of transition. It also enabled me to develop a positive working relationship with Christine, their Family Worker, which I believe was a key factor in her feeling able to be candid with her answers during our interview.

Use of video recordings

Video recording has been used as a successful method of data collection for many years at Pen Green because 'Video recording creates permanent primary records as resources that can be shared between researchers and practitioners whose activities are recorded, facilitating reflective review by both' (Jordan & Henderson, 1995: 52). This method of data collection therefore supports the belief at Pen Green that research should 'Provide data that are open to, accountable to and interpreted by all the participants' (Whalley and the Pen Green Centre Team, 2001: 13).

In my study, video was used to record Michael and Martin during their second day of the two-week settling in period, and again once they had been attending the Nursery for four weeks. This provided me with data that I viewed with the Family Workers, Valerie and colleagues at the Research Base to discuss the impact of the process of transition on Michael and Martin, heightening my understanding of their experiences as 'It is in the course of repeated viewing that previously invisible phenomena become apparent and increasingly deeper orders of regularity in actors' behaviours reveal themselves' (Jordan & Henderson, 1995: 52). This was certainly the case for us. We were able to return to the data many times and identify facial expressions and slight movements that may otherwise have gone unnoticed, particularly useful when considering Michael and Martin's levels of Well-being and Involvement (Laevers, 1997).

Use of interviews

While observations and video recordings enabled me to explore the process of transition from Michael and Martin's perspective, 'interviewing is a good way of finding out what the situation looks like from other points of view' (Elliot, 1991: 80), and the interviews gave me an insight into how the process was experienced by key adults.

Semi-structured interviews are consistent with a qualitative approach and attempt to 'portray and catch uniqueness, the quality of a response, the complexity of a situation' (Cohen et al., 2000: 272). I chose to use semi-structured interviews where I could ask each adult a series of open-ended questions that 'respondents can answer in their own way and in their own words, i.e., the research is responsive to participants' own frames of reference' (Cohen et al., 2000: 270).

Each interview was tape-recorded and subsequently transcribed. Although this was a lengthy and time-consuming process, it ensured that I did not miss any key words or phrases, and, as with the video recordings, I could go back to the interviewee for clarity or to explore specific responses further.

Research limitations

On reflection, although my intention was always that this would be a small-scale research project, there were other perspectives that I could have drawn on when interviewing that would have broadened my study. Michael and Martin live with Valerie in their grandmother's house, and it was Jill (their Gran) that spent the second week settling in the boys. Jill's perspective on the process of transition for Michael and Martin would have added another dimension to this project. In addition, I could also have interviewed their father to explore how he was feeling about the boys moving from the Baby and Toddler Nest into the Nursery. While tight timescales impacted in part on my decisions around who to interview for this project (the process of transition had already started for Michael and Martin, and I was keen to capture as much as I could of the process), my inexperience as a researcher also played a part.

I also realised that all of my interviews took place after Michael and Martin had already moved into the Nursery. This raises the question posed by Denscombe regarding the depth of my research: 'were the findings significantly affected by factors inherent in the approach which limited how far the research could deal with the complexities and subtleties of the situation?' (Denscombe, 2002: 127). Although all the adults I interviewed were extremely honest with their responses, I feel that had I interviewed throughout the whole process, I may have gained a deeper understanding of the emotional impact the process of transition had on all the parties involved.

Findings

My exploration of the processes of transition for Michael and Martin clearly demonstrated that there had been differences for them throughout the process. All three adults recognised that there were implications for twins undergoing the process of transition:

- Christine recognised that although Michael 'took the lead' in the exploration of the Den, this was actually enabling for Martin, who would then follow Michael's lead. Is this an integral part of their relationship as brothers that has developed naturally? And if so, what would the impact be if they were to experience the process of transition separately?
- Valerie stated that the boys are 'both very different personalities', and, although she was happy with how the transition had been managed for Michael and Martin, wondered about 'other ways of doing it . . . maybe take one down and see how he was on his own'.
- Margaret, too, recognised the boys as individuals, undertaking a separate home visit for Michael and Martin, but identified implications for practice when working with twins: 'they need twice the settling in amount because they are only getting 50% of the time.'

Interestingly, this study highlighted that there were significant similarities in the anxieties of Christine and Valerie during this process that linked back to one of the original questions raised in the working party discussions that took place after the Baby and Toddler Nest opened about the differences and similarities in the key worker/parent roles. Christine and Valerie both had concerns about whether or not Michael and Martin would be able to cope physically and emotionally in a bigger space with older children. Christine was reassured during her visits with Michael and Martin to the Nursery where she was able to explore the issues that she felt would be most challenging alongside the boys. Valerie had previous knowledge and experience of the Centre and workers, in particular Margaret, 'I just have a lot of confidence in her, I do, I trust her and I know the boys are safe' (Valerie, interview), and as a result of this, her anxieties were contained. This raises questions about how we manage to identify any anxieties that parents new to the Centre may be having and how we contain these emotions for individuals that have not yet developed trusting relationships with the staff.

Conclusions and implications for practice

My study showed that the process of transition for Michael and Martin was a positive experience. Both Family Workers supported both children to make a smooth transition; although their approaches were very different, they offered a good balance in terms of Michael's and Martin's emotional and cognitive development:

- As an experienced worker, Christine's emphasis was on Michael's and Martin's emotional well-being as she recognised that if this was not given due regard, the process of transition was unlikely to be successful for the boys.
- While ensuring that Michael and Martin were contained emotionally, Margaret also spent a considerable amount of time exploring their new environment with them, offering support as necessary but teaching them strategies

that empowered them within this environment, encouraging their autonomy and independence.

Having made these points, I believe that the implications for adults involved in the processes of transitions have to be considered. Peter Elfer discusses how a 'triangle of trust' (Elfer et al., 2003: 49) develops between the child, parent and key person. We have to consider how this *triangle* develops during the process of transition to include the new Family Worker, particularly with adults who are less familiar with the Centre than Valerie was. The study raised questions about how we address the issue of 'loss' within settings. To ensure sustainability in private provision, it is vital that childcare places remain filled. Therefore, where possible, as one child moves on from a family group, that place is immediately filled by another child. How does this enable staff to 'grieve' for children who have left their family group? As an experienced worker Christine has been through the process of transition many times before and was able to acknowledge and articulate this 'loss':

> I had prepared myself for that, that's what happens, people move on, we've got new children in so my focus is building up relationships with those now . . . it was hard . . . it can be quite hurtful knowing that you've been such a big part of their lives . . . I don't think there is a way I could have prepared myself any better . . . I knew it was going to be difficult.

What would this have felt like for a Family Worker experiencing 'losing' children from her family group for the first time, and would she have been able to express her feelings?

Drawing on Elfer's discussion around 'primary task' (2007), we need to be clear about the emotional commitment of Family Workers to the children in their family groups and the impact that the process of transition may have on them. If the 'primary task' is to be an effective key worker, we need to consider what policies and procedures are in place to support workers to ensure that they don't fall victim to emotional 'burn out'. Elfer argues that 'the question arises of what space may exist in a nursery to think about primary tasks and how these may conflict; indeed to address the two questions, what is it we are trying to do here together and what is our experience of doing it?' (Elfer, 2007: 116).

Bringing things into the present: A case study 2011–12

I have provided an account of research I carried out in my current place of work. I articulate how what I did with a family there was informed by the learning I took with me from the research into transitions I have described above.

I currently work full time in a 65-place nursery, which opened initially in 1995 as a 40-place nursery as part of a primary school. In 2008, the school achieved children's centre status, creating a 'learning community' for families and children pre-birth to 11 years old. As part of this designation, a new, purpose-built nursery opened on site in 2009 offering an additional 25 places. I joined the nursery team in 2010 initially on a part-time basis; however, a few months after joining I accepted a full-time position in the team. As a result, for the first time in many years, I was back in full-time practice as a key worker. In 2011–12, I completed a research project focussing on parental involvement, during which I was able to reflect on the learning from my earlier work on transitions.

How has my earlier research changed my practice?

Without any hesitation, if asked, I would describe myself as a reflective early years practitioner who has a child-centred approach to her work. Although I have always understood the importance of developing trusting and responsive relationships with children and parents, my research project on transitions provided an insight into "what the situation looks like from other points of view" (Elliot, 1991: 80) points of view that, if I am completely honest, I have not always given equal consideration. Particularly during periods of transition, I now purposefully make time to consider the likely impact for all involved, rather than focussing solely on the effect on the children. Like the children, I now recognise that adults draw on their previous experiences of transition, too, and that for many parents and key workers, transitions can provoke anxiety. I interviewed Sarah as part of a research project that I undertook in nursery. Although the focus of the project was to identify the meaning of parental involvement, as with my earlier work on transitions, the need for trusting and responsive relationships was identified as a fundamental aspect of the role of the key worker in supporting successful transitions.

Sarah's story

Sarah and her husband live at home with their five children, of whom her twin sons, Alfy and Lenny, are the youngest. During our interview, Sarah identified the need for parental involvement to be a two-way process: 'I am not putting my children into nursery and it's all over to you guys . . . it's between both of us.' The importance of positive relationships recurred throughout the interview, and Sarah identified the key times when she felt that the development of these relationships had been supported – transition day, the settling-in sessions and home visits. Transition day is a day in July when all parents and children due to begin nursery the following September are invited in to the setting to spend some time with their key worker and to explore the environment. While Sarah felt that 'it was fine that . . . we got to come round and have a look', she commented that 'that was more for the parents I felt than it was for the children' who 'don't take that in'. During the taped interview, Sarah described the settling in sessions as 'brilliant' but added 'mummy was still the primary carer there that day'. Later in a conversation that took place following the taped interview, Sarah described her experience of transition with her older daughter, Laura, who is now at school. Laura attended nursery in the original building, and Sarah explained how Laura had continued to be upset every morning for the whole school year as Sarah left her. Sarah recalled that prior to the boys beginning nursery she had felt 'really anxious that it would be the same experience – and there are two of them!' What Sarah found most reassuring about the settling-in sessions this time was the option to be flexible and attend for more than the minimum two sessions if she felt that this was necessary, giving her 'more options'. In particular, the home visit was identified as an integral part of the relationship-building process, and Sarah commented on the value of home visits for her own emotional well-being as well as that of the boys:

> There is no way I could have put the twins into nursery with them not know-ing any of the adults that they were going in to see. The fact that they had already had the home visit and that . . . they already had two familiar faces at least, yeah, without that I think it would have been a massive struggle . . . I did think that the home visit was the best of all.

During the course of the taped interview and the subsequent conversation, Sarah identified some key features for effective parental involvement:

- Communication – 'I am talking to you as often as I can'
- Personal relationships – 'until you've got names and faces to the teachers'
- Responsiveness and availability – 'no matter how upset they were, there was always a member of the nursery team to come and help me to ease them in . . . I wouldn't think that I would have to make an appointment to come and see anybody'.

Sarah's comments reiterated many of the findings from my original research proj-ect as key strategies to 'contain' both herself and the boys emotionally during the transition into nursery (see Bion, 1962). The critical difference for me as a practi-tioner was that I gave equal consideration to Sarah's emotional well-being at the end of the school year as Alfy and Lenny were preparing to transition into Foun-dation Stage Two. Remembering Sarah's vivid description of how she had felt about Laura's less successful transition, I recognised that it was likely that Sarah would have some anxiety about Alfy's and Lenny's moves from nursery into 'big school'. As Christine had done with Michael and Martin, I adopted a flexible approach to the transition process, involving Alfy and Lenny in the decision-making process about how often and when they visited their new classroom and teacher. All of the children spent time with their new teacher during a session in nursery (a safe space) before visiting their soon-to-be classroom for a story with their new teacher. During the visits photographs were taken of Alfy and Lenny exploring their new environment, which we discussed at group time. During this process Sarah was kept informed about the visits, the activities in which the boys had shown an interest and any concerns that they had expressed. Equally, Sarah kept me informed about discussions that were taking place at home regarding the transition process. Holding the family in mind on the first day of term, I made a point of being outside as Sarah, Alfy and Lenny came past nursery on their way into school. Sarah acknowledged that she was already finding the process difficult, so as she emerged being comforted by another parent, I invited her to join me for a cup of tea on the sofas in reception. Sarah accepted the invitation, and, along with the other parent and another key worker, we sat together for about 15 minutes until, after we had checked that Alfy and Lenny had settled in their new classroom, Sarah felt able to leave. Later in the school year, I asked Sarah if she felt as though she had been given as much consideration as the children during the transition process into and out of nursery.

Sarah's reflections

> I would say I was very well supported – I mean, the evidence speaks for itself doesn't it? Laura still had to be taken off me in Year Two. I still had memories of Laura and thought they (Alfy and Lenny) would still be being dragged off me in Year Two like Laura. The boys had settled by the end of the first term. So in just four full weeks they had settled. That's because of what you did in nursery and how well you worked with settling them in . . . I felt equally supported at both ends (of the school year). The way you stood in the school playground and waited for me . . . you knew there was a good chance I would be in a state and they wouldn't go in well, and you were there.

References

Bailey, K. D. (1978) *Methods of Social Research*. Basingstoke: Collier-Macmillan. In Cohen, L., Manion, L. & Morrison, K. (2000) *Research Methods in Education* (5th Edition). London: RoutledgeFalmer.

Bion, W. (1962) *Learning from Experience*. London: Heinemann.

Cohen, L., Manion, L. & Morrison, K. (2000) *Research Methods in Education* (5th Edition). London: RoutledgeFalmer.

Denscombe, M. (2002) *Ground Rules for Good Research: A 10 point guide for social researchers*. Maidenhead: Open University Press.

Elfer, P. (2007) 'Babies and Young Children in Nurseries: Using Psychoanalytic Ideas to Explore Tasks and Interactions'. *Children & Society*, Vol. 21, No. 2, 111–122.

Elfer, P., Goldschmied, E. & Selleck, D. (2003) *Key Persons in the Nursery*. London: Fulton.

Elliot, J. (1991) *Action Research for Educational Change*. Milton Keynes: Open University Press.

Freire, P. (1996) *Pedagogy of the Oppressed*. London, Penguin Books.

Homan, R, (1991) *The Ethics of Social Research*. Longman: London.

Jordan, B. & Henderson, A. (1995) 'Interaction Analysis: Foundations and Practice'. *The Journal of the Learning Sciences*, Vol. 4, No. 1, 39–103.

Laevers, F. (1997) A *Process-Oriented Child Monitoring System for Young Children*. Leuven: Centre for Experiential Education.

Middlewood, D., Coleman, M. & Lumby, J. (1999) *Practitioner Research in Education: Making a difference*. London: Paul Chapman Publishing Ltd.

Richardson, L. (2000) 'Writing: A Method of Inquiry'. In Denzin, N. K. & Lincoln, Y. S. (Eds), *Handbook of Qualitative Research* (2nd Edition). Thousand Oaks, CA: Sage Publications.

Roberts, R. (2007) *Self Esteem and Early Learning*. London: Paul Chapman Publishing.

Whalley, M. & the Pen Green Centre Team (2001) *Involving Parents in Their Children's Learning*. London: Paul Chapman.

Chapter 2

Multiple perspectives

Colette Tait and Penny Lawrence

The first section of this chapter focuses on work carried out by Colette Tait and her colleagues at the Pen Green Centre some ten years ago. She describes what they did and then focuses on one small aspect of a research project concerned with looking at 'Children's Well-being and Resilience', which was carried out between 2001 and 2003 (Pen Green Research Team, 2004). The project was initially funded by a grant from the Esmee Fairbairn Foundation and then by the Pen Green Research Base. The methodologies employed provided them, and others, with 'multiple perspectives' (Cherryholmes, 1993) on the children who were participants in the study; i.e., the gathering of data on a child from a range of important people in that child's life (Tait, Lawrence, & the Pen Green Team, 2001). Colette's section includes a description of how the methodology was used to gather multiple perspectives and discusses how this information can be used to help parents, nursery workers and researchers more fully understand the complexity of individual children and their lives. This is followed by a con-temporaneous case study of one child who was part of the Children's Well-being and Resilience project, illustrating multiple perspectives as a method that leads to a deeper understanding among those who take part in it. No real names are used, and minor details have been changed to respect confidentiality.

The second section, by Penny Lawrence, closely examines the ways in which video filming of children and their parents and those who work with them fur-nishes the practitioner-researcher with a body of data that they can view, review and analyse in many different ways and to good effect. Drawing on her back-ground in TV and filmmaking, Penny applies the thinking to be found in post-modern film theory (Spencer, 2011) to the analysis of video datasets of children, parents and practitioners.

The third section consists of an account of how the multiple perspectives ap-proach has been used to investigate an aspect of practice as opposed to focusing on a particular child. This example comes from Kirsty Forster, a practitioner who works in a setting in Northamptonshire. Kirsty graduated with her Foundation Degree in Early Years having completed the course at the Pen Green Research, Development and Training Base in 2012. This is followed by some guidelines from Penny Lawrence as to how readers can carry out a multiple perspectives research project in their own setting.

Section 1: Colette Tait

Background information

Since the inception of the Pen Green Centre, video material, taken in the Pen Green Nursery and by families in their own homes, has been used as both an observational tool and a training tool. This is a sensitive area to work in, so staff at Pen Green worked hard throughout the Children's Well-being and Resilience project to ensure the research was participative by asking the parents and workers to be co-researchers and enabling the research process to be as iterative as possible.

Throughout the three-year project, which was concerned with children's emotional well-being and resilience, workers and researchers made video clips of children 'settling-in' to nursery at the beginning of a session when separating from their parent/carer and at the end of the nursery session when reuniting with their parents or carers. This material was then used as a discussion point with parents/carers and workers. From these discussions, critical themes were identified (Strauss & Corbin, 1998), and questions were raised with parents and the children's key workers in the Nursery.

It became increasingly clear that for young children attending the Nursery there were many issues that needed to be addressed, including

- coping with major changes, e.g. divorce, death, physical and emotional abuse, drug and alcohol abuse; and
- coping with daily transitions, e.g. living in more than one home, attending more than one day care setting, coping with parents' complex shift patterns.

As a result of these findings, interviews were undertaken with the following:

- many of the important adults in the children's lives
- their peers in the Nursery
- their siblings.

These 'multiple perspectives' helped researchers, Nursery workers and parents to understand more fully how children coped with some of these issues and events and enabled workers to plan more effectively for them in the Nursery.

The following case study focuses on one child, whom I shall call James, and the many different viewpoints gathered from important adults and children in his life.

Theoretical influences

Workers and researchers at Pen Green were influenced by a paper titled 'Reading Research' (1993) by Cleo Cherryholmes in which he gives an interpretation of one paper through three different lenses – a critical reading, a deconstructive reading and a pragmatic reading. Cherryholmes's approach demonstrates that any one piece of data is potentially open to multiple perspectives on it. Another study that was influential on the thinking of people at Pen Green at that time was that of Joseph Tobin et al. (1989) who carried out a comparative study of pre-schools in China, Japan and the USA, within which there is 'a telling and retelling of the same event from different perspectives' (p. 68).

Workers and researchers were fascinated by the idea of 'multiple perspectives'. As practitioner researchers it was important to both engage with the literature as well as dialogue directly with families, enabling staff to come to deeper understandings about individual children. Staff did not want to dismiss what they already knew, but built on their knowledge at that time so that they could think more deeply. Raban et al. (2003) say that 'when fresh perspectives are articulated, then researchers and practitioners will be able to conceptualise the complexity more clearly'. This is what we aimed to do with James: to gain a more in-depth and more holistic picture of James in order to understand him and the complexity of his life as completely as we could.

Case study: Contemporaneous background information

James is 3 years old. He lives with both of his parents, Maureen and Adam, and his younger sister, Susan, who is nearly 2 years old. James also has an older step-sister, Heather, and stepbrother, Wayne, from his mother's earlier relationship, and another older stepsister, Sally, from his father's earlier relationship, all of whom spend some days and nights each week in James's family home. Sometimes his home life can be, in his father's words 'quite chaotic', with five children in the family and at other times just two or three children. Over the last two or three years, there has been some animosity between Maureen and her ex-partner in relation to access and custody of Wayne and Heather, therefore there has not been a consistent arrangement about the amount of time they spend in each household. We wonder what James's understanding of this inconsistency might be?

James has recently been diagnosed as being on the autistic spectrum. Whilst this may be useful in terms of getting James the resources he needs, as researchers and nursery workers, we have some concerns about this early labelling.

James currently attends the Pen Green Nursery for four days each week; last year he had a 1:1 support worker within the Nursery for four morning sessions each week, and prior to this James was in the Nurture Group within the Nursery

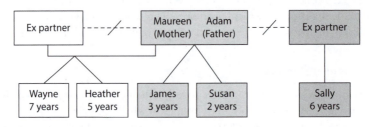

Figure 2.1 James's genogram.

setting, a provision that children attend when families need additional emotional support.

Methodology

After gaining permission from James's parents, we gathered multiple narratives about him. As well as asking his immediate family (his parents and siblings) to be interviewed, we also approached other adults who had played a role in James's life. Some of these adults had spent considerable amounts of time with James and were very close to him; others were professionals who had been instrumental in watching and assessing him in terms of his additional needs. We interviewed all of these people on film. Each person was asked to

- tell the interviewer about James;
- talk about a specific memory they had of James, perhaps something he liked to do with them;
- tell the interviewer something that would give them an idea of James's character if they had never met him; and
- give the interviewer three words that they thought described James.

The multiple perspectives

All of the interviews were transcribed verbatim, and we carried out an open coding (Strauss & Corbin, 1998) on them. Several themes emerged and were identified during this process and agreed by those who co-coded the material:

- James's determination
- James's interests
- James's interest in functional dependency
- James's increasing ability to communicate.

1. James's determination

    - Dad – 'he's very determined'
    - Mum – 'it's all got to be the same, if you change anything then he gets in a paddy, or in a uproar'
    - Dad – 'they can't force him to join in, he just won't have any of it!'
    - Family Worker – 'he has his own little rituals you have to follow'
    - Home Start volunteer – 'if he picks up on something he works really, really hard to get it finished'.

2. James's interests

One of James's favourite things was to have a clothesline, pegs and clothes to peg onto it:

- Mum – 'an example is his pegs and his controller . . . he has to take that everywhere . . . hanging pegs out – hanging washing out coz he's got his own washing line'
- Family Worker – 'a string with pegs on it that he brings into nursery every day . . . clothes for him to wash and for the washing line'
- Community paediatrician – 'grossly involved with his pegs because he likes using clothes pegs'
- Home Start volunteer – 'his washing line is the classic example that he takes everywhere'.

3.   James's interest in functional dependency

- 1:1 worker – 'he wanted to play at the water tray and we got jugs, erm, and bottles, and then I hid a doll, a little toy plastic doll in a bottle and he was, he realized if he poured the water in, the water would come up and bring the doll up with it and it would pop out the top'
- Nurture Group worker – 'he had a real interest in "cause and effect", so why things happen, and if I do this what happens next . . . he was fascinated by the light coming on and off in the fridge, so he'd go in there and check it out every day, see if it still happened'
- Family Worker – 'I was watching him in the discovery area with the water run and he went and he rummaged about and found the box that had the boats in it and he took the boat up to the beginning of the run, put it in where the flow of water enters the system, and then he just ran all the way around the steps and around all the pieces of equipment to where he knew it would come out – and I hadn't even noticed before that he'd taken any notice of that but he had obviously sussed where it had gone'.

4.   James's increasing ability to communicate

- Mum – 'One day we were in the town and there was a boy in a wheelchair – he was disabled and James just walked straight up to him and was stroking his hand, and the boy was, like they were communicating with each other. James couldn't speak but they were going "erh erh", and the boy was smiling'
- Dad – 'a couple of months back we were on a camping trip with the fathers group, and like, a big guy there, Fred I think his name was, he had a skinhead and James just went straight up to him – touched his head, touched his face and gave him cuddles'
- Researcher – 'through encouragement he began to lean across and just put my hand on his yoghurt carton if he wanted the lid off, or if he wanted a spoon he would indicate it by touching my hand, or bringing my hand across'
- 1:1 worker – 'we stood at the water tray he pulled me over, if he wants to let me know what he wants me to do, he can't communicate verbally, but he does communicate – he'll pull my hands where he wants to go'

- Home Start volunteer – 'he actually wants you to be involved with it, coz he'll get you to hold the other end of it while he sorts out his pegs, his little bits of washing then as the game goes on he'll actually let you hang washing on his line, which is a big step for him and that's his way of trying to get you involved'
- Researcher – 'his mum told me that he plays it with his dad at home, so I started trying it out at lunchtime and then he would face me, hold my hands, and rock back and forth quite vigorously, and he loved to do that, and I just had to say "row your boat" and he would start doing it'
- Home Start volunteer – 'just in the last six months, he'll come across and he'll actually give me a kiss and a cuddle now when I go in, he waves to me, if I see him in the street and I shout on him he does acknowledge that he knows me'
- Head of Nursery – 'I put the phone on the top and James took it, picked the phone up, put it down and said "Bye, bye", gestured, so when he put the phone down I picked it up and said "Hello" at which point he then said, er made an attempt to say "Hello" and we had this game of "Hello", "Bye bye", "Hello Mummy", "Hello Daddy"'
- Stepsister – 'yeah, like if we are at Daddy's we usually just ring up and then sometimes James grabs the phone off of Mummy and goes "ga ga"'
- Head of Nursery – 'peeped his head out into the nursery, and his Family Worker was out there and another Family Worker and at this point he said "Hello" to them outside'.

Adjectives to describe James

"happy . . . happy boy . . . he's an excited one as well . . . he's intelligent, very intelligent, and very clever as well . . . very loving, and very attentive to detail . . . well, very intriguing, and one to watch and see . . . curious, and demanding . . . interesting, lively, persistent . . . I think James, unique, determined . . . very determined . . . persistent, determined . . . determined . . . stubborn, clever . . . lovable, very cheeky personality . . . endearing . . . very appealing . . . great fun, great fun . . . and I think he's really intelligent"

Key questions, insights and implications for practice

- How could this methodology be used to support children in different situations, for instance
  - when being assessed in relation to special educational needs?
  - in their transition from nursery to reception class?
- How useful would it be to share this material as empirical evidence with the 'professionals group' who observe and assess James? Of course, the caveat for this group would be 'what was filmed, and what was edited out of the film?'

- It may be easy to lose sight of James's cognition when there is so much interest in his emerging sociability. A fascinating future research project might focus on the co-ordination of cognition and affect in James.

Section 2: Penny Lawrence

Theoretical decisions

How we work with video depends on our theoretical framework. Do we seek a single unchanging truth about the child we are studying? Using multiple perspectives is a constructivist approach and not a positivist 'one measurable truth' ontology. In this study our chosen methodology allowed for the construction of understanding about the child between contributors and also aimed to engage viewers in the process of meaning making (Jonassen, 1999). A word of caution is needed at this point – the knowledge we created was based on each contributor's perspective *on that day*. It would need revisiting because this view would not remain the same over time, just as the child would not remain the same over time. Here, there is an underlying assumption that a person changes in time, and this assumption goes beyond 'a once and for all' fixed-in-time 'temporal production' (Denzin, 1989: 63). Wittgenstein also argued that a genuine understanding of another person would arise 'in a far less neat reality . . . in a thousand different forms' (1958: 31). Hagberg (2008) valued a swathe of interconnected thoughts, speech and action to make a person intelligible. Using video itself is a form of multiple perspectives; compared to solely using text data, it can make our engagement more complex. 'Individuals who shine at the creation of a film or story might have little competence using the modes of thought and the forms of representation used in conventional types of research' (Eisner, 1997).

Our study of a person is also in accord with Gardner's thinking on the knowledge generated through multiplicity: 'Approach the core, to convey the central understandings of the topic, using multiple representations' (1999: 71). With multiple perspectives the person in the middle, the 'core', is defined by all those around him or her. It is a negative space of sorts in artistic terms, a form defined by other forms, by other people, that is, unless the multiple perspectives include the perspective of the person him or herself and the person at the centre of a case study becomes a social actor, a participant in the research about him or herself. This will depend on the circumstances of the child being studied. In James's case, he was not using speech at this time. In that central space is also the observed experience of the person within a context, e.g. James playing with his reflection. Including observations allowed the viewer of all the perspectives to construct his or her own overview and interpretation. An identity was established. Deleuze (1986) would say the person was 'materialized' through the construction of different aspects of subjectivity.

People can form their opinions about the personality of another very quickly watching 'very thin slices' of video (Miller & Zhou, 2007: 328), even as quickly as 10 to 30 seconds. Providing more context for the viewing and providing multiple perspectives can provide more information in those moments of opinion forming, and Miller and Zhou acknowledge there may be no single ideal perspective (2007: 330). They conclude that what makes videoed cases compelling is the partly real, partly illusory ability to convey complexity. The more views one sees of the child, the more wide ranging the contexts with which the viewer can construct his or her understanding of the child. This thinking mirrors that of Laurel Richardson (2000) and her 'imaginary' of 'crystallization' as a way of conceptualising the complexity of modern family life, and of individual children, and the multifaceted ways in which both need to be studied. For Richardson, the image of the crystal combines 'multidimensionalities and angles of approach' (2000: 934); what we see when we look at a crystal, 'depends on how we view it, how we hold it up to the light or not' (Janesick, 2000: 392).

'Crystallization', as a way of conceptualizing complexity, helps us to understand that 'there is no single truth' and instead we need to develop a 'deepened, complex, thoroughly partial, understanding' of any child accepting that 'we know more and doubt what we know' about the child because 'we know there is always more to know' (Richardson, 2000: 934).

Figure 2.2 A highly multifaceted halite crystal from the Wieliczka Salt mine, Poland; a UNESCO World Heritage Site.

QUESTIONS FOR PRACTITIONER-RESEARCHERS

Consideration needs to be given to the following:

Are we working with interviewees, respondents, contributors or participants? In TV/film, we refer to contributors.

If we consider that we are working with participants, at what level of participation are they involved?

Multiple perspectives viewed through film theories

This section is based on the full record of the video-taped evidence about James and not only the videos that were the focus for the case study about him, i.e., videos of a range of people answering questions about James and giving their own impressions of him. Consequently, some of the examples and illustrations used relate back to the case study, while others do not.

When we decide to use a camera, we make decisions about the direction we point it in and what is framed within the shot. Multiple perspectives can be understood in the language of film as the equivalent of using multiple camera shots to create a scene. Each contributor represents a point of view of the child. The research questions frame the knowledge explored from these points of view in a similar way to the framing of a scene:

Figure 2.3 James pulls the pegs along.

1. How do you spend time with (child's name?) *This is an orientating question similar to establishing the geography of the scene the action takes place in, in a wide shot.*

    e.g.
    Researcher Question: What does James like doing best?
    'Hanging pegs out, hanging um his washing out, 'cos he's got his own washing line, his own prop so he likes to put the washing out on the line'.

2. What is a strong memory for you of a time you have shared with (child's name)? *This is another contextualizing question, but this is comparable to a mid-shot with a close focus on a particular event that the contributor selects as significant.*

    e.g. Community paediatrician
    'The nice thing was of course that he used the tissues and didn't insist on having real clothes to put on there. So he can use his imagination and pretend that the tissues are clothing I suppose, which I take as a very positive thing'.

3. How would you describe him/her to someone who had never met him/her? *This is a close-up focus question about the view the contributor takes of the child.*

    e.g. Medium close-up: Michele – Family Worker
    'I think James is a lively little boy who has a good set routine and has his own little rituals that you have to follow'.

Figure 2.4 James stretches the cable out.

Figure 2.5 James connects the cable to his handlebars.

4. How would you describe him/her in one word? *This is an extreme close-up focus question. It is not 'essentialism' attempting to reduce what is multifaceted and shifting to a fixed essential identity (Crabtree et al., 2009), but a focused detail that has emerged from experience.*

    e.g. 'determined'

5. Make a selection from your own photographic and/or video observations of the child. Share these observations with the contributors and ask for their view of them. *This question shifts the focus to the viewpoint of another person's subjectivity. What do we see in somebody else's observation? The contributor and the researcher co-construct meaning about the child.*

    e.g. Mid-shot of James winding a piece of paper into a shredder held by Sharon. James attempts to feed shredded pieces in the top; this is difficult because they bend in different directions. Vocalises frustration, looks up, fleetingly at Sharon. She offers him a sheet of paper. James carefully puts the shredded strips down before starting to shred the sheet.

6. What would you like to know about him/her? *This question returns to a wide view and implies that not all is known about the child, and there are scenes yet to play out in the child's experiences.*

Figure 2.6 Close up of James's games controller with the pegs clipped onto the cable.

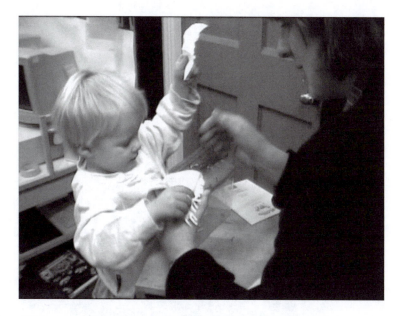

Figure 2.7 James putting a sheet of paper through the shredder.

Figure 2.8 Another view of James reorganising objects.

Figure 2.9 James's point of view of the pegs lined up on his controller cable.

e.g. Community paediatrician: 'Very intriguing and one to watch and see'. There is an additional perspective to consider. If we include the child as a contributor, we could include the subjective shot representing the child's point of view, which may have looked something like Figure 2.9.

Movement, mobility and point of view

The essence of work in video lies in the mobility of the camera and the freedom, even 'the emancipation of the viewpoint' (Deleuze, 1986: 33). It transforms from being only spatial, like a stills camera, to being in time, too, which is a much more open and multiple way of thinking that Deleuze and Guattari (1987) later call *rhizomatics*. It is not hierarchical, not structured according to beginning and end (linear), and it does not necessarily have segmental or oppositional divisions (binary) (Deleuze, 1986: 11); it is more an 'assemblage' of heterogeneous views or aspects of a person. This may seem confusing compared to clear binary logic – a less stable and recognizable form, and a less safe form of representation formed in a similar way to the brain circuits assembling movement-images and time-images on a screen (Deleuze, 1986: 13). These ideas have only come into English language film theory since 2000 and will complement the pedagogical applications that are already becoming established (McClaren & Kincheloe, 2007).

The interpretation of the responses requires a considered combination of the points of view. This study has not ranged the responses in a linear representation of the child, with polarized 'good' and 'bad' aspects of a character. It is more complex than a binary structure for an autobiography. Neither is there one eye seeing who or how a person is in a conclusive way. This research presented in video is also an open invitation to the viewer to contribute to constructing meaning as part of the process. In film theory combining the views may create a synthesized interpolated view from synchronized frames from different input cameras. Perhaps this is a stronger voice than a single one (Jackson, 2003) using the diverse subjectivities of the contributors. Directors like Jean Luc Goddard, Andy Warhol and Peter Greenaway have attempted multiple splits of the screen to show all views simultaneously. The pioneering French director Abel Gance called this Polyvision and there was an explosion of juxtaposing video in the 1990s and early 2000s (Spencer, 2011). The clips could also be controlled by the viewer in non-linear DVD navigation. Whichever way we arrive at our own view, it is not a fixed or permanent view.

Section 3: An example of multiple perspectives from practice

Kirsty Forster successfully completed the sector-endorsed Foundation Degree in Early Years in 2012 at the Pen Green Research, Development and Training Base. This is an edited version, with some commentary, of the information that Kirsty produced for her assignment on Evidence Based Decision Making at Work to Support Change.

KIRSTY FORSTER'S ANALYSIS OF HER INVESTIGATION INTO MULTIPLE PERSPECTIVES WITH PARENTS AND THE PROFESSIONALS WHO WORK WITH THEM AND THEIR FAMILIES

Do professionals and parents have a shared understanding of how children learn?

In her Foundation Degree assignment, Kirsty Forster was interested in gathering perspectives from a range of parents and professionals with regard to investigating whether they had a shared understanding of how children learn. It had become apparent to Kirsty in a previous assignment that parents were getting mixed messages about how children learn from the range of professionals they were engaging with.

Kirsty engaged with a range of professionals from the Health Visiting Team, a private day nursery, Children's Centre staff and parents attending the Children's Centre in which she works.

Initially she asked all the professionals to complete questionnaires with the following questions:

- What type of setting/organisation do you work in, or does your child attend?
- What age are your children or the children you care for or work with?
- What is your professional background?
- How do you think children learn?
- What do you feel is important to a child before learning can take place?
- How do you evidence children's learning? Or if your child/children attend(s) a setting, do you know how they record children's learning?
- When children's learning is being assessed, are there any kinds of targets for them to meet? How do you feel about this?

The questionnaires were analysed by a validation group of fellow Foundation Degree students. During the process of grouping the common words together, moving the data from 'heaps to sets', Kirsty realized that she had generated far more data than she needed to answer her research question in the timescale she had.

She planned to follow up the questionnaires by carrying out a more in-depth interview with one person from each profession and a parent. In order to do this Kirsty used the following questions as the main prompts for the interview:

- How do you think children learn?
- What do you feel is important to a child before learning can take place?

Kirsty ensured that the person she interviewed had responded in a way that was largely indicative of that practitioner group's responses. It was also important that the person had enough time to give to undertaking the interview so that they and Kirsty had the opportunity to explore their values and practices in depth.

Findings

The word used by the majority of professionals and parents to the question, 'How do you think children learn?' was 'play'. In addition to the word 'play', Children's Centre workers also said 'exploring', 'first hand experiences' and 'investigating'. Kirsty, through prior knowledge of this group of workers, assumed that these words also described 'play'. As Tina Bruce claims, 'without firsthand experiences, we cannot wallow in ideas or feelings and relationships. Without direct and real experiences we have no opportunities to develop our competence or technical prowess in a variety of ways' (1991: 83).

The worker from a private day nursery when interviewed responded differently to all the other participants by saying that she believed 'children learn by following instructions'. The responses via questionnaire were also in this vein from the professionals from the private day nursery.

In relation to the question 'what do you feel is important to a child before learning can take place?', the responses from all participants were similar, with the words 'safe' and 'comfortable' being the most common.

Kirsty concluded that within the cohort of professionals and parents she worked with, the perspectives were generally quite similar and in keeping with her own beliefs about how children learn. The only disparity appeared to be the more didactic approach from the nursery worker. Consideration needs to be given to the fact that the parents and health professionals who completed questionnaires, and the parent and health professional who were interviewed, attended or worked closely with the Children's Centre where Kirsty works, no doubt contributing to a shared ethos and understanding of how children learn and what the optimum conditions would be for that to happen most effectively.

However, by gathering these multiple perspectives, Kirsty was able to conclude that there were many commonalities in understanding and beliefs in the groups she worked with and that developing a 'shared language', possibly though multi-disciplinary training, might ensure that fewer 'mixed messages' are received by parents with young children from the range of professionals who support them and their families.

As Kirsty Forster's work shows, these are the kinds of things that it would be good for parents and practitioners to talk about, to share their multiple perspectives about, so that they can support the learning of children more effectively:

The roles of professional experience and parent's everyday experience are seen as complementary and equally important. The former constitutes a 'public' (and generalised) form of 'theory' about child development, whilst the latter represents a 'personal theory' about the development of a particular child. An interaction between the two 'theories' as ways of explaining a child's actions may produce an enriched understanding as a basis for both to act in relation to the child. Only through the combination of both types of information could a broad and accurate picture be built up of a child's developmental progress. (Easen et al, 1992: 282–296).

Penny Lawrence has provided a step-by-step set of points to follow if you want to carry out a multiple perspectives study in your own setting.

    A. Identify and agree about a child to study.

    B. Identify people around the child who could contribute their experiences of him or her.

    C. Aim for a minimum of five contributors. They could be in the following relationship to the child: parent, key worker, sibling, child friend, other member of nursery staff, other multi-agency worker, or family friend.

    D. Depending on the nature of your study, then the child him or herself could be included.

This approach could also be used with text data.

Interview each one separately. The following questions may be a guide:

1. How do you spend time with (child's name)?
2. What is a strong memory for you of a time you have shared with (child's name)?
3. How would you describe him/her to someone who had never met him/her?
4. How would you describe him/her in one word?
5. Make a selection from your own photographic and/or video observations of the child. Share these observations with the contributors and ask for their view of them.
6. What would you like to know about him/her?
7. Ensure you do all of the above, and what follows, in an ethical manner using your own setting's code of ethics or guided by those of a reputable organization such as the British Psychological Society. Pen Green employs a set of ethics that say that research should always

    • "be positive for all the participants
    • provide data that are open to, accountable to and interpreted by all the participants

- focus on questions that the participants themselves (parents, children and staff) are asking
- be based on a relationship of trust where people's answers are believed
- produce results which are about improving practice at home and at nursery, or at least sustaining it". (Whalley & the Pen Green Centre Team, 2007: 12)

8. Collate the responses according to the interview questions. Framing is wide then close-up then wide.
9. Decide if you are going to meet with the contributors separately or together to consider this overview. What is the level of participation going to be? Who will write an interpretation of the responses? Does it require an interpretation, or will you be leaving it open for the viewer/reader to interpret?
10. Accompanying notes, with some interpretation/guidance would aid the useful application of the research in practice.

References

Bruce, T. (1991) *Time to Play in Early Childhood Education*. Abingdon, England: Hodder and Stoughton.

Cherryholmes, C. (1993) 'Reading Research'. *Journal of Curriculum Studies*, Vol. 25, No. 1, 1–32.

Crabtree, R., Sapp, D. & Licona A. (Eds) (2009) 'Introduction'. *Feminist Pedagogy: Looking Back to Move Forward*. Baltimore: The John Hopkins University Press.

Deleuze, G. (1986) *Cinema 1: The Movement Image*. Minneapolis: University of Minnesota Press.

Deleuze, G. & Guattari, F. (1987) A *Thousand Plateaus: Capitalism and Schizophrenia*. Minneapolis: University of Minnesota Press.

Denzin, N. (1989) *Interpretative Biography*. London: Sage.

Easen, P., Kendall, P. & Shaw, J. (1992) Parents and Educators: Dialogue and Developing through Partnership. *Children and Society*, Vol.6, No. 4, 282–96.

Eisner, E. (1997) 'The Promise and Perils of Alternative Forms of Data Representation'. *Educational Researcher*, Vol. 26, No. 6, 4–10.

Forster, K. (2012) Unpublished Foundation Degree assignment.

Gardner, H. (1999) 'Multiple Approaches to Understanding'. *Instructional Design Theories and Models: A New Paradigm of Instructional Theory*, Vol. 2, 69–89.

Hagberg, G. (2008) *Describing Ourselves: Wittgenstein and Autobiographical Consciousness* [online]. Oxford Scholarship. Available from: http://www.oxfordscholarship.com/oso/viewoxchapbook/10.1093$002facprof:oso$002f9780199234226.001.0001$002facprof-9780199234226;jsessionid=EB3E7C7C89886D31485BE1CEE086956B [Accessed 6 August 2012].

Jackson, A. (2003) 'Rhizovocality'. *Qualitative Studies in Education*, Vol. 16, No. 5, 693–710.

Janesick, V. (2000) 'The Choreography of Qualitative Research Design'. In Denzin, N. K. & Lincoln, Y. S. (Eds), *Handbook of Qualitative Research* (2nd Edition). Thousand Oaks, CA: Sage.

Jonassen, D. (1999) 'Designing Constructivist Learning Environments'. *Instructional Design Theories and Models: A New Paradigm of Instructional Theory*, Vol. 2, 215–239.

McClaren, P. & Kincheloe, J. (2007) *Critical Pedagogy: Where Are We Now?* New York: Peter Lang.

Miller, K. & Zhou, X. (2007) 'Learning from Classroom Video: What Makes It Compelling and What Makes It Hard'. In Goldman, R., Pea, R. & Denny, S. (Eds), *Video Research in the Learning Sciences*. London: Lawrence Erlbaum.

Pen Green Research Team (2004) *A Research and Development Project to Promote Well Being and Resilience in Young Children: A series of papers produced over 4 years to illustrate the ongoing research and development work involving children/ parents, workers and researchers at the Pen Green Centre*. Unpublished. Pen Green Centre for Children and Families, Corby, England.

Raban, B., Ure, C. & Waniganayake, M. (2003) 'Multiple Perspectives: Acknowledging the Virtue of Complexity in Measuring Quality'. *Early Years*, Vol. 23, No. 1, 67–77.

Richardson, L. (2000) 'Writing: A Method of Inquiry'. In Denzin, N. K. & Lincoln, Y. S. (Eds), *Handbook of Qualitative Research* (2nd Edition). Thousand Oaks, CA: Sage.

Spencer, S. (2011) *Visual Research Methods in the Social Sciences: Awakening Visions*. Abingdon: Taylor and Francis.

Strauss, A. & Corbin, J. (1998) 'Basics of Qualitative Research: Techniques and Procedures for Developing Grounded Theory'. In Robson, C. (Ed.), *Real World Research* (2nd Edition). Crewe, England: Blackwell.

Tait, C., Lawrence, P. & the Pen Green Team (2001) *Multiple Perspectives*. Paper presented at the European Early Childhood Education Research Association (EECERA) 11th Annual Conference, *Early Childhood Narratives*. Alkmaar, The Netherlands.

Tobin, J. J., Wu, D. & Davidson, D. (1989) *Preschool in Three Cultures*. New Haven, CT: Yale University Press.

Whalley, M. & the Pen Green Centre Team (2007) *Involving Parents in Their Children's Learning* (2nd Edition). London: Paul Chapman.

Wittgenstein, L. (1958) *Philosophical Investigations* (2nd Edition). Oxford: Basil Blackwell.

Chapter 3

Using attachment theory to inform practice in an integrated centre for children and families

Natasha Charlwood and Howard Steele

In this chapter the authors describe a research-in-practice project conducted by medical student Natasha Charlwood, undertaking her psychology project at University College London, and her tutor Howard Steele, working in collaboration with group leaders and researchers at Pen Green. An earlier version was published in the European Early Childhood Education Research Association's journal (EECERJ, 2004, Vol. 12 No 2). The empirical component of the research project that follows concerned the use of the Adult Attachment Interview (AAI) with mothers using therapeutic support groups at Pen Green.

The proposition was that mothers' responses to the AAI would correlate with independent ratings of the children's social and emotional well-being as measured previously by a set of Pre-School Rating Scales (Erickson et al., 1985). The outcome was that emotional insecurity and past experience of loss and trauma in childhood figured predominantly in the interviews. It proved to be the case that ratings of mothers' probable past experiences and current states of mind regarding attachment were powerfully correlated with their children's well-being. This was the first time that Pen Green researchers had engaged in a formal research partnership with a university. Pen Green researchers attended seminars on the application of the AAI but did not themselves undertake the interviews. Their role was to actively support both the university researcher and the parents before and after the interview and in the Growing Together groups that were subsequently set up.

Growing Together provides a 'focussed' drop-in group to support parents with children from 0-3 years of age. Group leaders and parents develop a shared language through the informal discussion of child development concepts, such as the schema theory of Chris Athey and the work of Ferre Laevers on Well being and Involvement (Athey, 1990; Laevers, 1997). Psychodynamic concepts such as John Bowlby's 'attachment' theory, and William Bion's ideas on 'holding in mind' and 'containment' are also shared with the parents (Bion, 1962; Bowlby, 1969). The shared language is a combination of the workers' knowledge of the concepts and the parents' knowledge of their children. The aim of Growing Together is to help parents develop a deeper understanding of their children's cognitive and emotional development and the underlying processes which shape their children's play behaviour.

This research-in-practice project has had an enormous impact on work undertaken at Pen Green. It is our belief that children's centres constantly work at the interface of infant and adult mental health. It would clearly be beyond the reach of most children's centres, and that includes Pen Green, to train staff to administer the AAI routinely. However, we see it as essential to equip all staff to have a strong understanding of the emotional roots of learning and development, to offer all staff effective supervision and support and to offer the opportunity for work-based discussion groups with expert facilitators.

Practitioner perspective: The development of integrated services to support the needs of young children and their families

The rapid expansion of the development of integrated services for children and families in the first two terms of the Labour Government in the UK has been a complex and challenging task (Atkinson, 2002). Programmes that support the development of the most vulnerable children and that promote the education and development of all the children have been established through a number of key initiatives: the Early Excellence Centres (DfEE, 1997), the Sure Start Programme (DfEE, 1999) and, most recently, the Children's Centre Programme (DfES, 2003).

Poverty has received the greatest focus as "the most immediate injustice" (Esping-Anderson, 2002), and most of these initiatives have targeted the 20% poorest communities in England. Developing 'the cultural capital' that is needed to equalise children's life chances is seen as the central task, and this has meant that services, whilst retaining a central focus on children's needs, are also required to engage with parents and the wider community (OECD, 2003). The links between a poor start, as opposed to a Sure Start, and later social exclusion have been made (Glass, 2003). The challenge for integrated settings and services is to encourage all the important adults in the child's life to be aspirational and to share an image of the child as 'rich in potential, strong, powerful, competent and, most of all, connected to adults and other children' (Malaguzzi, 1993).

The parent's role in encouraging the development of high self-esteem, a sense of agency, and a strong disposition to learn is seen as critical if children's life chances are to be transformed (Feinstein, 2003). What is less clear is how children's centre staff can be most effective in supporting parents in their role. Parents whose own experience of parenting has been less than positive may struggle to use services effectively (Shaw, 1991). Early childhood educators in these settings need to have a very clear understanding of relevant theory if they are to effectively engage with vulnerable parents. In this study, early childhood educators worked with developmental psychologists to deepen their understanding of attachment theory. The AAI was initially used as a research tool, the outcomes of which are reported later in this chapter. Subsequently, the practitioners were able to develop a number of focused interventions, including insights gained from the AAI, to support parents more effectively.

Ethics

This study and all research undertaken at Pen Green complies with British Education Research Association (BERA) guidelines and the Pen Green ethical code (Whalley & the Pen Green Team, 2007: 12).

Origins of attachment theory and its relevance to early childhood and the clinical domain

Mary Ainsworth (1982) recounts how the idea of attachment came to Bowlby 'in a flash' when, in 1952, he read Lorenz's and Tinbergen's work on ethology (Holmes, 1993). The ethological approach provided a scientific grounding that Bowlby believed was needed to update psychoanalytical theory. At the time, psychoanalysis was the leading influence on clinical (psychiatric and psychological) training and practice, and thus attachment theory, with its emphasis upon real-word interactions between mothers and their children (as opposed to unconscious fantasies linked to instinctual drives), was seen as a radical departure from psychoanalysis (Bowlby, 1969, 1973, 1980). When Bowlby first presented his ideas to the British Psychoanalytic Society in the late 1950s and early 1960s, he was met with hostility and disapprobation (Steele & Steele, 1998). This contributed to Bowlby's ideas initially having minimal influence upon clinical practice with children and adults (Holmes, 1993). Another reason why attachment theory was taken up so reluctantly by the clinical world was because it was perceived as having too narrow a focus; attachment for Bowlby was 'A psychological bond in its own right, not an instinct derived from feeding or infant sexuality' (Holmes, 1993: 63). Clinicians found this conceptual framework more difficult to work with because clients reported multiple conflicts and motivators. There was also no focus on its direct clinical application. Attachment theory in the beginning, and for some 25 years through the mid-1980s, was therefore largely perceived as having academic rather than clinical relevance. This situation changed somewhat dramatically after the development and validation of the AAI with its stated aim of 'surprising the unconscious' and eliciting narrative evidence of a range of emotional and mental conflicts stemming from early attachment experiences (George, Kaplan & Main, 1985; Main, Kaplan & Cassidy, 1985).

Ultimately, the contribution of attachment research over the last 15–20 years to understanding child development, and promoting personal and family wellbeing, may arguably be seen to derive from the development of the AAI (George et al., 1985) and a corollary rating and classification manual (Main & Goldwyn, 1998). The AAI provides a thorough assessment of the meaning (to the respondent) of attachment experiences, including painful childhood experiences that have happened to everyone (e.g. separation, rejection and emotional/physical hurt), as well as painful experiences that have happened to some people (i.e., loss and abuse). The reliability and validity of the AAI has been extensively explored, with many studies in diverse cultural contexts demonstrating that the mothers' responses to the AAI are highly predictive of infant-mother patterns of attachment at one year of age (see van Ijzendoorn et al., 1995). These infant-mother patterns of attachment were first identified by Mary Ainsworth and her colleagues based on their 20-minute procedure involving two brief separations from the mother and two reunions with her – the widely used Strange Situation Procedure (Ainsworth, Blehar, Waters & Wall, 1978). For Ainsworth, close study of reunion behaviour permits the identification of secure and insecure patterns of infant-mother attachment. If a child is happy to see mother upon reunion, this indicates a secure pattern, whilst other children who avoid the mother upon reunion, or who cry inconsolably, are said to have insecure patterns of attachment. The importance of being able to predict these infant-mother attachment patterns at one year of age is underscored by the vast developmental literature showing that infant-mother attachment patterns predict various social and cognitive outcomes at later ages (Cassidy & Shaver, 1999).

Attachment patterns and their outcomes for children

There are robust findings concerning the long-term social, emotional and cognitive consequences of infant-mother patterns of attachment (Ainsworth et al., 1978; Ainsworth, 1982; Cassidy & Shaver, 1999; Sroufe, 1988; Steele, 2002). This previous work has documented both short- and long-term developmental outcomes of these infant-parent patterns of attachment. For example, secure attachments during infancy predict optimal patterns of peer relations and adjustment in the pre-school years, high levels of academic achievement in the school years, and adaptive coping in the adolescent years. Correspondingly, the insecure (avoidant, resistant and, the more recently discovered, disorganised) infant patterns have been shown to predict much less favourable, sometimes psychopathological, developmental outcomes.

A series of studies conducted in Minnesota are of direct relevance to the current study. In this work, securely attached children were more compliant at age two (Erickson, Sroufe & Egeland, 1985), were found to be more sociable with peers (Pastor, 1981), and were less dependent on their teachers (Sroufe, 1983). In the 1983 study, Sroufe observed 40 children in a special laboratory pre-school over a number of months. He found that securely attached infants demonstrated more ego-control; greater levels of independence, compliance and empathy; and higher levels of social competence. Children who were insecurely attached were found to display more negative affect, less positive affect and lower self-esteem than children with secure attachments (Sroufe, 1983).

Of particular relevance to the current study was work reported by Erickson and colleagues (1985) when they followed up a group of children, whose attachments to mother had been observed at one year of age, now at pre-school. Their theoretical proposal was that those pre-schoolers who had been insecurely attached at one year would show maladaptive patterns in the early years, manifesting in pronounced difficulties with impulse control, aggression, antisocial behaviours, emotional dependency and difficulties in relating to peers. This 1985 study was an extension of Sroufe's work; however, 56 extra subjects were included. Pre-School Ratings of children's agency, dependency, ego control, social skills, positive affect, negative affect and compliance were taken. The results of these Pre-School Ratings were used to identify children who were functioning well in pre-school and those with marked deficits in well-being. This latter group were found to demonstrate more negative affect, and their mothers were less supportive, gave less encouragement during laboratory problem-solving tasks, gave less clearly structured directions, and were less firm and less confident in setting limits. Quality of infant attachment was a predictor of behaviour at pre-school. Only 2 of the 16 anxiously attached children were in the well functioning group compared to 15 of the 22 securely attached children. The 1985 Erickson et al. study was concerned with identifying the discriminating factors that contributed to anxiously attached children functioning well and securely attached children having behaviour problems.

Conclusions drawn from the Erickson et al. study substantiate the findings of Ainsworth and colleagues in 1978, in that quality of attachment is an assessment of the quality of care and support in the first year of life. Erickson and colleagues found that differences between attachment status and expected functioning in pre-school accompanied changes in the quality of care: children who in infancy were securely attached but who at age 4–5 were experiencing behaviour problems in pre-school had experienced inadequate maternal care during their subsequent developmental stages. Factors that were thought to help children who were anxiously avoidant in infancy move towards healthy functioning were the level of mother's emotional support and overall sensitivity. The effects of mother's support and sensitivity were enhanced if they were accompanied by a stable family environment and improved support from family and friends (Erickson et al., 1985).

A possibly important variable that the Erickson et al. study did not include was the attachment status of the mothers. The present study aimed to extend the work of Erickson and her colleagues on a similar but smaller-scale project. In the present study, no measurements of mother-child interaction or infant security were taken; instead the AAI was administered to the mothers for comparison with ratings of the pre-school-aged children's well-being. The central questions guiding this research project were as follows:

• Would patterns of maternal response to the AAI predict their children's social and emotional well-being as measured by the Pre-School Ratings used in the Erickson et al. study?

- Would mothers' probable attachment history *and* their current state of mind regarding attachment both correlate with children's Pre-School Ratings?

The question of whether gender affected children's scores on the Pre-School Rating Scales and any possible inter-correlations between each of the rating scales would also be examined.

Our method

Sample

The Pen Green Centre for Under Fives and Their Families is situated in an area where there are high levels of perinatal mortality, high teenage pregnancy and high morbidity, particularly among women. Most families come to Pen Green from three wards, one of these is amongst the 30% most deprived wards in England. The population of Corby at the time of this study was predominantly Caucasian; less than 1% of families came from minority groups. For the current study, 15 mothers who attend the Pen Green Centre were involved. Of these, 8 (53%) were unemployed, 3 (20%) were living alone (i.e., without a partner) and 11 (73%) were in receipt of government benefits. They were aged between 20 and 38 (median age = 30). The children of these 15 mothers comprised a group of 17 (i.e., two mothers had two children each in the study), and 11 (73%) of these 17 were boys. All the children were aged between 2 and 4 years.

Measures

Two principle measures were used in this study:

- an interview-based measure of the mothers' internal representations of attachment relationships, i.e., the Adult Attachment Interview (George et al., 1985)
- an observation-based rating of each child's adaptation provided by two members of the Pen Green Staff, i.e., the Family Worker and the Nursery Head and Deputy Head. A previously validated instrument was used. This was the Pre-School Rating Scales (Erickson et al., 1985).

The Adult Attachment Interview (AAI)

The AAI is a structured interview designed to elicit childhood memories from which inferences can be drawn about relationships with parents and other attachment figures during childhood (George et al., 1985). There are approximately 20 questions each with standardised follow-up questions or 'probes'. Participants are asked for five adjectives to describe their relationship to each parent during their childhood and then for anecdotes to substantiate these adjectives. Coding of the interview is not about assessing whether the subject grew up in adverse or favourable conditions, rather it depends on the 'goodness of fit' between the generalised descriptions and specific memories. Participants are asked whether they felt closer to one parent and why, and what they used to do as a child when they were upset. Other issues such as rejection, separation and loss are also discussed. Finally, participants are asked why they think their parents behaved as they did, and the effects these early relationships have had on the participant's adult personality.

The technique has been described as one of "surprising the unconscious" (George et al., 1985). The interview format has been designed so that there are plenty of opportunities for the subject to contradict or fail to support statements. The interview is transcribed verbatim, including all indications of speaking difficulty and genuine speaking errors of the subject and the interviewer. The words, phrases, speech errors, and hesitations are key to the analysis, where deviations from truthfulness (or credibility), economy (saying neither too much nor too little), relevance (to the topic of past attachment relationships) and manner (politeness) are noted in the process of rating and classifying the interviews into one of four distinct groups (Main & Goldwyn, 1998). The basic classification system assigns interviews to one of three groups: two insecure (dismissing or preoccupied) and one deemed autonomous-secure. An insecure-dismissing narrative is brief but incomplete, marked by a lack of fit between memories and evaluations, often punctuated or sustained by an unrealistically positive evaluation of parents and/or self. An insecure-preoccupied narrative is neither succinct nor complete and contains many irrelevant details, together with much passive (weak, nonspecific) speech or highly involving anger towards one or both parents. By contrast, the autonomous-secure narrative robustly fulfils all or most of the criteria of coherence, *whether or not* the speaker was well cared for during childhood. In other words, a narrative that refers to neglecting, rejecting, or even abusive experiences during childhood may be judged autonomous-secure if these malevolent relationship patterns are clearly relegated to the past, with the narrative conveying understanding and acceptance of how these have influenced the individual's development.

A further important consideration when rating and classifying attachment interviews concerns past loss and trauma. When there is clear evidence of a significant loss or trauma (physical and/or sexual abuse), the judge follows a number of specified guidelines (Main & Goldwyn, 1998) for assessing the extent to which the past trauma is resolved. In sum, this comes down to determining the extent to which the overwhelmingly negative experiences are (a) identified as such and (b) spoken about in such a way as to indicate that they have acquired the characteristics of belonging to the past. Unresolved mourning is most notable when there are lapses in the monitoring of reason or discourse when discussing the past loss and/or trauma. For example, where loss has occurred, it is important for the speaker to demonstrate full awareness of the permanence of this loss. And, where abuse has occurred in speakers' childhood experiences, it is important for speakers to at once acknowledge the abuse, and also show that they understand they are not responsible for the maltreatment they suffered. Important clues as to the extent of resolution in the speaker's mind follow from careful study of the narrative for a logically and temporally sequenced account of the trauma, which is neither too brief, suggesting an attempt to minimise the significance of the trauma, nor too detailed, suggesting ongoing absorption.

The interview pro forma touched on a number of sensitive issues. It was the first time that some participants had talked openly about their childhood, and in some cases this involved participants recollecting painful topics. A significant number of participants had experienced abuse or neglect in childhood. Hollows (1994) suggests that 1:10 of the UK population has experienced some form of sexual abuse and that that is a conservative estimate. A more recent report estimated that 59% of young women and 27% of young men had been sexually abused (Hollows, 1994: 2).

For this reason a number of extra measures were put in place to make the interviews as supportive an experience as possible for the subjects:

- two hours were allowed for the interviews to take place
- crèche and/or nursery facilities were offered to the parents so that they had time and space to take part in the interviews, and a physical space was provided for such purposes
- a debriefing session was offered to participants with a social worker or senior member of staff
- a member of the Pen Green research team was available on the premises during all of the interviews in case extra support was needed.

All of the 17 interviews were rated and classified by the first author, and 8 were independently coded by the second author, who had been trained to high standards of reliability with the established guidelines (Main & Goldwyn, 1998). There was 100% agreement as to the insecure vs. secure and resolved vs. unresolved assignment of all eight interviews coded independently by both authors. Thus, the first author's classifications of the interviews were assumed to be reliable. Of the 17 interviews, 3 (17%) were judged autonomous-secure, 1 (6%) dismissing, 1 (6%) preoccupied, and 12 (71%) were judged to be unresolved with respect to past loss or trauma. Of these unresolved interviews, where the judge assigns a best-fitting alternative, 3 were autonomous-secure, 4 were dismissing and 5 were preoccupied.

In addition to the classification, each interview was scored using the 9-point rating scales specified in the Main and Goldwyn (1998) manual. These pertain to

- description of past childhood experiences (whether in the coder's opinion attachment figures were: loving, rejecting, neglecting, involving, pressuring);
- the language used to describe these experiences (overall coherence of transcript, vague discourse, insistence on lack of recall, fear of loss). Scores are

assigned on the basis of key sentences and upon the study of the transcript in its entirety. After this has been carried out a third coding is made;

- this assesses the subject's ability to give an integrated, coherent, believable account of experiences and their meaning;
- the extent to which each past loss or trauma was resolved, i.e., located convincingly in the past as opposed to continuing to occupy and drain emotional and mental resources.

The two authors' ratings of these 9-point interval scales of probable past experience and current state of mind concerning attachment were in strong agreement. Further, these 9-point rating scales were normally distributed, and therefore preferred (over the uneven distribution of interview classifications) for use in comparing the interviews with the ratings obtained of the children's emotional and social well-being and dispositions to learn.

Children's Pre-School Rating Scale

The scale used in this study to assess infant and child emotional and social well-being was a Pre-School Rating Scale that had not been used before in the Pen Green Nursery. The Pre-School Rating Scales (Erickson et al., 1985) consist of seven, seven-point scales that were designed to be used by project observers and pre-school classroom teachers to assess children on the following issues:

- **agency and self confidence.** A child who is high in agency will demonstrate a high level of confidence in asserting his/her will over events in almost every situation. He/she demonstrates high levels of assertiveness and has a sense of what he/she wants to do and will make every effort to do it. On the other hand, a child with a low agency score seems to want to 'fit in' with what others are doing and would rarely take the role of leader.
- **ego control.** This is defined as a broad characterisation of the way a child controls his/her responses to situations and his/her engagement in the environment. A child with high ego control is able to regulate his/her approach to events to such a degree that they may show an excessive modulation of feelings to events, displaying flat affect and little spontaneity. A child with optimum ego control would score 3–4 on the scale by showing the ability to 'work well and play well'. A child with low ego control would rarely show thoughtful or organised behaviour or restraint. Instead, such a child would be easily distracted or disorganised by competing stimuli or difficult tasks.
- **dependency.** This is a measure of the child's dependency to rely on others for emotional or physical assistance and approval. It is described as taking both a positive form (showing off to peers and the teacher, being the teacher's self-appointed assistant) or a negative form (whining, clinging, making demands for assistance). A child with high dependency will regularly seek support and

becomes upset without the comfort of such attention, whereas a child with low dependency will tend to rely mostly on him/herself.

- **social skills with peers.** This scale represents the degree to which the child is able to interact well with peers. A child with low social skills would find it extremely difficult to interact with peers and would seem to have no friends or playmates. He/she would tend to alienate other children when playing through his/her arbitrary behaviour and lack of social responsiveness. The child would tend to play on his/her own or be included by other children only in a limited capacity. A child with high social skills is able to modulate his/her behaviour in ways that contribute to good social interactions; he/she seems able to understand another child's perspectives and desires.
- **positive affect.** This is a scale that rates the degree to which the child 'radiates' positive emotion. A child with low positive affect would characteristically approach events with a flat expression or may be overwhelmingly negative. A child with very high positive affect seems to radiate happiness and spreads his/her joy to surrounding peers.
- **negative emotional tones.** This scale is based on a clinical judgment of the degree of negative emotional baggage the child 'carries around' with him/herself. It is characterized by signs of hostility, coldness towards others and deliberate and noncompliant behaviour. A child with high negative affect may provoke confrontations or may withdraw from the 'social world'. The character of either behaviour is said to involve anger and hostility.
- **compliance.** This scale measures the degree to which the child listens to instructions and complies with them. A child with high compliance would actively listen to instructions and comply quickly with what was said; the child may question an instruction or direction but does so in a way that reflects autonomy within a compliant manner rather than direct negativism. A child with low compliance ignores all instructions and displays total negativism towards the teacher.

Nursery staff at Pen Green routinely make detailed observations on children's emotional well-being and cognitive concerns. For the purposes of this research, each child's key worker filled in a Pre-School Rating Scale. Subsequently, the Nursery Head or senior teacher independently filled in a Pre-School Rating Scale on each child in the study. The ratings of the Nursery Head and the key workers were highly positively correlated, and an average set of ratings for each child was computed.

What we discovered

The results are organized into two sections. The first section of results compares the Pre-School Ratings with the ratings of the probable past attachment experiences of the mothers. The second section of results compares the Pre-School

Ratings with the ratings of the state of mind concerning attachment reflected in the interviews from the mothers.

1. *Results from the correlational analyses for mothers' past experience and children's well-being*

In order to compare Pen Green staff members' ratings of the children's well-being with mothers' probable past experience, these two sets of ratings were correlated in Table 3.1.

Table 3.1 includes 48 correlations, 30 (63%) of which were significant, 11 of these (~20%) at the $p < 0.01$ level. Four main results are evident in Table 3.1:

- **loving parents:** Children whose mothers had the experience of a loving mother throughout *their* childhood had significantly higher agency/self-confidence ratings and greater social skills. Children's positive affect correlated to their mothers having had the experience of a loving mother but not significantly. Mothers' experience of having a loving mother also decreased the degree of negative affect demonstrated by their children. Mothers'

Table 3.1 Correlations between Children's Pre-School Ratings and mothers' probable experiences scores

	Agency	Dependency	Social Skills	Positive Affect	Negative Affect	Compliance
Mother loving	.662**	−.450	.561*	.480	−.435	.179
Father loving	.689**	−.550*	.519*	.425	−.680**	.503*
Mother rejecting	−.657**	.497*	−.586*	−.423	.457	−.264
Father rejecting	−.493*	.503*	−3.12	−.225	.568*	−.430
Mother involving	−.679**	.342	−.593*	−.400	.620*	−.562*
Father involving	−.666*	.388*	−.647*	−.653*	.603*	−.075
Mother neglecting	−.730**	.537*	−.692**	−.628**	.664**	−.342
Father neglecting	−.645**	.425	−.628**	−.458	.539*	−.388

Note: Ns are variable due to list-wise deletion of subjects with any missing data and the varied set of variables in each of the analyses (min N = 5, max N = 17).

*p < .05
**p < .01

experience of having a loving father correlated more strongly with her children's Pre-School Ratings than her experience of having a loving mother. Compliance in children is significantly correlated with mothers having had a loving father, and both dependency and negative affect show significant negative correlations with mothers' experience of having had a loving father during her childhood.

- **rejecting parents:** Children whose mothers had experienced rejection by their mother throughout *their* childhood had significantly lower self-confidence and social skills, were more highly dependent and displayed an increased negative affect. Children whose mothers had experienced rejection by their mother throughout childhood also tended to display less positive affect and less compliance. Children whose mothers had experienced rejection by their father throughout their own childhood had significantly higher negative affect.

- **involving/reversing parents:** The experience of a mother having an involving/reversing mother significantly decreases her child's agency, social skills and compliance. Children whose mothers had experienced an involving/reversing mother had significantly higher negative affect. A mother's experience of an involving/reversing father correlates significantly with increases in her children's dependency and negative affect. A mother's experience of having an involving/reversing father significantly correlates negatively with her child's agency, social skills and positive affect.

- **neglecting parents:** Children whose mothers had experienced neglect by *their* mother during their childhood had significantly lower Pre-School Ratings of self-confidence, social skills and positive affect; these children also displayed significantly higher negative affect and were more highly dependent. Children whose mothers had experienced neglect by their father during their childhood had significantly decreased self-confidence and social skills.

2.   *Results from the correlational analyses for mothers' current state of mind regarding attachment and children's well-being*

In order to compare the mothers' state of mind regarding attachment with the independently obtained ratings of their children's well-being, we correlated these two sets of ratings in Table 3.2.

Table 3.2 includes a total of 72 correlations carried out, 14 (19%) of which were significant, 6 (8%) of these at the $p < .01$ level. These results are described in further detail here:

- **coherence:** Coherence is the degree to which the mother presents a believable, reflective and easy to understand impression of her own childhood experiences. Table 3.2 reveals that mother's coherence of mind and the coherence of the interview transcript are both positively correlated at a significant level with child's agency, social skills and positive affect. Mother's

Table 3.2 Correlations between Children's Pre-School Ratings and mothers' states of mind

	Agency	Dependency	Social Skills	Positive Affect	Negative Affect	Compliance
Coherence of mind	.658**	−.430	.701**	.681**	−.618**	.537*
Coherence of transcript	.534*	−.363	.678**	.586*	−.410	.398
Highest unresolved mourning re loss	−1.67	.297	.226	.114	.145	−.241
Idealisation of mother	.171	−.246	.061	−.161	−.224	.217
Idealisation of father	.035	−.099	−.040	−.349	−.088	.176
Involving anger with mother	−.655**	.478	−.453	−.401	.441	−.484*
Involving anger with father	−.201	.034	−.467	−.187	.305	−.199
Derogation of mother	−.453	.252	−.403	−.388	.539*	−.480
Derogation of father	−.470	.340	−.376	−.313	.533*	−.446
Derogation of attachment	−.408	.185	−.472*	−.409	.491*	−.445
Lack of recall	.474	−.173	.343	.226	−.269	.350
Passivity of thought	−.212	.021	−.356	−.219	−.021	−.111

Note: Ns are variable due to list-wise deletion of subjects with any missing data and the varied set of variables in each of the analyses.

*p < .05
**p < .01

coherence of mind is also positively correlated to compliance and negatively correlated to negative affect to a highly significant degree

- **unresolved mourning re loss:** The results of the correlations between the children's Pre-School Ratings Scale and mother's scores for highest unresolved mourning re loss produced no results that were significant. However, some of the trends were in a meaningful direction, for example, higher scores for unresolved mourning re loss seemed to be negatively correlated with children's scores for agency and compliance, and positively related to a child's dependency.

- **idealisation of parents:** No significant relationships were found when the Pre-School Ratings of children were correlated with the idealising state of mind with respect to the mothers' mothers or mothers' fathers. However, several meaningful trends were suggested by the results. Both the idealisation of mother and father seem to decrease the positive affect of the child. Idealisation of father correlates negatively with children's social skills.

- **involving anger:** Involving anger relates to the degree to which the mother expresses a preoccupying anger that she directs towards her parents during the interview. When the scale for involving anger with mother was correlated with the Pre-School Ratings of their children, significant results were obtained. Involving anger with mother is negatively correlated with both agency (p < .01) and compliance (p < .05) in the child: as involving anger of the mother decreases self-confidence and compliance of the child increases. Correlations of this scale with the other Pre-School Ratings suggested meaningful relationships. As involving anger with mother increases, the results imply that dependency and negative affect of the child would also increase, and the child's social skills would decrease; however, these results did not reach significance. Correlations of involving anger with father and the Pre-School Ratings gave no significant results; however, trends in the predicted direction, as described previously, were observed in Table 3.2.

- **derogation of parents:** Derogation is a scale that reflects the degree to which a mother dismisses attachment relationships and experiences and the influence of attachment on her own growth and development. When the children's Pre-School Ratings were correlated with derogation of mother, derogation of father and overall derogation of attachment, the direction of the correlations were very similar. A greater derogatory state of mind in the mother seems to correlate with decreased agency, social skills, positive affect and compliance in her child. The results of the correlations also suggest that derogation is positively correlated to a child's dependency and negative affect. A number of these correlations produced significant results; these were that derogation of mother, father and attachment were all significantly associated with negative affect in the child (p < .05), and overall derogation of attachment was negatively correlated to a child's social skills.

- **lack of recall:** The results in Table 3.2 show correlations between mothers' lack of recall of childhood experiences and children's Pre-School Ratings. None of these correlations are in a meaningful direction.

- **passivity of thought processes:** None of the correlations between mother's passivity of thought processes and children's Pre-School Ratings were significant; however, most of the correlations were in a meaningful direction. Passivity of thought processes seems to be negatively correlated to child's agency, social skills, positive affect and compliance. When passivity was correlated with dependency, a positive relationship was found; this would suggest that as the passivity of a mother's thought processes increased, so does the dependency of her child.

Discussion

The statistical correlations that have been presented in the previous sections show important links between the mothers' narrative accounts of their attachment history and their children's directly observed Pre-School Ratings. Both the probable childhood experiences of the mothers and their current state of mind concerning relationships were meaningfully associated with children's Pre-School Ratings, thus providing affirmative answers to both questions posed by this investigation. This discussion reviews the main findings and points to clinical and educational applications of the results.

In the present study, mothers' probable experiences with their parents in childhood as assessed by the AAI were strongly linked to children's Pre-School Ratings. A mother's experience of having a loving mother and father was strongly correlated to higher levels of agency, social skills, positive affect and compliance in her child. If a mother experienced rejection, reversal and neglect from her parents, then it was likely to be the case that her child scored lower on the index of emotional well-being. That is, lower scores for agency, social skills, positive affect and compliance were noted when mothers had impoverished attachment histories, while their children had higher scores for dependency and negative affect. These results suggest that interventions such as the Ann Arbour/San Francisco Infant-Parent Project, which emphasises the links between parents' early childhood experiences and their current behaviours towards their children, might well be effective (Lieberman & Zeanah, 1999). As a result of this study, Pen Green set up two groups for parents wanting to explore how their own experiences of being parented have impacted on their current relationships with their children.

However, as Cromwell and Feldman suggested, 'meanings and interpretations given to experiences in childhood contributed as much to parenting behaviour as did actual experiences' (1988: 1283). Results from the correlations between mothers' states of mind with respect to attachment and children's Pre-School Ratings suggest the strongest correlation is between coherence of mind and children's Pre-School Ratings. Coherence is positively related to children's scores for agency, social skills, positive affect and compliance; it is negatively correlated to children's scores for dependency and negative affect. The only scale that was not significantly correlated to mother's state of mind was child dependency. Erickson suggests that dependency can manifest in many ways and that the Pre-School Rating Scale for dependency is not comprehensive enough to obtain significant results (Erickson et al., 1985). Main and Goldwyn state the importance of coherence of mind quite simply as: 'the overall "state of mind" score with respect to adult attachment. It is expected to predict an infant's overall security of attachment better than any other single score, and also to predict, better than any other single score, a subject's overall functioning insofar as it is related to attachment' (Main & Goldwyn, 1998: 91). Results from the present study clearly support this statement.

Coherence of mind implies a lively sense of self, organised and capable of reflecting upon past relationship adversities in such a way that limits the possibly malevolent influence of these experiences upon parenting, with consequent ill-effects on children's well-being. But, invariably, one does not arrive at a coherent mind regarding past attachment experiences all on one's own – there must be at least one supportive relationship in one's life to compensate for earlier adversity. This may arise in the context of relationships with the other parent, a grandparent, or, in adulthood, a therapist, a partner, or possibly an early years professional in the nursery setting attended by one's child.

The results of the present study suggest that the role of the early years professional may be critical. This is because of the complicated intergenerational issues facing the majority of parents in the current study. Although the importance of grandparents cannot be overestimated, the majority of mothers in the current study faced complicated intergenerational issues. Many families in Corby will have at least two generations living fairly closely – principally, families who moved down from Scotland between the 1930s and 1950s who have remained relatively isolated in the East Midlands. Some children will therefore benefit from close relationships with supporting, loving parents and loving grandparents. However, the only family support available to some children was from parents who were unsupported in childhood and from grandparents who were unable to appropriately support their own children and might continue to find it difficult to support their grandchildren. The implication is that the effects of parents' probable experiences with these older adults may be very complex, and appropriate intergenerational support may not be readily available. Additional support to help mothers make optimal use of the resources available to them, and within them, is clearly an important role for early years workers in children's centres such as Pen Green. Early childhood practitioners working in this way are developing the role of *key worker* to embrace not only the child but also the parent (Elfer, 1976; Manning-Morton & Thorp, 2001). Whilst early childhood educators have for some time understood that their role is to support the children's emotional needs, particularly at times of transition, there is not yet a deep understanding of the role of the key worker in supporting the child's parents.

The necessity for such support is underlined by the observation in the current research that a majority of mothers interviewed reported some experience of abuse during their childhood. It could be that the levels of abuse experienced by this cohort and the high scores for rejection from both parents experienced by subjects accounted for the very significant correlations between mothers' probable experience and children's well-being. Pen Green has a highly developed and comprehensive groupwork programme, including a group for adult survivors of abuse. As a children's centre, Pen Green can also offer parents counselling and support from trained social workers and psychotherapists.

It has long been presumed that parents' representations of their life history shapes the way in which the infant is conceptualised in the mind of the parent and therefore the way the infant is treated (Freud, 1940; Fraiberg, Adelson & Shapiro, 1975). With the development of the AAI it has become possible to reliably measure the extent to which ghosts from the past may be haunting particular parents in the nursery (Fonagy, Steele, Moran, Steele & Higgitt, 1993). Research with the AAI has helped to refine thinking about how mothers' attachment histories may influence their children and has provided explanations as to why this should be the case.

Main, Kaplan and Cassidy (1985) suggest that parents with an insecure attachment status find the need to restrict attachment-relevant information and that this may result in an inability to perceive and interpret the attachment signals of their infant accurately. They suggest that these adults may find that they need to alter the infant's signals or inhibit them. This means that the caregivers with insecure AAIs were not in tune with their children and were not answering the emotional needs of their child. Cromwell and Feldman (1988) found that sensitive and responsive patterns of maternal behaviour were more frequently found where mothers' AAI were classified as autonomous-secure. In a separate study, Haft and Slade (1989) found that mothers with insecure AAIs demonstrated a lack of attunement in mother-infant interactions. Fonagy et al. (1993) suggest that attachment security in infants is based on parental sensitivity to, and understanding of, the infants' mental world.

Results from the present study endorse the results of the Erickson et al. (1985) study based in Minnesota. It does seem that attachment can be used as a measure of the quality of care and support provided by a caregiver. It also seems that the AAI is a suitable measure that can be used to infer children's attachment patterns and probable parent-child interactions.

Implications for the Centre

It has not been possible to build the use of the Adult Attachment Interview as an integral part of the intake process into our groupwork programme. This is in part because of the high levels of staff training required to administer and analyse the AAI outcomes and because of the high levels of support that must be available to parents undertaking the AAI.

Groups offered at Pen Green are generally universally open to local families. However, within 'open' groups, such as our Growing Together groups, there are also targeted interventions for parents and children experiencing greater vulnerability. Parents can be referred by other agencies or can self refer. If parents then find that they need additional support, we do have specialist groups for parents who have had or are currently experiencing severe postnatal depression, drug and alcohol abuse, domestic violence and sexual abuse.

References

Ainsworth, M. (1982) 'Attachment: Respect and Prospect'. In Parkes, C. M. & Stevenson-Hindem, J. (Eds), *The Place of Attachment in Human Behaviour.* London: Routledge.

Ainsworth, M., Blehar, M. C., Waters, E. & Wall, S. (1978) *Patterns of Attachment: A Psychological Study of the Strange Situation.* Hillsdale, NJ: Erlbaum.

Athey, C. (1990) *Extending Thought in Young Children: A Parent Teacher Partnership.* London, Paul Chapman.

Atkinson, M. (2002) *Multi Agency Working: A Detailed Study.* Slough, England: NFER.

Bion, W. (1962) *Learning Through Experience.* London: Heinemann.

Bowlby, J. (1969) *Attachment and Loss. Vol.1: Attachment.* New York: Basic Books.

Bowlby, J. (1973) *Attachment and Loss. Vol.2: Separation.* New York: Basic Books.

Bowlby, J. (1980) *Attachment and Loss. Vol.3: Loss.* New York: Basic Books.

Cassidy, J. & Shaver, P. (Eds) (1999) *Handbook of Attachment.* New York: Guildford Press.

Charlwood, N. & Steele, H. (2004) Using attachment theory to inform practice in an integrated centre for children and families. *European Early Childhood Education Research Journal,* Vol. 12, No 2, 59–74.

Cromwell, J. A. & Feldman, S. (1988) 'Mothers' Internal Working Models of Relationships and Children's Behavioural Developmental Status: A Study of Mother Child Interaction. *Child Development,* Vol. 59, 1273–1285.

DfEE (1997) *Early Excellence Programme* [online]. Available from http://www.dfes.gov.uk.

DfEE (1999) *Report on Excellence Programme* [online]. Available from http://www.dfes.gov.uk.

DfES (2003) *Children's Centre Programme/Sure Start* [online]. Available from http://www.dfes.gov.uk.

Elfer, P. (1976) 'Building Intimacy in Relationships with Young Children in Nurseries'. *Early Years,* Vol. 16, Spring, 30–40.

Erickson, M. F., Sroufe, L. A. & Egeland, B. (1985) 'The Relationship Between Quality of Attachment and Behaviour Problems in Pre-School in a High Risk Sample'. Monographs of the Society for Research in Child Development, 50, 147–166.

Esping-Anderson, G. (2002) *Why We Need a Welfare State.* Oxford: Oxford University Press.

Feinstein, L. (2003) 'Not Just the Early Years. The Need for a Developmental Perspective for Equality of Opportunity'. *New Economy,* Vol. 10, No. 4, 213–218.

Fonagy, P., Steele, M., Moran, G., Steele, H. & Higgitt, A. (1993) 'Measuring the Ghost in the Nursery: An Empirical Study of the Relation Between Parents' Mental Representations of Childhood Experiences and Their Infants' Security of Attachment'. *Journal of the American Psychoanalytic Association,* Vol. 41, 957–989.

Fraiberg, S., Adelson, E. & Shapiro, V. (1975) 'Ghosts in the Nursery: A Psychoanalytic Approach to the Problem of Impaired Infant-Mother Relationships'. *Journal of the American Academy of Child Psychiatry,* Vol. 14, 387–422.

Freud, S. (1940) 'An Outline of Psycho-analysis'. In Strachey, S., Freud, A., Strachey, A. and Tyson, A. (Eds), *The Complete Psychological Works of Sigmund Freud.* London: Hogarth Press.

George, C., Kaplan, N. & Main, M. (1985) *Adult Attachment Interview.* Unpublished manuscript, Department of Psychology, Berkeley, University of California.

Glass, N. (2003) *Sure Start 5 Years On: The Early Years of the Early Years Programme.* Unpublished lecture. City University of London.

Haft, W. L. & Slade, A. (1989) 'Affect Attunement and Maternal Attachment: A Pilot Study'. *Infant Mental Health Journal,* Vol. 10, 157–172.

Hollows, A. (1994) 'Who Are They?' *Community Care*, 30 June, Supplement, 2.

Holmes, J. (1993) *John Bowlby and Attachment Theory*. London: Routledge.

Laevers, F. (1997) A *Process Oriented Child Monitoring System for Young Children*. Leuven: Centre for Experiential Education, University of Leuven.

Lieberman, A. F. & Zeanah, C. H. (1999) 'Contributions of Attachment Theory to Infant-Parent Psychotherapy and Other Interventions with Infants and Young Children'. In Cassidy, J. & Shaver, P. (Eds), *Handbook of Attachment* (555–574). London: The Guilford Press.

Main, M. & Goldwyn, R. (1998) *Adult Attachment Scoring and Classification System*. Unpublished manuscript, Department of Psychology, Berkeley, University of California.

Main, M., Kaplan, N. & Cassidy, J. (1985) 'Security in Infancy, Childhood and Adulthood: A Move to the Level of Representation'. Monographs of the Society for Research in Child Development. 50 (1–2, Serial No, 209) 66–104.

Malaguzzi, L. (1993) 'For an Education Based on Relationships'. *Young Children*, Vol. 11, 9–13.

Manning-Morton, J. & Thorp, M. (2001) *Key Times a Framework for Developing High Quality Provision for Children Under 3 Years Old*. Obtainable from University of North London / Camden LEA.

OECD (2003) Learning for Tomorrow's World. Pisa Study [online]. Available from http://www.oecd.org.

Pastor, D. (1981) 'The Quality of Mother-Infant Attachment and its Relationship to Toddlers' Initial Sociability with Peers'. *Developmental Psychology*, Vol. 17, 326–335.

Shaw, J. (1991) *An Investigation of Parents' Conception of Development in Light of the Dialogue with a Community Teacher*. Unpublished, PhD Thesis, University of Newcastle upon Tyne.

Sroufe, L. A. (1983) 'Infant-Caregiver Attachment and Patterns of Adaptation in PreSchool: The Roots of Maladaptation and Competence'. In Perlmutter, M. (Ed.), *Minnesota Symposium in Child Psychology* (41–81). Hillsdale, NJ: Erlbaum.

Sroufe, L. A. (1988) 'The Role of Infant-Caregiver Attachment in Development'. In Belsky, J. & Nezworski, T. (Eds), *Clinical Implications of Attachment* (18–38). Hillsdale, NJ: Erlbaum.

Steele, H. (2002) 'State of the Art: Attachment'. *The Psychologist*, Vol. 15, 518–522.

Steele, H. & Steele, M. (1998) 'Attachment and Psychoanalysis: Time for a Reunion'. *Social Development*, Vol. 7, 92–119.

van Ijzendoorn, M. H., Juffer, F. & Duyvesteyn, M.G.C. (1995) 'Breaking the Intergenerational Cycle of Insecure Attachment: A Review of the Effects of Attachment-Based Interventions on Maternal Sensitivity and Infant Security'. *Journal of Child Psychology and Psychiatry*, Vol. 36, 225–248.

Whalley, M. & the Pen Green Centre Team (2007) *Involving Parents in Their Children's Learning* (2nd Edition). London: Paul Chapman.

Chapter 4

Polyvocal ethnography
Making sense of practices

Cath Arnold and Carmel Brennan

Introduction

This chapter explains polyvocal ethnography as a research methodology and briefly describes its use in two small-scale research projects. The first project on polyvocal ethnography as a means of developing inter-cultural understanding of pedagogy and practice subsequently informed the second project, 'Making Children's Learning Visible', aimed at developing and enriching the reflective practice of teachers. The first research study explored similarities and differences in pedagogical practice between two pre-school settings, one in Ireland and one in England. While the project began with a focus on identifying and sharing 'best' practice, it evolved into engagement with a more critical analysis of pedagogical practice as the researchers were encouraged to question the cultural agendas embedded in the practices and theories of both groups of practitioners. It was a small-scale study that used the polyvocal ethnographic approach (Tobin, Wu & Davidson, 1989) in the following way. Two local 'practitioner' researchers, one from the Pen Green Centre for Children and Families (Cath Arnold [CA]) and the other from the Irish Preschool Playgroup Association (IPPA), now Early Childhood Ireland (Carmel Brennan [CB]), worked with the staff in an Irish (CB) and an English setting (CA). CA worked in Pen Green, within a disadvantaged community in England. CB engaged with a community playgroup in a disadvantaged suburban Dublin area. Each researcher organised the production of two videoed vignettes of practice, one that profiled an adult engaging with a child and one of children engaging with each other. Following Tobin et al. (1989), they then used the video vignettes to stimulate discussion with the practitioners in both settings and to gather data from and between settings.

What is 'polyvocal ethnography'?

To begin with, ethnography is a qualitative research approach in which the aim is to provide a rich and detailed description of the life, practices and values of a group of people. Because ethnography strives to gain insight into why people do what they do, the ethnographer not only closely observes but also seeks explanation. Denzin (1989: 83) tells us 'It goes beyond mere fact and surface appearances. It presents detail, context, emotion and the webs of social relationships that join persons to one another'. In capturing lives as they are lived, ethnography aims to allow the insider view to emerge so that the reader can also interpret what is happening. Polyvocal ethnography introduces another dimension. It aims to share the observed experience with others, particularly the research participants, and to give them a voice in how events are interpreted. It wants to allow for different perspectives – for more than one 'truth'. The use of video supports this because viewers can see what is happening as opposed to hearing a second-hand account.

The methodology is largely informed by Tobin and colleagues (1989) and their study of 'Pre-school in Three Cultures'. Their approach has been much acclaimed in enabling workers to reveal to themselves, and to others, the values underpinning their work with children and to reflect on and to be critical of their own practice (Tobin et al., 1989). They described their study as a 'cross-cultural comparison' of American, Japanese and Chinese pre-school practice. The team made videos of a typical day in an early childhood setting in each of the three countries. The video was then edited and shown to groups of workers in the 'home' country to establish typicality before being shown to workers in the other two countries. Their aim was to 'facilitate a dialogue between insiders and outsiders, practitioners and researchers', a coming together of a broad range of voices (Tobin et al., 1989: 4). The video itself is not the data but rather the cue that stimulates discussion. The response of the video-observers is the data, and this was analysed by Tobin and his colleagues to show how our perspectives and our image of the child is informed by our culture. Originally there was no intention to use the video material as more than a stimulation to dialogue. However, video is powerful, and despite its grainy nature, many scholars are keen to view some of that original material. With that in mind, the study has been revisited and a video is available of some of the original material and also of the newer material (Tobin, Hsueh & Karasawa, 2009). This allows a comparison both between countries and of change over time.

In this chapter we describe the two small-scale studies in which we drew on the method used by Tobin et al. (1989) to facilitate reflection and discussion of practice.

Study one: Methods and techniques

A researcher in England in partnership with a researcher in Ireland carried out the first study. Each researcher worked with a small team of staff from a setting in their own country. We wanted to video practice in the settings and to generate discussion that would give us insight into the practices and thinking of the practitioners. Our aim was not to compare in an evaluative way but to identify differences and to understand the thinking and values behind the different practices. We were interested in cultural differences but did not expect practice in the two settings to be significantly different as they were both English speaking and belonged to very similar communities of practice (the early years). This is a community that has established much shared practice and language in the Western world.

We looked for definitions of 'culture' and defined it as a system of social relationships, concepts and symbols through which people 'communicate, perpetuate and develop their knowledge about and attitudes towards life' (Geertz, 1973) and thereby 'arrive at satisfactory ways of acting in given contexts' (Bruner, 1986). As the work of Tobin et al. (1989) shows, we live and think within culture, and we are not aware of differences and other perspectives unless we make the effort to see things from another perspective.

Tobin is clear that when he films, he is not looking for the mundane; he intends to be provocative. We, however, were only interested in sharing some examples of practice. We did not set out to be provocative. We focussed on just two aspects: first, adult/child interactions, and second, child/child interactions. Workers in the two settings volunteered to take part. Parents gave their written consent for their children to be involved. Workers ensured that children were comfortable with being filmed. Any analysis was shared with workers on an ongoing basis. Rather than filming 'a day in the life of . . .' we asked the teams to select two five-minute clips, one of an adult and child and a second of a child interacting with other children. These were used, first with the 'insiders', to stimulate discussions of practice, then the videos were swapped and we reviewed each other's episodes.

An interesting aspect was how we supported the two small groups of workers to engage in a discussion of their practice. The English group, who were considered to be highly trained professional workers, had a number of demands on their time, and, although they chose to take part, this was just one more thing to fit in. The English researcher asked the group of workers what would help. Their response was, 'a room booked with tea and coffee made and the computer/TV set up ready to roll as soon as we get together'. This worked, and with their permission, the discussions were recorded using a digital sound recorder. The recording proved to be a very important tool in reflecting on the discussions. This group of workers really appreciated the chance to reflect on practice with a focus. The group of workers were experienced in using video, so they filmed and selected the clips to be viewed for the study. We held a series of meetings in order to view the four video clips (two from the English setting and two from the Irish setting). Each meeting was held at the end of the day and lasted just 30 minutes. The researcher cleared up the dirty cups afterwards so that the team could return to any other duties in the setting, e.g. planning. There was a feeling of recapturing something lost because of other demands. Once some workers got over seeing themselves on film, they were highly reflective.

The Irish group facilitated morning and afternoon playgroup sessions and could not be released from their work for meetings. They organised three extended lunch breaks over a month and then gave up their lunchtime so that they could meet with the researcher. This group had little experience of using video, so the Irish researcher did the filming and the group of workers selected two five-minute clips to be used in the study. The researcher was also able to make a short film to show parents about practice in the setting, which was greatly appreciated. This group of practitioners, while holding the necessary qualifications, tended to draw more on their extensive experience as parents rather than on their professional training during discussions. Again, the discussions were recorded, and this allowed us to revisit elements of the discussions as we proceeded.

Facilitating or guiding the discussion?

As partners in the research process, we, the researchers, were aware of the power dynamics between us and between each of us and the groups of workers, and we wanted to share both power and participation. This process was only useful if it uncovered some 'taken-for-granted' assumptions. Our hunch was that the groups would look to us for answers and information. We felt sure that we could discover more in dialogue with them. As Freire points out, when thinking about 'problem-posing education', 'The students – no longer docile listeners – are now critical co-investigators in dialogue with the teacher. The teacher . . . re-considers her earlier considerations as the students express their own' (1996: 62). The English researcher was explicit with the group about her role as 'facilitator' and told them right at the beginning that she was going to try not to talk too much or dominate with her views. This helped the discussion and meant that when there was silence, different people broke that silence at different times, and what happened at those times also became part of the discussion.

The Irish researcher saw her role as facilitating the discussion and helping the group to stay focussed on the video episodes. What is happening here? What is good about the interactions? What are the problems? – these were the kind of questions she posed to guide the discussion. Again, she wanted the views of the practitioners, which she summarised at intervals in order to ensure their agreement with what she was documenting.

We each needed to 'tune in to' the group we were working with and to hear and represent their voices authentically, so we checked back with them in order to confirm each group's meaning.

Ethical considerations

We needed to make sure that we were behaving ethically at all times. It was comparatively easy to gain written permissions to embark on the study from workers and parents and from the children when they were filmed. It was important to us, as researchers, that the workers opted in to the study and knew that they could opt out at any time. They also knew that we would not use information unless they agreed to it being used for a particular purpose. If we were aware of any sensitivity, we checked back with individual workers. However, we were under no delusions about the balance of power and realised that it took courage for workers to request changes. We had to make sure that both workers and children benefitted from the process. Tobin and Davidson critiqued their own method in a 1990 paper and found that workers were not always happy about how they were represented in written form and also that sometimes decisions about taking part were made on their behalf (Tobin & Davidson, 1990). We tried to make sure that the people participating made the decisions about taking part and about how they were represented.

What was filmed

1. English film of adult and Polish child playing 'The Billie Goats Gruff' with figures and animals
2. Irish film of adult and child with Down Syndrome playing with colour pegs and boards
3. English film of 'Home Play in the Sky House', a group of children going to bed, having medicine, etc.
4. Irish film of boys dressed up and engaged in 'Superhero Play Fighting'

Both adult/child scenarios involved children with individual needs. We questioned whether the adults felt more useful when interacting with children that might obviously need some special attention.

The discussions

Film 1 was well received by both groups. The practitioner and Polish child were both equally involved in telling and enacting the story, although they did not share a common language. At the same time, both groups noticed another child wanting the adult's attention that she had not noticed in real time. The Polish child, we were informed by our Polish worker, was 'babbling', but when we shared the film with her family, her Dad was quite clear that she was 'pretending to speak English'. This information from home shifted our view of her actions and language considerably, as so often happens when we listen to the knowledge of parents about their own children. This clip elicited a discussion about learning English as an additional language and what is known about that process. In between meetings, as a facilitator, I was able to gather information about learning English as an additional language and to feed the research findings of other writers into the discussion (Olshtan & Horenczyk, 2000).

Film 2 was, again, well received by both groups, with a lot of admiration for the relationship between adult and child. Both groups noticed that the little girl with Down Syndrome was 'teasing' her worker and that teasing was part of their close relationship (Reddy, 2008). Again, a child the adult had not noticed in real time was trying to gain the adult's attention, and this was only picked up on film. In critiquing her own practice, the Irish practitioner noticed that in focussing solely on one child, she had 'excluded' others. She identified that she needed to have a 'looser' neck (Aarts, 2000) so that she could see and respond to more children around her.

The English group found the experiences offered in the Irish adult/child sequence very 'structured' and 'adult-led'. They expressed surprise that the children were 'all doing the same thing' at 'work' time. They talked about their preferred practice of 'offering choices to children in a workshop environment' and building on their schemas and schematic play (Athey, 1990). They saw the provision of choice as a way of sharing power with children and encouraging individual expression and difference. The Irish film seemed to show a much stronger lead by adults in arranging children's activities. There seemed to be little choice for the children at that time of day. The Irish group were less concerned about the kind of activity offered or who led the activity in this particular episode. They enthused about the progress the child had made in terms of communication and trust. They attributed her progress to the adult's relationship with her and the 'fun factor'. When pushed to say more about the engagement between them, time, building trust and the 'fun factor' were reiterated over and over again as the strengths and outcomes of both the teaching and learning. They identified that the little girl was learning to read and understand another person's interactions and to respond knowingly. They explained that they only structured activities at the beginning of each session to help children settle in so that parents could see how focussed and disciplined the children can be. They also thought it prepared children for 'big' school. On reflection, they realised the need to reconsider not the structure, but the activities, and to engage the children in more challenging tasks.

This gave rise to questions about choice. Should children have choice all the time? Should some activities be adult led? It was interesting to see how the child in this particular episode skilfully managed to divert the adult from the task and lure her towards fun. Could it be that children learn to manage other people and their agendas in these situations? Is this important learning? Could it be that giving children endless free choice robs them of opportunities to resist and/or manage control? These questions generated much debate and strong feelings.

Film 3 was typical of the role play of 2, 3 and 4 year olds. All were agreed on this. There was one tense moment when a child corrected the adult filming because it seemed she had got his name wrong, but it turned out that he wanted to be called 'Ben', the character he was playing. He also wanted to bring in a more aggressive storyline but was discouraged from doing this by the worker, demonstrating not complete 'choice' but a subtle form of control during which the group play was protected by diverting 'Ben' to another area where he could continue his play. The Irish group felt they needed to know more about the characters involved to comment on this diversion strategy, but they wondered how the children might have managed the intrusion, if allowed.

Film 4 elicited the most discussion in both groups, with a focus on gender differences; how to facilitate safe rough-and-tumble play and what different observers might think about children in settings being allowed to play fight. As female workers, we often find it difficult to understand boys' play when we have not had those experiences ourselves.

This episode led to the most discussion on the image of the child. On a previous visit to Pen Green, the Irish group were impressed with how quiet and focussed on their activities the children were during their visit. They now noted that, in contrast, their children, particularly these boys playing superheroes, were quite 'wild' and energetic, and they liked that 'wildness'. 'When we went to Pen Green – they were so busy, all the children doing their own thing – when we look at that now . . . there's so much more interaction between the children – the children in Pen Green were more focussed on their own activities – so calm and relaxed – but there's so much interaction between the three there – they're wild . . . (she laughed) but not really'. Again they talked about the 'fun factor', the pleasure of shared pretence and the companionship. They wanted to show the video to parents so that they could see how well the boys played together and how cleverly they encouraged one another to engage.

The fact that the Irish group selected the 'Superhero Play Fighting' scenario gave a strong message about what they valued. One worker had helped the children to dress up and encouraged their pretence, calling them by their pretend names and feigning fear and shock and horror when they showed their pretend fierceness. The adults were pleased with the play they had facilitated.

The Irish group repeatedly mentioned relationships and the 'fun factor' when thinking about what the children were gaining from their play, whereas the English group were more analytical, bringing in schema theory and trying to work out which concepts children were developing. What does this tell us about what each group sees as the role of early childhood education and about the kind of development we are trying to promote? Is one more valuable than the other? These questions are worth reflecting on because they lead us to question our values and what we see as children's rights.

We watched each piece of film more than once and each time noticed more, so allowing time to view and re-view is important (Jordan & Henderson, 1995; Brennan, 2009).

Researchers' discussions

As researchers, we were looking for possible conflicts in the views and practices of practitioners and trying to be open to understanding the differences. We had to deal with the conflict in our own views, and that was often challenging and troubling. We not only discussed the conflict, we felt it and were anxious about it. Most of the time, we were conversing through email, so we were not able to see each other's reaction to our latest thinking. When we did meet up, we each seemed to want to convince the other that our way was best. Coming to appreciate that the conflict was good and helpful to us in questioning our own beliefs and teachings was a journey that required sustained effort.

On reflection, we describe this journey as having three stages. In the first stage, we were in 'teaching' mode, which unintentionally positioned one setting as teacher and the other as learner and where we alternated as teachers and learners ourselves. We moved to 'narrative' mode, where each setting and researcher narrated and reflected on their own setting's practice but without necessarily engaging with the perspective of the other. Finally, we engaged with 'argumentation' mode (Shotter, 1993), where we began to look for conflicts and to defend differences. We recognised the need to challenge, as Moss (2007: 231) says, 'taken-for-granted truths'. We have learned that this can be an uncomfortable and uncertain place, but it is also a place where, with trust and commitment, conflict can occur and differences can be explored.

Other lessons

We have also learned lessons about the research methodology and about pedagogy. We summarise them here:

- The polyvocal ethnographic approach acted as a powerful reflection tool. Practitioners could see what was happening in another setting and get feedback from others about their own practice. They were invited to explain their practices and argue their case. Emerging from this process, they can choose what they continue to value and what they want to change. As researchers and practitioners, it offered the opportunity to share experiences and learn from one another.
- Pedagogy is a complex and uncertain science. Living with uncertainty, dealing with dilemmas and engaging in reflection is essential to the work of the pedagogue and practitioner researcher. This research gave us an opportunity and a way of doing this.
- We need to learn to argue. In argumentation mode, we have a responsibility to question rather than accept. We have to value and defend difference. Our experiences and reflections can inform one another's thinking – they are not the only way of thinking about things and not the only truth.
- In presenting their practice for critique, the pedagogues in both participating services in this research took brave steps, the Pen Green staff no less than the Community Playgroup staff in Dublin. They have taken reflective practice to a new level. They have helped us to question our practice and our image of the child. We need to learn to respect and listen to not only children but to each other as educators.
- In the process of this practitioner research, we realised that there is not 'one way' of providing for children in early childhood settings. The way we see and understand children is different, and what we want for our children is different. Whilst we all argued that we want children to be respected and powerful and to reach their potential as learners and citizens, our 'image' of the child was subtly different.

This became the starting point in study two the following year.

Study two: Methods and techniques

This study was carried out in Northamptonshire and involved workers, children and families from seven nursery schools. The study was designed to encourage reflection and action through collaboration across the schools. The technique drew again on Tobin's method of using video as a tool to stimulate multi-vocal dialogue. An innovation was for each staff group to begin the process by discussing and articulating the 'image of the child' they were trying to promote in their setting by considering the shared values of the staff group and parents. Following on from this discussion, staff identified the pedagogical approaches that supported their image of the child. This data provided some starting points for discussion, when viewing video from their own and a partner's setting.

In this instance staff were trained to lead the project in their own setting. Drawing on what we had learned during study one and from other similar studies, we put on two days of initial training at the Pen Green Research Base and supported the project with visits and meetings with the leaders. During the two-day training, workers discussed the 'image of the child' that they were currently promoting in their setting and pedagogical approaches and frameworks for discussing pedagogy. They practised gathering video sequences of each other and reflected on video material of adults and children, as well as video of children in nursery settings. The local authority funded the project in order to increase reflection and to improve practice in settings. This occurred at a time when local authorities were beginning to consider how to 'narrow the gap' between the most and least advantaged in our society.

METHOD

Beginning by discussing the 'image of the child' held by workers in each of the seven settings was a new way of approaching this polyvocal dialogue. We hoped that encouraging workers to state their beliefs about children and what they wanted for children would

1. convey the message that differences are expected and accepted and that we do not expect everyone to hold a universal view of what is good for young children; and
2. encourage workers to think deeply about why they do what they do and surface some of their 'taken for granted' ideas about pedagogical approaches.

After selecting a child or children (who lived in the 20% most disadvantaged areas served by their setting) to film for their two 5-minute video sequences, the discussion was inevitably about using differentiated pedagogical approaches that might benefit all children, including those considered to be at a disadvantage.

Narrowing the gap

In the UK, both government and early childhood workers were becoming increasingly aware of the gap in achievement between our most and least advantaged children and families (Feinstein, 2003). Since 1997, through a range of initiatives, including the Sure Start Project and Children's Centres, the government has focused on trying to narrow that gap (Department for Children, Schools and Families [DCSF], 2008a; Department for Education [DfE], 2010). The focus of this study was on stimulating dialogue among workers about the differentiated pedagogical approaches that we currently use or can adopt in order to support *all* children's development and learning more effectively. We asked workers to focus on the 20% most vulnerable children and families in each setting. Our local authority was interested in funding research that would 'promote equality' and 'help the poor' by challenging workers to consider their pedagogical approaches (Holman, 1987: 699).

Following the training, the lead people met with their teams and discussed and articulated the 'image of the child' that each team agreed they were promoting in their setting. They also 'teased out' together the pedagogical approaches that supported their 'image of the child'. Workers in each setting then filmed and selected two 5-minute video sequences, first, of a child alone or children engaging with each other, and second, of an adult engaging with a child or children. The workers chose as their focus children from the 20% most disadvantaged using their setting. In order to select the children, workers used either the categories in the 'Together for Children Toolkit' produced by the DCSF in January 2007 (DCSF, 2007) or the categories used in the 'Performance Management Update for Sure Start Children's Centres' published in July 2008 (DCSF, 2008b). Indicators of disadvantage included 'being a lone parent', 'living in poverty' and 'being from a minority ethnic community' (DCSF, 2007: 4). Drawing on the technique used by Tobin and others (1989), the video sequences were viewed by the staff team ('insiders') and then swapped with a buddy setting ('outsiders') to stimulate dialogue about pedagogical approaches and underpinning beliefs. The data consisted of those discussions. The lead people met up for one day after going through this whole process.

Although members of the Pen Green research team could not be available for all the resulting discussions about pedagogy and practice, we attended many of those meetings. We needed to use our skills as facilitators to encourage workers to be more critical and to voice any reservations about what they were seeing and feeling. We were aware that our andragogical approach could make a difference to what they were able to voice and that we could be simultaneously studying our role in facilitating their learning. One setting filmed their discussions and most of the others sound recorded theirs, so the rich data gathered was available to be analysed by the participants and the research team.

A critique of our approach

Most leaders of the project reported that everyone in their setting seemed to enjoy discussing their 'image of the child'. In some settings workers involved parents and governors in the process. When the Heads were interviewed, several expressed the view that they and their staff had found this process affirming and positive. Moving on from their 'image of the child' to discuss the pedagogy they used to support their image of the child was also reported as being quite affirming.

What was more challenging for workers was choosing a child or children from the 20% most disadvantaged as the focus of their filming. Most workers wanted to be honest with parents about why their child was the focus but were worried about expressing this idea about disadvantage to the parents. Many workers had worked really hard at not seeing children and families within a deficit framework of thinking and celebrating what children can do rather than what they cannot as yet do (Athey, 1990), and this approach seemed to some workers to be going against the idea of and belief in the 'competent child and family' (Rinaldi, 2006). However, we discussed that people are in circumstances of disadvantage and also that we need to demonstrate that we are including all children and that disadvantage does not necessarily determine what will happen to a child within the education system. In future studies, it would help to include discussions of this issue during the initial training and perhaps practise with each other different ways of approaching what workers perceive as these more difficult conversations with parents.

In some settings, using video and transferring film onto DVD or memory stick was a major barrier to overcome when carrying out the study. A few workers relished the challenge and learned a great deal from the process. In some settings, the workers did the filming but handed over the editing process to an in-house Information and Communications Technology (ICT) expert.

Everyone agreed that watching video stimulated dialogue and that those discussions about pedagogy continued and extended towards other workers in the setting. There seemed to be something very immediate and 'live' about watching oneself or colleagues on video. Judgements could be suspended, questions could be asked and a rationale could be given. This idea of 'holding the question of meaning open', conceptualised by Jensen (2009), seemed significant to most participants.

In most cases, workers have gained an insight into the use of video, and many intend to continue using video, especially in peer-to-peer observations. The process for some was very uncomfortable, but as one worker commented, 'We need to get over seeing and hearing ourselves and do it more regularly in order to benefit from the learning this process provides'.

Findings

Our approach to making sense of the data was to read and discuss all transcribed discussions, as a research team, and to dialogue with participants and with each other about the themes we could draw from the data. These themes are listed under the headings that follow. It is important to note that the subtle changes in pedagogy and related learning continued well beyond that year. We limited our discussions to Heads of the nurseries and leaders of the project, who, in some cases, were the same people. So, although we have data on the discussions in each staff group, our partners in dialogue, in this instance, were the co-leaders of the project.

Leadership issues

We identified across the data a resistance and reluctance by workers in some settings to engage in the process of learning through critiquing practice. Staff seemed unsure about taking risks and moving outside of a safe and secure comfort zone. It was difficult for some leaders of the project to 'galvanise others into action'. One Head described 'an emotional day' when she and her co-leader had to start at the beginning and reassure workers that nothing awful was going to happen and that they would survive and learn from this process. She found that she needed to 'contain' workers' anxieties about what would happen (Bion, 1962).

Some leaders of the project struggled with leading for what felt like the first time. One worker described the role as having 'high stakes' and 'trying to be someone else'. She felt quite 'isolated'. Another leader found the project 'difficult to put across'. She found that there was a feeling of 'please join us' for a project. In terms of future actions, the leaders, who were not Heads, and did not feel confident, realised that *they needed the Head to be the driver, even in setting deadlines and strongly supporting them.* One Head found that staff 'deferred' to her during the video discussion, even though she was not leading this project. This raised questions about real and perceived hierarchical structures in organisations and how to shift those structures. However, in other settings workers reported on a 'more positive leadership experience' and that the leader of the project felt 'empowered'.

Leading the discussions with each staff group provided data on how to effectively lead a discussion without dominating or telling participants what to say and how to think. As researchers and leaders of the project, we are continuing to reflect on the amount and nature of support and challenge that we offered others and how that was received by them. Often, either the researcher or the Head was expected to 'lead' the discussion, or there was some discomfort when there were silences.

Language used both by the leaders and workers sometimes revealed thinking, so phrases like 'getting staff on board' and 'getting parents on board' revealed whose project this was.

There was a real discomfort with describing vulnerability, particularly to those people who were considered to be disadvantaged. Each setting seemed to have a set of words in common use to describe children who are vulnerable in some way. When the leaders met up, we noticed that some people adopted the other setting's words in order to communicate their ideas about individual children. We think that it would be really *helpful for the use of language to be up for discussion* and that researchers and Heads could facilitate those sorts of discussions.

Pedagogy

Our intention was to stimulate discussion about pedagogy, so a common theme was to do with insights about pedagogical approaches. Holding the camera meant that some workers were less likely to intervene and more likely to watch carefully when children got into conflict. Workers were surprised to discover that *some children were capable of resolving conflicts and that standing back*, rather than 'nipping things in the bud', *gave children a chance to learn how to resolve conflicts.*

One worker, who felt she talked too early during an interaction with a child on video, talked about 'the pause' and the 'tension' that created in her. It seemed to be important to experience and to acknowledge that tension. It may be helpful for other workers to reflect on how pausing before intervening feels for them. Similarly, when Heads paused and waited during staff discussions, this too caused tension.

Method

One barrier to fully participating for some workers was the ICT challenges. In some cases a lot of time was spent trying to solve these, sometimes to the detriment of the project. Our impression from a few workers was that they were all trying to come up with a perfect product. Within our experience, as long as you can point and switch on a camera, you can engage in dialogue with video. In this project, they did have the extra challenge of making a copy to share with their buddy. People tackled this in different ways, some relishing the challenge of learning how to do this and others relying on so-called experts. It was important if group discussions involved more than three or four people to show the film on a large screen. Sometimes this was possible. Most of the settings have a Smartboard for the children to use, but sometimes the quality or lighting interfered with being able to view anything in detail, and the detail was a necessary part of this method.

Most participants could see the benefits of a dialogue using video, especially for peer-to-peer observations. One worker commented, 'To see what other people see is very striking'. In one instance, a practitioner researcher described herself as being 'on edge' as she could identify with a worker desperately trying to support a child who was quite needy and not very interested in doing what she was suggesting and offering. This shows the power of video in helping us to draw on our own earlier experiences when viewing similar scenarios. With regard to peer-to-peer observations, *power could be more equally shared* than when one worker observes, notes down and makes judgements about the performance of another worker. Some settings have made a plan to introduce this technique in the near future.

Image of the child

We received most of the positive feedback from leaders about this part of the process. Thinking about and articulating their image of the child in each setting brought staff (and governors and parents, in some cases) together. It was quite a simple way of sharing pedagogy without using the word 'pedagogy', which some leaders of the project felt might be off putting to workers.

When we interviewed the Heads, there was a strong theme of 'togetherness', wanting to keep people together and unified in some way. People used phrases like 'singing from the same hymn sheet'. The Heads were keen to have a strong setting ethos, which was shared and owned by everyone working in their setting.

On reflection, as a research team, we realised that this idea might result in wanting a 'conforming child'. One worker commented that in her setting they were promoting this idea of a 'feisty child', but what about a 'shy and quiet child'? Would that child not be equally valued by workers? Were we moving away from the idea of difference as strength?

Another question raised in the research team was about whose voices were heard when discussing the image of the child. We have all been in group situations where one or two voices dominate and others go unheard. How could the newest worker challenge the view of the head teacher?

Caution needs to be used with regard to 'standardising' the image of the child in a setting. It is critical for Heads to find ways that all voices are heard and acknowledged in staff discussions. We would not see the image of the child as static but *part of a dynamic ongoing staff discussion, which is constantly revisited and open to challenge.*

Language used

We began to consider the language used in all of our discussions, and this is a fascinating part of the study that will require more time, attention and discussion. However, we can already see the huge significance of the language we all use during our discussions. Writers on Bakhtin, who is a language theorist, comment,

> Language carries as part of its nature the viewpoints, assumptions, experiences of its speakers, and it does this because it is personally and socially situated, not an abstract system . . . It is clear, then, that Bakhtin believes that one can think only what one's language allows one to think. (Brock University, 2013).

We have already noticed instances where we and others have led the discussion and defined the content by the language used, particularly professional language; for example, an initial comment by a researcher on schemas observed resulted in an ongoing discussion about children's schemas and how to support and extend them. This was worthwhile but resulted in everyone following a researcher's interest rather than creating the space for the different interests that may have emerged from the group.

The language in use in each setting to describe vulnerability in children varied enormously. All participants, including the researchers, seemed to struggle to find the right words to respectfully acknowledge the difficulties of individual children and families. Words like 'strong-willed' and 'determined' seemed to convey something of those difficulties along with different perceptions of what a 'challenging' child or 'challenging' behaviour might mean. *Workers seemed to be struggling to describe a whole situation, including their feelings about individual children.* This study seemed to bring the necessity of developing and discussing respectful language to the fore.

In contrast, much of the language generally used in the early years field with children and in discussions is extremely positive and affirming. We are beginning to question and to think about the almost dominant use of positivity in discourse within the early years field. Across the data we have gathered, we have noticed an avoidance of any behaviour or attribute that might take people anywhere they consider less positive. It may be a false dualism to consider positive language versus authenticity, but there does seem to be a sort of 'sanitising' taking place. If we cannot express and talk about the unkind things that children do as well as the nice things they do, then do we pretend that the whole range of behaviours does not exist?

Bringing things up to the present

These two small studies carried out in 2008–2010 paved the way for conceptualising a project titled 'Making Children's Learning Visible' (MCLV), which local authorities and settings can engage in. The programme has four strands:

- establishing the 'Image of the Child' within a staff team, which includes selecting and discussing a video clip of that image as a team and reflecting on the pedagogy that supports this image;
- identifying the most vulnerable children in a setting and reflecting on the differentiated pedagogy needed to support these children;
- using video to record peer observations, which can support team members to reflect together on the pedagogy in the setting and how effectively workers are supporting children's learning; and
- making assessment judgements with parents and discussing children's progress and how each child can be most effectively supported at home and in the setting. These assessments are displayed on individual graphs to aid the discussion, and parents and workers use them to share their understanding of the child with other professionals. They are also used by parents and workers at transition to support dialogue about how to effectively engage the child in their learning.

References

Aarts, M. (2000) *Marte Meo: Basic Manual*. Harderwijk: Aarts Productions.

Athey, C. (1990) *Extending Thought in Young Children: A Parent Teacher Partnership* (1st Edition). London: Paul Chapman.

Bion, W. (1962) *Learning Through Experience*. London: Heinemann.

Brennan, C. (2009) *Making Children's Learning Visible*. Symposium V9 at the 19th European Early Childhood Education Research Association Annual Conference, *Diversity*. Strasbourg, 28 August. Contribution to a post-presentation discussion in the symposium.

Brock University (2013) *Department of English Language and Literature* [online]. Brock University, St Catherines, Ontario. Available from: http://www.brocku.ca/english/courses/4F70/bakhtin.php [Accessed 15 January 2013]

Bruner, J. (1986) *Actual Minds, Possible Worlds*. Boston: Harvard University Press.

DCSF (2007) Together for Children. *Toolkit for Reaching Priority and Excluded Families*. www.tda.gov.uk [accessed 04.02.13]

DCSF (2008a) *Narrowing the Gap*. London: Department for Children, Schools and Families.

DCSF (2008b) *Performance Management Update for Sure Start Children's Centres*. London: Department for Children, Families and Schools.

Denzin, N. K. (1989) *The Research Act: A Theoretical Introduction to Sociological Methods* (3rd Edition). Englewood Cliffs, NJ: Prentice Hall.

DfE (2010) *The Single Equality Scheme*. London: Department of Education.

Feinstein, L. (2003) 'Inequality in Early Cognitive Development of British Children in the 1970 Cohort'. *Economica*, Vol. 70, No. 227, 73–97.

Freire, P. (1996) *The Pedagogy of the Oppressed*. London: Penguin.

Geertz, C. (1973) *The Interpretation of Cultures: Selected Essays*. New York: Basic Books.

Holman, B. (1987) 'Research from the Underside'. *British Journal of Social Work*, Vol. 17, 669–683.

Jensen, J. (2009) Meeting at the Pen Green Research Base, Corby, Northants.

Jordan, B. & Henderson, A. (1995) 'Interaction Analysis: Foundations and Practice'. *The Journal of the Learning Sciences*, Vol. 4, No. 1, 39–103.

Moss, P. (2007) 'Meetings Across the Paradigmatic Divide'. *Educational Philosophy and Theory*, Vol. 39, 229–245.

Olshtan, E. & Horenczyk, G. (Eds) (2000) *Language, Identity and Immigration*. Jerusalem: The Hebrew University Magnus Press.

Reddy, V. (2008) *How Infants Know Minds*. London: Harvard University Press.

Rinaldi, C. (2006) *In Dialogue with Reggio Emilia: Listening, Researching and Learning*. London: Routledge.

Shotter, J. (1993) *Cultural Politics of Everyday Life*. Milton Keynes, England: Open University.

Tobin, J.J. & Davidson, D. (1990) 'The Ethics of Polyvocal Ethnography: Empowering vs. Textualising Children and Teachers'. *Qualitative Studies in Education*, Vol. 3, No. 3, 271–283.

Tobin, J.J., Wu, D. & Davidson, D. (1989) *Preschool in Three Cultures*. New Haven, CT: Yale University Press.

Tobin, J., Hsueh, Y. & Karasawa, M. (2009) *Preschool in Three Cultures Revisited*. Chicago: University of Chicago Press.

Chapter 5

Making Children's Learning Visible

Uncovering the curriculum in the child

Kate Hayward and Eddie McKinnon

Making Children's Learning Visible (MCLV) is a pedagogical approach that has grown over several phases of professional development work with early years settings and schools. Initially MCLV was a co-constructed research project with nursery schools designed to show that they were 'making a difference' to outcomes for children and families and 'narrowing the gap'. The project's underpinning methodology, 'polyvocal ethnography', originated in the work of Tobin et al. (1989, 2009) and was further developed by Taylor (2007) and Arnold and Brennan (2008, 2013; see Chapter 4 by Arnold and Brennan).

Polyvocal ethnography means 'many voices' discussing what children and workers are doing. It is an approach that enables practitioners to 'make sense' of their practice through the collective identification of what constitutes the 'image of the child' in their setting and the viewing of selected video clips of pedagogical interactions between children and themselves. The discussions generated by the clips support deeper reflection on practice. These reflections, alongside assessment judgements of each child in dialogue with parents, promote the differentiation of pedagogy so that the specific learning needs of children can be met more effectively, thereby 'making children's learning visible'.

Practitioners are supported in focusing on outcomes for children and families by completing the following steps:

- Generating their 'image of the child' through a negotiation exercise in which all members of staff write down what they believe are the characteristics they are supporting in children and discuss and debate these ideas to form an agreed 'image of the child' for their setting.
- Identifying the vulnerable children in their setting in relation to national data on vulnerable groups (Together for Children, 2009) and their own reflections on vulnerability in their context.
- Reflecting on their own pedagogy through selecting and reviewing video clips from their own practice to illustrate this 'image of the child'. These clips can then be shared with a partner setting in the project, which stimulates discussion.
- Using a new assessment data gathering process (the Pen Green MCLV software package, MCLV Course Materials Training Pack; Pen Green Research

Base [PGRB], 2012a) that allows them to look at, and evidence, the progress of individual children at three times in the year. They are also able to look at cohort data on children within each academic year and to use this data to inform their practice and their discussions with other professionals and parents when the child moves on to another setting or class.

- Reflecting on the effectiveness and differentiation of their pedagogical interactions through peer observations using video to raise questions about the nature of pedagogical support for children with different learning needs.

The MCLV methodology has been used successfully in nursery schools, children's centres, and in a combined primary school and children's centre, enabling pedagogical reflection across all year groups. MCLV has also been used in the Early Years Teaching Centres project (PGRB, 2012b; Whalley & Riddell, 2013) as a tool for gathering data on outcomes for children and to focus staff teams on the evaluation of early intervention.

In this chapter we will outline two case studies. One detailing the use of MCLV at Pen Green and one illustrating how MCLV was used effectively in a combined primary school and children's centre.

Case study I: MCLV at Pen Green

Developing the Pen Green 'Image of the Child'

Following the use of 'polyvocal ethnography' in a project with a setting in Ireland (see Chapter 4 by Arnold and Brennan), Pen Green Nursery workers were well placed to consider their 'image of the child'. This language was familiar to staff through the work of Loris Malaguzzi in Reggio Emilia (1993:9), which challenges the deficit view of children that can be created by detailing what they cannot do. He instead introduces pedagogues to the 'hundred languages of children', seeing children as active agents in their learning and as capable and competent learners (Edwards et al., 1998). The Pen Green Curriculum Document, written in 1983, states that at Pen Green we encourage children

- to feel strong
- to feel in control
- to feel able to question
- to feel able to choose.

The Pen Green 'image of the child' has been carefully considered over the years, and this thinking has informed our discussions about our beliefs and values in relation to how children learn and how we can best support them.

In developing the MCLV methodology, we have supported workers to engage in a negotiation exercise to enable them to consider their 'image of the child'. We encourage teams to devise a 'community learning contract' before they embark on this exercise so that they have negotiated an ethical approach. This involves recording what people think is important about how individuals relate to each other during the task so that everyone has a visible set of 'group rules' that help them to feel safe and supported enough to be able to engage effectively.

The 'Image of the Child' negotiation exercise

The negotiation exercise involves each staff member, on their own, writing down on six index cards six things that they think they are trying to support in children; their 'image of the child'. They then join up in pairs and negotiate which of the twelve statements between them they most value; they agree on six of them and discard the rest. They then join together in a group of four and, in the same way, negotiate down to six cards and statements they all agree on. In this way they are able to come up with a negotiated list of six statements that illustrate the 'image of the child' in the setting.

Pen Green staff revisited their 'image of the child' during a MCLV project completed with the nursery schools in the county. Their statements were that they wanted children to be

- confident and strong
- able to question
- able to choose
- able to assert themselves
- to be empathetic
- to be secure.

The negotiation exercise is used every year now by different teams at the Centre as a means to collaboratively and democratically discuss beliefs and values. It is also a way of ensuring that these discussions are kept alive and involve all staff, including those who may be newly appointed.

Identifying the most vulnerable children

In this methodology the discussions around vulnerability have a dual purpose: to focus on identifying those children who may need the most support, and to enable practitioners to challenge each other and themselves about the language used and judgements made around vulnerability. Initially the Government list of criteria for vulnerable families (Together for Children, 2009) was used to stimulate a focus group discussion on this issue. Practitioners were alarmed at the use of such categories, arguing that there was a clear danger of parents and families being labelled in some way as being 'inadequate' due merely to their circumstances, for example, being a 'lone parent'. Several of the workers at Pen Green were, or had been, lone parents and did not see themselves, nor were seen by others, as having some kind of 'parenting deficit' as a result. However, during discussions it was stressed that descriptors such as 'lone parent' in the guidance were never intended to be pejorative, or support a crude deterministic relationship between membership of one of these groups and negative outcomes. Workers were able to challenge themselves on the provision for some children who may find accessing the learning opportunities at Pen Green more difficult. These included children who spoke a home language other than English, children who had complex lives, children who faced challenges in relating to others or children who had low self-esteem. The focus on vulnerability enabled the team to think about individual children and to raise questions. Was a child more vulnerable when their parents were not involved in their learning? When their dad was not actively involved? When it had not been possible to do the usual three home visits to the family and their worker did not know the family so well?

Selecting a video clip to illustrate the 'Image of the Child'

The team then used their 'image of the child' to select a five-minute video clip to illustrate this image. In the project with the local nursery schools, they were also asked to select a clip illustrating their pedagogy in support of a vulnerable child. This raised many issues. When practitioners think of their 'image of the child', they tend to have in mind the children who Laevers (1997) would describe as acting like 'fish in water' in the setting. It was an additional challenge to select a clip that illustrated a vulnerable child displaying the 'image of the child' characteristics. The Pen Green team selected a clip at first that was so subtle in the pedagogical approach that they thought anyone else watching it would not be able to understand the effectiveness of the approach. This raised a lot of discussion about context and the narrow view a five-minute clip gives of a way of working with vulnerable children. The important factor in this methodology was that it raised a lot of discussion that helped practitioners to reflect on practice.

Reflecting on pedagogy: Watching your own, and another setting's, clips

Pen Green and the other nursery schools in the project swapped video clips with a 'buddy' setting, and the discussion that took place when they were viewed was recorded. Some practitioners felt it was easier to critique their own videos, while others were more stimulated by watching the videos selected by other teams. Many practice issues were raised. The general themes from these discussions were analysed and deconstructed by the groups of practitioners engaged in the project during a study day at Pen Green. Practitioners shared their learning and the practice questions that had been raised, which they were keen to address. The reflection on pedagogy and improvements in practice were seen as a team effort. The emphasis was on what they were able to provide as a setting and as a team, and in this way, practitioners described the project as a team-building exercise.

Developing the assessment tool to support reflection on each child's progress

Numerous electronic systems have been developed to track children's progress through the Early Years Foundation Stage (EYFS). Usually, the Development Matters statements are presented in ways that can be 'ticked off' or highlighted when achieved. We felt that this promotes a deficit view of children's learning, concentrating on what children are *not yet* able to do, rather than the progress children have made. Charged by the knowledge that there is a differential at 22 months, especially between children from a disadvantaged background and those from a more privileged background (Feinstein, 2003; Feinstein et al., 2007), we knew as early years practitioners that we needed to be more aware of children who were not making progress. We wanted a system where we could celebrate children's learning but also know that *all* children were making progress. We knew we needed to grasp the assessment nettle, but in so doing, many practitioners who admired our rich celebratory documentation at Pen Green felt that we had 'gone to the dark side'. Gradually, as we have worked with settings to use our assessment tool, we have been able to show that we have not gone against any of our hard-won principles. We have been able to maintain a principled approach because of the following:

- our rich documentation remains vital and forms the basis for all assessment judgements
- our rich documentation is only possible through a continuous two-way dialogue with parents where knowledge is shared and acted upon between home and the setting
- it is only possible to make an accurate assessment if the worker knows the child and the family well and if the parents are involved in the assessment process
- the assessment judgement we make is a professional judgement at a point in time. It does not involve highlighting or ticking off skills on a sheet. Rather, it is a judgement based on all that is known about the child.

Using the MCLV software

Each Family Worker (key person) gathers all the information and observations they have made on each child through discussions with their parents. The Family Worker, together with parents, then makes a professional assessment judgement against the Development Matters statements in the EYFS (British Association for Early Childhood Education [BAECE], 2012). They record whether the child is emerging 'E', developing 'D' or confident 'C' in which age band and for each aspect of each area of learning and development. The programme has now been updated to correspond to the revised EYFS, and an example of a recorded assessment is set out in Figure 5.1.

| Childs Name | Child 1 | | | | | | | | | | | | | | | |
| Date of Birth | 01/11/2007 | | | | | | | | | | | | | | | |

To return to the top of the page press Ctrl & Home together

| Assessment | Autumn Nursery 1st Year | Prime Areas | | | | | | | | | | Specific areas | | | | |

Date of Assessment Age in months at Assessment		Personal, Social & Emotional Development			Communication & Language			Physical Development		Literacy		Mathematics	Understanding the World			Expressive Arts & Design	
		Making Relation-ships	Self Confidence & self-awareness	Manging feelings & behaviour	Listening & attention	Understan-ding	Speaking	Moving & handling	Health & self care	Reading	Writing	Numbers	Shape, space & measure	People & communities	The world	Technology	Exploring & using media & materials	Being imaginative
0 - 11 months																	
8 - 20 months																	
16 - 26 months																	
22 - 36 months																	
30 - 50 months																	
40 - 60+ months		D	E	E	E	D	E	D	D	E	E	E	E	E	E	D	E
Early Learning Goal																	

Figure 5.1 Inputting Sheet for MCLV Assessment Data

Figure 5.1 shows the recording sheet of a child's assessment in the Autumn term of their first year in nursery: E = Emerging, D = Developing, C = Confident.

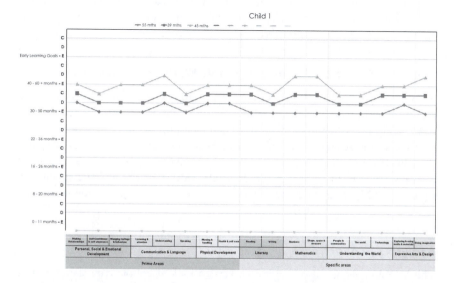

Figure 5.2 Example of individual child's assessment graph generated by the MCLV software

Figure 5.2 shows a line graph of assessments of a child made at 35 months (bottom line), at 39 months (middle line) and at 43 months (top line).

Once the assesement has been recorded, the software produces an individual graph that shows where the child 'is at'. This is a snapshot in time. When two assessment have been made the child's progress can easily be seen, so making the child's learning 'visible'.

This graph is used by workers and parents to analyse the child's progress and to raise questions about pedagogy and how to support the child's learning. Workers reflect on the child's graph with parents to celebrate the strengths children demonstrate, and they discuss ways to support the child's learning effectively. This is not an exercise in 'teaching to the gaps' but rather an exercise in knowing the child well and introducing the child to experiences that offer appropriate learning, linked to their interests. In this child's graph (Figure 5.2) you can see that progress has been made in all areas, but some aspects are showing as strengths (e.g. numbers and shape, space and measures).

During the Pen Green MCLV nursery schools project, Trudy (worker), Holly (mother) and David (father) talked about Michael's learning (NB – these are not their real names). They had assessed his learning in writing (CLL) as emerging in the 30–50 month age band when he was 40 months old. Four months later, as he was about to start school, they reflected on how his writing had progressed; he was interested in drawing pictures to describe what he liked to do at nursery and beginning to write his name. Michael drew a representation of the monkey bars so that his teacher would understand what he meant. His learning had been supported by giving him opportunities to 'mark make for meaning' (i.e., make marks that had a meaning and significance for him), supporting him in recognising his name and in exploring the shape of some of the letters.

Analysis of children's graphs in Family Workers' groups

Family Workers are also able to examine the graphs of children in their family group and engage with the data, raising questions about their pedagogy and their assessment processes and moderation. These questions focus on why some workers were seeing strengths in children as a group in a particular area of learning. Was this because they supported children effectively in this area? Because they assessed children differently in this area? Or because of the way the statements were written? Workers begin to reflect on their own pedagogy and become open to learning from each other.

Analysis of cohort data

The MCLV software also enables workers to look at cohort data. Practitioners can study trends across assessments and the progress different groups of children have made between assessments, e.g. boys/girls, English as an additional language or children who have attended nursery for five terms. In the Pen Green Nursery Schools project (using the EYFS 2011 version) the following cohort graphs were produced (see Figure 5.3).

The team identified particular aspects, such as calculating and linking letters and sounds, as areas for development, given that a larger percentage of children were assessed in the lower age bands in these aspects. They responded by reflecting on their pedagogy in these areas and by moderating their assessment judgements.

Studying the cohort data on the second assessment, the team reflected on the assessment judgements. The 11 children who had been assessed at 22–36 months in Calculating and the 9 children who were assessed at 22–36 months in Linking Letters and Sounds and Language for Thinking all had either additional needs

Number & Percentage of Children in Each Age Band

1st Assessment   Nov-10

	Personal, Social & Emotional Development					Communication, Language and Literacy							Problem Solving, Reasoning & Numeracy			Knowledge & Understanding of the World						Physical Development			Creative Development			
	D & A	SC & SE	M R	B & SC	Self care	S of C	L for C	L for T	L S & S	R	W	HW	N as L & for C	C	S S & M	E & I	D & M	ICT	Time	Place	Com	Mov & Sp	Hlth & BA	Use E & M	B C	Ex M & M	C M & D	Devi & IP
Blank	26	26	26	26	26	26	26	26	26	26	26	26	26	26	26	26	26	26	26	26	26	26	26	26	26	26	26	26
0-11mths	0	0	0	0	0	0	0	0	0	0	0	0	0	0	0	0	0	0	0	0	0	0	0	0	0	0	0	0
8-20mths	0	0	0	0	0	0	0	0	0	0	0	0	0	0	0	0	0	0	0	0	0	0	0	0	0	0	0	0
16-26mths	1	1	2	2	2	2	2	2	2	1	1	1	2	2	2	1	1	1	1	1	0	1	1	1	1	1	0	2
22-36mths	9	11	9	9	10	11	12	13	15	12	13	11	13	15	14	10	10	12	11	12	12	12	11	11	11	11	11	10
30-50mths	80	80	82	79	81	77	74	74	74	75	76	75	80	79	78	81	80	75	82	81	80	74	79	77	82	80	81	78
40-60+mths	12	10	9	12	9	12	14	13	11	14	12	15	7	6	8	10	11	14	8	8	9	16	10	13	8	10	10	12
Early Learning Goals	0	0	0	0	0	0	0	0	0	0	0	0	0	0	0	0	0	0	0	0	0	0	0	0	0	0	0	0
0-11mths	0	0	0	0	0	0	0	0	0	0	0	0	0	0	0	0	0	0	0	0	0	0	0	0	0	0	0	0
8-20mths	0	0	0	0	0	0	0	0	0	0	0	0	0	0	0	0	0	0	0	0	0	0	0	0	0	0	0	0
16-26mths	1	1	2	2	2	2	2	2	2	1	1	1	2	2	2	1	1	1	1	1	0	1	1	1	1	1	0	2
22-36mths	9	11	9	9	10	11	12	13	15	12	13	11	13	15	14	10	10	12	11	12	12	12	11	11	11	11	11	10
30-50mths	78	78	80	77	79	75	73	73	74	75	74	78	77	76	79	78	74	80	79	78	73	77	75	80	78	79	79	76
40-60+mths	12	10	9	12	9	12	14	13	11	14	12	15	7	6	8	10	11	14	8	8	9	16	10	13	8	10	10	12
Early Learning Goals	0	0	0	0	0	0	0	0	0	0	0	0	0	0	0	0	0	0	0	0	0	0	0	0	0	0	0	0

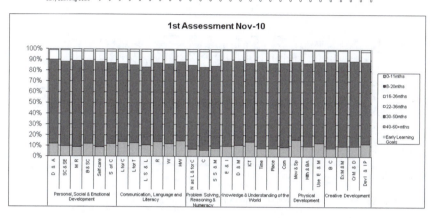

Figure 5.3 First Assessment of Children by Age Band 2010–11

Figure 5.3 shows the first MCLV assessment across the cohort of children: white = the proportion of children assessed as being between 22–36 months, black between 30–50 months and grey between 40–60 months.

or English as an Additional Language. This led staff to consider how to assess children's progress when the Family Worker does not speak the same language as the child and how we could use our language support workers more effectively, both with the child and with our engagement with parents in discussions about assessment. This second assessment, made in February, is particularly important as it not only shows where progress is being made, but it also allows workers an opportunity to respond to the data. Entry and exit data gives the progress that children have made in the year but not until the children have moved on and cannot benefit from the worker's and parents' reflection on their progress. The third assessment for the cohort studied in this year showed that all children had made progress in all areas of learning. Looking at whole cohort data allows practitioners to see, and reflect on, what is happening for all of the children across all of the aspects. As in the example given previously, using children's individual assessment

Number & Percentage of Children in Each Age Band

2nd Assessment   Feb-11

	Personal, Social & Emotional Development					Communication, Language and Literacy							Problem Solving, Reasoning & Numeracy			Knowledge & Understanding of the World						Physical Development			Creative Development			
	D & A	SC & SE	M R	B & SC	Self care	S of C	L for C	L for T	L S & L	R	W	HW	N as L & for C	C	SS & M	E & I	D & M	ICT	Time	Place	Com	Mov & Sp	Hlth & BA	Use E & M	B C	Ex M & M	C/M & D	Dev I & I P
Blank	34	34	34	34	34	34	34	34	34	34	34	34	34	34	34	34	34	34	34	34	34	34	34	34	34	34	34	34
0-11mths	0	0	0	0	0	0	0	0	0	0	0	0	0	0	0	0	0	0	0	0	0	0	0	0	0	0	0	0
8-20mths	0	0	0	0	0	0	0	0	0	0	0	0	0	0	0	0	0	0	0	0	0	0	0	0	0	0	0	0
16-26mths	1	0	1	2	1	1	0	1	0	0	1	1	0	0	0	1	1	1	1	1	0	1	0	0	0	0	0	1
22-36mths	2	4	2	1	2	2	7	9	9	7	7	5	7	11	8	3	2	4	4	5	5	3	4	3	4	5	5	3
30-50mths	50	54	61	59	56	60	51	49	60	53	56	52	66	66	65	59	57	43	61	68	64	51	57	50	58	56	61	56
40-60+mths	41	36	30	32	35	31	36	35	25	34	30	36	21	17	21	31	34	46	28	20	24	40	32	41	32	33	28	34
Early Learning Goals	0	0	0	0	0	0	0	0	0	0	0	0	0	0	0	0	0	0	0	0	0	0	0	0	0	0	0	0
0-11mths	0	0	0	0	0	0	0	0	0	0	0	0	0	0	0	0	0	0	0	0	0	0	0	0	0	0	0	0
8-20mths	0	0	0	0	0	0	0	0	0	0	0	0	0	0	0	0	0	0	0	0	0	0	0	0	0	0	0	0
16-26mths	1	0	1	2	1	1	0	1	0	0	1	1	0	0	0	1	1	1	1	1	0	1	0	0	0	0	0	1
22-36mths	2	4	2	1	2	2	7	10	10	7	7	5	7	12	9	3	2	4	4	5	5	3	4	3	4	5	5	3
30-50mths	53	57	65	63	60	64	54	52	64	56	60	55	70	70	69	63	61	46	65	72	68	54	61	53	62	60	65	60
40-60+mths	44	38	32	34	37	33	38	37	27	36	32	38	22	18	22	33	36	49	30	21	26	43	34	44	34	35	30	36
Early Learning Goals	0	0	0	0	0	0	0	0	0	0	0	0	0	0	0	0	0	0	0	0	0	0	0	0	0	0	0	0

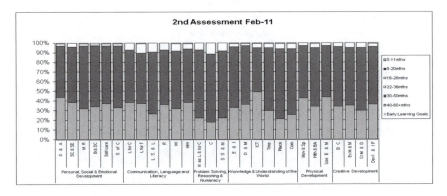

Figure 5.4 Second Assessment of Children by Age Band 2010–11

Figure 5.4 shows the second MCLV assessment across the cohort. The proportion of assessments at 22–36 months (white) has reduced in most areas while the proportion of assessments in the 40–60 month range has increased (grey). Displaying the cohort data in this way allows the kind of reflection by practitioners reported on below, where areas of strength across the cohort can be identified as well as those areas where there is a need for development.

graphs (as in Figure 5.2) allows the children whose assessments contribute to the pattern in each aspect to be identified. This furthers practitioners' understanding of how the learning of both individual children, and children across the cohort, can be most effectively supported.

Gender disparities in the cohort data

In the 2010–11 cohort, the graphs for boys and girls (see Figure 5.5) showed that in the area of Linking Sounds and Letters (Communication, Language and Literacy), 28% of boys were below their chronological age compared to only 18% of the girls at the first assessment. Workers were able to raise questions about their practice. Was the difference due to different levels of their engagement with girls and boys, or was it that they engaged with them in different ways? Was there a difference in the pedagogical support offered to girls and boys? Was the

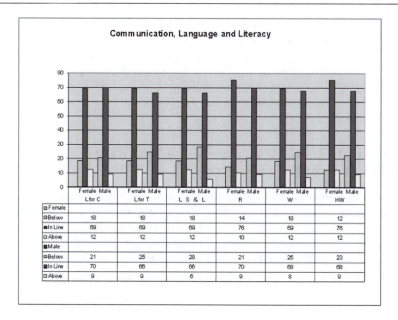

Figure 5.5 Children Below, In-line and Above in 1st Assessment split by Gender

Figure 5.5 shows the assessments across the cohort for girls and boys showing whether they were below (first column), in line (second column) or above (third column) their chronological age.

difference in assessments due to an underlying difference in the developmental levels of boys and girls or the ages of girls and boys in this particular cohort?

Using MCLV on transition to school

The MCLV assessment graphs have been a useful starting point in a dialogue between parents, nursery (FS1) workers and reception (FS2) teachers as children transition to school. It has been difficult in the past for reception teachers to access all the rich detailed nursery documentation on each child due to the size of each child's record of achievement. The MCLV graph has allowed the dialogue to begin with an overview of the child's learning and progress. It has provided a 'way in' to look at some aspects of the child's achievements in more depth. It has also promoted respect by reception teachers for the assessment judgements made by nursery staff, and it has promoted a professional discussion about moderation. The summer assessments made by nursery workers, who by the summer know children well and are assessing children in a familiar environment with people they know and trust, and the autumn assessments made by reception teachers as the children transfer to the new environment of school are likely to differ. The MCLV graphs have enabled a respectful discussion to take place about these differences, which has also stimulated all workers and parents to think about the transition process.

Sharing data and data analysis in this way has supported workers to focus on the child and the support for their learning, rather than focusing on whether assessment data at transition between settings has been suppressed or inflated. Three of the primary schools attended by Pen Green children are now using the MCLV software to measure the progress children make through FS2 as a continuation of assessments made in FS1 at Pen Green.

Case study 2: MCLV at a combined primary school and children's centre

A combined primary school and children's centre (the school) were looking for a research project that would enable staff across the setting to learn together, support the building of the whole staff team and reflect on outcomes for children and parents and also for themselves as learners. As a school with more than 800 pupils on roll, 120 full- and part-time staff, a DSP Nurture Group and a children's centre, this was a considerable challenge. The head teacher (HT) expressed the needs of the setting:

> We needed a way of understanding each other's experiences and thinking, both within year groups, and right across the setting, from the Children's Centre to Year 6. We were looking for a way that allowed us to have a professional dialogue and discussion that led to a more informed view of learning and teaching at our school. (personal interview, 2010)

What was needed was something that would support leaders, teachers and support staff to coalesce around a shared ethos about what the school wanted to offer to its pupils, parents and its community. As the HT expressed it, 'What we needed was a methodology that facilitated the dialogue and reflection. Working with Pen Green on Making Children's Learning Visible seemed to be the ideal vehicle for gaining that clarity around our pedagogical approach.'

The aims of this project were challenging.

- Could time spent reflecting on their individual and agreed 'image of the child' in each year group help staff to think deeply about what they are promoting for children?
- Could the assessment processes and pedagogical reflection support staff in articulating how they are 'making a difference' for children and families?

The research team carefully considered how they could identify 'vulnerable children', and they were supported by using the school's own Child and Young Person Screening Tool. The intention was that the learning gained by practitioners about their own pedagogy was key to developing a differentiated pedagogy that recognised and met the needs of individual children as being 'the best basis for reducing inequalities between young children, because the characteristics of high quality early learning for all children are those that enable a focus on meeting the needs of every individual child' (Department for Children, Schools and Families [DCSF], 2008: 29).

The ethics of the MCLV project

The ethical approach adopted for the project was one that focussed on the 'ethics of care' (Tronto, 1993). This meant that everyone involved in the project could expect to be treated in ways that safeguarded them as participants:

- the school and Pen Green were equal partners in the research project
- senior staff at the school would make themselves available to colleagues wanting to know more about the project and/or express any concerns
- all practitioners being videoed would do so voluntarily as far as this was practical and this would be part of a process of discussion and consultation within Year Group teams
- parents of children involved in the research needed to be made aware of the staff's plans, be consulted, agree that their child could be filmed and have information arising shared with them
- children needed to be informed of what was happening in language they would understand and if any child said or indicated that they were not happy being videoed then the filming must stop
- a 'learning contract' approach would be adopted whereby participants could contribute to discussions about acceptable boundaries and conditions under which they would agree to be part of the project; typical learning contract items are that people treat each other with respect, that everyone is entitled to their opinions and to express them and be listened to and that confidentiality will be ensured by agreeing that 'what is said in the room, stays in the room'.

Polyvocal ethnography in the combined school and children's centre

Each year group team produced two five-minute video clips, one featuring child-child interaction and the other child-adult interaction. Year group teams watched their own video clips and discussed them, facilitated by a member of the Pen Green Research team. Year group teams then swapped their video clips with the teams in the year groups immediately adjacent to them for viewing; for example, the Year 1 team watched the video clips produced by FS2 and Year 3. These discussions were also supported by a team member from Pen Green Research.

The emphasis in these video watching/discussion sessions was on raising critical questions in relation to the practices seen in the video clips and how these

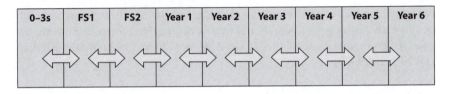

0–3s	FS1	FS2	Year 1	Year 2	Year 3	Year 4	Year 5	Year 6

Figure 5.6 Polyvocal ethnography between the school and children's centre year groups.

related to the wider practice of practitioners as individuals and as members of a team. These recordings formed the project's initial dataset; i.e., the discussions that teams had about their own pedagogy and that of their colleagues. Each year group team, before further distribution, checked the transcriptions of the discussions and the questions raised and noted by researchers. In addition to this, the Pen Green researchers gathered more data when they ran a half-day session with practitioners who had been involved in the MCLV project. All members of each year group team were able to record their experiences of the project and how they felt it had impacted on their thinking, actions and practice.

Research data: Pedagogical learning from the MCLV project

What follows is a digest of the most illuminating comments that teachers and support staff who had participated in the MCLV project had to make about what they felt they had gained as a result. Some commentary is also included.

Individual and team pedagogy and their knowledge and understanding of their children

Some practitioners reported how tentative they had been about the whole enterprise:

> *Think we were initially quite apprehensive but found the process very useful.* (Year 2)

Others appreciated that the project work had helped them to share their own ideas about the children they taught:

> *It was nice as a whole team; there were lots of different perspectives and different views of the child . . . the project made us reflect on our own practice and how we need to be constantly aware of the different needs of individuals.* (FS2)

Another team understood that these discussions had given them '*more time to get to know individuals*'. (Year 4)

Defining, identifying and working with 'vulnerable' children

It has challenged our views in terms of 'what is a vulnerable child?' We've all been very clear on our vulnerable groups: Free School Meals, white boys, looked after children . . . because we have had to think very carefully about who our vulnerable children are, it has highlighted some other groups of vulnerable children which has been extremely useful. (Head Teacher)

Several teams clearly articulated their view that 'vulnerability' took many forms and should not necessarily be associated with children or families whose circumstances 'located' them somewhere in an official classification:

We felt strongly that a child could not be categorized . . . a child receiving free school meals, from a single parent family or living in a particular street or area would not necessarily be seen as vulnerable for this reason alone. A child living with both parents and being cared for adequately could be vulnerable in other ways. (FS2)

Using video as a tool to support reflection on practice and pedagogy

To discuss and reflect upon their practice . . . to just take that five minute clip . . . but to really unpick what's going on there; and to have the discussion in a way that is safe. To really be able to challenge one another in a safe way. And also, to celebrate. There's been a lot of celebration around what's been going on. (Head Teacher)

Year group teams reported that using video had generally been a positive experience; even those who had initial misgivings saw, literally, the benefits of using video in this way:

Initially, I thought being videoed was nerve racking but upon reflection I found the experience useful. Especially when looking back over the video to see how the pupils interacted with me and each other. (Year 3)

Other teams' comments reflected the same kind of experience and learning:

It made us more aware of changes in free flow, friendship groups etc. (FS2)
  Helped us to reflect on our own practice and gain valuable experiences from others. (Year 2)

'Image of the Child' characteristics across the year groups

What was our 'image of the child'? What would a (name of school) child look like? That was very interesting, because, for example, our Early Years staff and our parents talked about wanting children to be 'fearless'. However, for Year 6 staff, for example, use of the word 'fearless' meant that you would have anarchy and chaos. (Head Teacher)

Comments made by the year group teams on their 'image of the child', after viewing their own and other teams' video clips, showed that their awareness of their own assumptions had been raised and evidenced critical reflection on their previous thinking:

> *We used the term 'compliant' and realised this was not what we actually meant. After discussion we decided 'flexible' was a more suitable word.* (Year 1)

Pedagogy across the year groups

> *I certainly think it's developed awareness across year groups, which I think is always invaluable. It gets people away from the attitude of 'Well, that's what they do in Year 2 and that's what they do in Year 3'. I think it's built a deeper and greater understanding of that.* (Head Teacher)

Responses from teams on their understanding of each other's pedagogy, based on viewing each other's video clips included the following:

> *There's a commonality of language throughout the school . . . a deeper understanding about learning and teaching than has gone before.* (Year 2)
>   *A consistency in expectations and standards across the school.* (Year 4)
>   *See progression in the child on the video in year 5 . . . in terms of my own view of the 'ideal child'.* (Year 4)
>   *It was beneficial to work in Year 3 and Year 5 to see the links that were apparent within both years regarding the image of the child.* (Year 5)

Working effectively with parents

> *These are children who, on the surface, might not have been defined as vulnerable . . . one of the next strands for us will be our engagement with the parents of children who we define as vulnerable – who may not fit within an already defined group.* (Head Teacher)

Practitioners' comments across the year group teams showed their understanding of the importance of working with parents to better understand the family's circumstances and help children achieve.

Implications for practice

While the following points are those that were given in the MCLV project report written for the school's Head Teacher, Senior Leadership Team and Governors, we would argue that they would equally apply to any setting wanting to make effective use of video, promote better relationships and authentic partnerships with parents, support the learning of their most vulnerable children and develop a differentiated pedagogy in order to achieve this.

- Using video as a tool for

  - supporting practitioner reflection on their own and each other's practice through making video the medium for peer-peer observations in the classroom
  - recording the learning of children as individuals and in group/class contexts for viewing by practitioners in teams or on their own
  - focused work with children in terms of an identified Special Educational Need (for example, the articulation of a child requiring or being supported by a Speech and Language Therapist)
  - sharing knowledge about children with parents and supporting an ongoing dialogue about home learning and the celebration of children's progress.
    The use of video has the following implications:
  - resourcing – purchasing cameras, computers, film, disks
  - training – so that practitioners can feel confident about operating cameras, transferring the footage to computer, editing, transferring to DVD disks, etc.

- Engagement with parents

  - Being more accessible to parents at times and in ways that address their needs and fit in with their timescales and availability
  - Conducting case studies on individual children that involve their parents as partners in the work
  - Using video as the medium for sharing and exchanging information about what the child is doing and learning at the school and at home (The Pen Green PICL Approach – Parents Involved in their Children's Learning).

- Defining, identifying and supporting the learning of vulnerable children

  - Make use of classifications provided by government to raise staff's awareness of the correlations between risk factors and poor outcomes for children in the identified categories
  - It is made clear that these reflect statistical relationships between recognised risk factors and poor outcomes for children and are not deterministic
  - Make full use of the school's own Child and Young Person Screening Tool to promote discussion in teams about who is a 'vulnerable' child and why, monitor their educational progress and devise strategies to support their learning if needed.

- Developing a differentiated pedagogy

  - Supporting practitioners to reflect on how they monitor children's progress through assessments and then respond to the individual learning needs of all children, in particular those who may be described as 'vulnerable'
  - Finding ways for staff to get to know children as they 'move through' the school; for example, using a portfolio, produced and developed by the child and their family, as they transition between Year Groups
  - Ensuring that 'standing back' and 'being quiet' are seen to be legitimate adult pedagogic strategies that can support children's learning and development.

Continuing use and development of the MCLV methodology

The MCLV methodology has now been developed into a three-day professional development programme that includes project work by staff teams. It has been used successfully in the DfE funded Early Years Teaching Centre project (2011–2013) by many centres and is now being developed as part of Pen Green Accountable Practice: The Two Year Old Project. MCLV provides a comprehensive way of measuring outcomes for children while enabling workers and parents to reflect on the processes that promote progress in children's learning. In this way it provides an evaluation tool that is both developmental (Patton, 2011) and illuminating in that it is able, in a very straight forward manner, to 'make children's learning visible'.

References

Arnold, C. & Brennan, C. (2008) *Using Polyvocal Ethnography to Examine Adult and Child Engagement in an English and an Irish Setting.* Paper given at the European Early Childhood Education Research Association Annual Conference, *Reconsidering the Basics.* Stavanger, September.

Arnold, C. & Brennan, C. (2013) 'Polyvocal Ethnography as a Means of Developing Inter-Cultural Understanding of Pedagogy and Practice'. *European Early Childhood Education Research Journal,* Vol. 21, No. 3, 353 – 69.

BAECE (2012) *Development Matters in the Early Years Foundation Stage (EYFS).* London: British Association for Early Childhood Education.

DCSF (2008) Sure Start Children's Centres Update, July. Department for Children, Schools and Families [online]. Available from: shttp://www.surestart.gov.uk/publications/?Document=1852

Edwards, C., Gandini, L. & Forman, G. (1998) *The Hundred Languages of Children: The Reggio Emilia Approach – Advanced Reflections* (2nd Edition). London: JAI Press.

Feinstein, L. (2003) 'Inequality in the Early Cognitive Development of British Children in the 1970 Cohort', *Economica,* Vol. 70, No. 277, 73–97.

Feinstein, L., Hearn, B., Renton, Z., Abrahams, C. & MacLeod, M. (2007) *Reducing Inequalities: Realising the Talents of All*. London: National Children's Bureau.

Laevers, F. (1997) A *Process Oriented Child Monitoring System for Young Children*. Leuven: Centre for Experiential Education.

Malaguzzi, L. (1993) For an Education Based on Relationships. *Young Childern*. November 1993.

Patton, M. Q. (2011) *Developmental Evaluation: Applying Complexity Concepts to Enhance Innovation and Use*. London: The Guildford Press.

PGRB (2012a) *Making Children's Learning Visible: A Project Approach for Early Years Teams Focusing on Outcomes for Children*. Course Pack Training Materials. Pen Green Research, Development & Training Base & Leadership Centre, Corby, Northamptonshire. Unpublished.

PGRB (2012b) *Early Years Teaching Centre Progress Report 2012*. Pen Green Research, Development & Training Base & Leadership Centre, Corby, Northamptonshire. Unpublished.

Taylor, S. (2007) '*Is Breaking a Leg Just Another Experience?' Using Video to Gain a Bi-Cultural Perspective of Risk-Taking in the Natural Environment*. University of Leicester MA Dissertation. Pen Green Research, Development & Training Base & Leadership Centre. Unpublished.

Tobin, J. J., Wu, D. & Davidson, D. (1989) *Preschool in Three Cultures*. New Haven, CT: Yale University Press.

Tobin, J., Hsueh, Y. and Karasawa, M. (2009) *Preschool in Three Cultures Revisited*. Chicago: University of Chicago Press.

Together for Children (2009) *Toolkit for Reaching Priority and Excluded Families* (Version 6). Birmingham: Author.

Tronto, J. (1993) *Moral Boundaries: A Political Argument for the Ethics of Care*. London: Routledge.

Whalley, M. & Riddell, B. (2013) Pen Green Children's Centre – Standing the Test of Time. *Nursery World* 25 February–10 March, 34–35.

Chapter 6

Parent-to-parent interviewing at Pen Green

Voice, richness, depth

Eddie McKinnon

The Pen Green Centre for children under 5 and their families

As a lifelong Corby resident, looking back, it would be difficult to over-estimate the importance of the establishment of the Pen Green Centre in 1983. In 1980 the British Steel Corporation had announced the closure of the huge iron- and steel-making plant that had been the economic foundation of the town. In 1983 the community was still suffering the social and economic fallouts of high unemployment; in 1983 the adult male unemployment rate in the wards surrounding the Pen Green Centre reached 46%.

These factors hit the people of Corby very hard. The town had enjoyed a period of sustained economic growth and development for more than 30 years, and its shops and businesses had prospered on the spending of the 'working class aristocracy' based at Corby steelworks. The economic fortunes of Corby and its inhabitants remained difficult throughout the rest of the 1980s as unemployment remained high locally and nationally. The community experienced previously unknown levels of poverty and deprivation with their concomitant pressures on families and communities. The Pen Green Centre, and its multi-disciplinary team's philosophy and practice, combining high-quality care and education for children with provision and support for parents, could not have come along at a better time for the families of Corby.

During the intervening 30 years, Pen Green has worked hard with parents and families to develop innovative methods for assessing community needs and evaluating services. This chapter looks at one of these methods: parent-to-parent interviewing. At Pen Green we regard this method as having significant advantages in the way it can be used to both assess the needs of families in the community and to evaluate the effectiveness of the services that are offered to them.

The critical role of parents at Pen Green

Since its beginning, parents have played critically important roles in the ways in which the Pen Green Centre has grown and changed. Once plans to open a centre for children and families in Corby were announced, a group was immediately formed to oppose it (Whalley, 1994: 9). Corby parents feared that the local authority intended to set up a centre for 'problem' families and were concerned about what that could mean for the community. Pen Green Centre staff quickly engaged with the 'protest' group and recruited all but one of them to form the parents' steering committee for the Centre and its early development. On the surface this may appear to have been a piece of savvy opportunism. However, it was in fact an action deeply rooted in the belief that if you genuinely want to serve the needs of a community, then you have to engage with that community in authentic ways that see parents and children as powerful co-constructors of the services that are offered to them. The founding head brought with her from community work in the majority world a deep understanding of the needs of disadvantaged communities informed by the work and writings of Paolo Freire. Freire, a community educator who worked in some of the poorest neighbourhoods in Brazil in the 1960s and 1970s, emphasised that

> The teacher is no longer merely the-one-who-teaches, but one who is himself taught in dialogue with the students, who in turn while being taught teach . . . They become jointly responsible for a process in which they all grow . . . Here, no one teaches another, nor is anyone self-taught. People teach each other. (Freire, 1970: 61)

Parent-to-parent interviewing as a research method

Whilst training parents and supporting them to carry out needs assessments and service evaluations in communities is not exclusive to the Pen Green Centre in Corby (Weinberger, 2005), this approach has been used consistently at Pen Green throughout a number of years, resulting in successful changes to practice and provision for families. Isobel Brodie (2003) features a number of examples of this approach in her report on the critical importance of involving parents in the evaluation of services. Brodie argues that evaluation of services is vital so that those providing them can

- 'Understand how well their services are performing
- Keep track of progress in meeting the objectives and targets
- Make changes to their programme as a result of evaluation findings'. (Brodie, 2003: 4–5)

Brodie emphasises that, while service evaluations need to be done using robust methods, they also need to be carried out by people with the 'appropriate research skills' who are also in a position to enable 'parents to participate meaningfully in the evaluation activity' (Brodie, 2003: 5). Furthermore, this participation needs to be more than merely attending 'an initial planning session, or asking them to hear about results . . . Their involvement is important throughout the whole evaluation process'. However, if families are to engage in the evaluation of services in any authentic sense of the term, then, as Brodie expresses it, 'a shift in the traditional balance of power between those providing and those receiving services' (ibid.) would have to be made. Other benefits of involving parents and carers in needs assessments and service evaluations identified by Brodie (2003: 5–6) include the following:

- It is 'morally and ethically desirable'
- The 'quality of our understanding of services is improved'
- It ensures that 'the issues and outcomes which are important to . . . [parents and carers] . . . are identified and prioritised within evaluations'
- Their 'specific skills and knowledge' about their communities can help improve the 'overall quality of the evaluation . . . [such as] . . . extensive knowledge of cultures within the community, and of languages spoken
- They can 'acquire new skills and build on existing skills', contributing to their employability and potentially reducing 'the number of young children in workless households'
- They know which families in their communities are not using services and can more easily make contact with them, engage with them and gain their confidence so that their experiences can be documented; this may be particularly true of families who are vulnerable in some way, such as asylum seekers
- They can actively help to 'disseminate the results of evaluation and can work to ensure that changes are implemented'
- They can 'alert other parents about under-used services and encourage them to attend'.

Consequently, some parents and carers may be perfect candidates for the training required to carry out community-based surveys in flexible and efficient ways and at an optimum cost.

Parent-to-parent interviewing at Pen Green: The Corby Sure Start Local Programme evaluations

The model of parent-to-parent interviewing developed at Pen Green fulfils all of the key points identified by Isobel Brodie (2003) and has been used extensively in evaluations of services provided by Pen Green and throughout the Corby Sure Start Local Programme, which ran from 1998 until 2006. Pen Green was the lead partner for the Corby Sure Start Local Programme and worked closely with other agencies in the town, both statutory and voluntary, that were involved in family support. Pen Green has consistently used a semi-structured interview approach in its parent-to-parent evaluations. This is because a semi-structured interview schedule simultaneously allows those who devise it to ask the questions that they want answered, while giving the flexibility needed for the interviewee to lead the conversation into areas not thought about by the interviewer. In the kind of needs assessments and service evaluations carried out at Pen Green the latter point is crucial; parents being interviewed need to be able to bring their 'agenda to the table'. The training given to the teams of Parent-Interviewers emphasised the need to let the parent lead the discussion when it was fruitful to do so but to be able to bring it back to the interview questions with tact and sensitivity towards the parent.

The following section outlines how this approach was put into operation in each of the four annual Corby Sure Start Local Programme evaluations and discusses their key findings.

Corby Sure Start Local Programme evaluation 1999

Anticipating the setting up of the Corby Sure Start Local Programme in 1999 (Tait et al., 1999), meetings were held so that the project development group could discuss, plan and identify local targets and proposed interventions with parents in the community. The planning group was made up of both parents and professionals. To ensure that the needs and wants of the local community received close attention during this initial phase the planning group decided the following:

- the development group would always be chaired by a parent
- at least one-third of the group would comprise parents from the Sure Start catchment area.

It was clear that parent representatives and parents who attended the meetings to develop the plan wanted their voices to be heard. In the words of the report, 'parents were very vocal in expressing their views and concerns' (Tait et al, 1999: 1). Funds provided by the starter grant for the project were used to conduct a Parent Led Needs Assessment (PLNA), which, conducted by other parents, ensured a congruence between the priorities identified by the development group and those of people in the local community. A team of 13 'Parent-Interviewers' was recruited and trained because 'It was felt that parents as interviewers would be more likely to engage in an honest, open and critical dialogue with other parents' (Tait et al., 1999: 1).

Families with children under the age of one were the 'target group' for interviewing as their experiences would have been the most recent and most relevant to the aims and objectives of the Sure Start Project in Corby. The 1999 PLNA had four key aims in line with local and national objectives:

1. to produce evidence as to how effective ante- and post-natal services had been
2. to identify those needs of families that had not been met
3. to develop insights into the contributions made by Health, Social Services, Education and the voluntary sector to the reduction of stress and vulnerability of families with infants
4. to ensure that the interventions planned by the Corby Sure Start Local Programme, as developed by parents and professionals, were appropriate and matched local needs.

The parent-to-parent interview schedule

The Parent-Interviewers used a pro forma interview schedule to record the responses of parents. Two cards were used to help parents identify the services they had used. One card listed the range of ante-natal services offered, while the other listed the post-natal services. As parents identified the services they had used on the cards, the name of the agency was recorded, along with a rating between 0 and 10 (10 as highest) and a comment explaining why they had rated it in this way and how they thought the service could be improved for families.

Analysis of the interviews identified that the key needs for expectant mothers and new mothers and their families included the following:

- more emotional support from services
- access to transport and health services
- information on child development
- provision of childcare facilities such as crèches so that parents could have some 'free time' from their children when they could do something for themselves, or 'just have a break'. (Tait et al., 1999: 21)

Corby Sure Start Local Programme evaluation 2001

The second survey, conducted in 2001, focused on how parents evaluated services in the light of patterns of parental employment and the accessibility of early years childcare (Tait et al., 2001). This study followed the model established in 1999, and Parent-Interviewers were once again recruited, including several parents who had carried out interviewing in the initial study. As many of the original cohort of interviewees as possible were contacted, as their children would by then have been about two years of age. This was done so that

- comparisons could be made
- levels of support from local services experienced by these families could be ascertained
- an accurate assessment of how many families had used the Corby Sure Start Local Programme could be made
- focussing on parents with children aged 18 months to 2 years would allow assessment of the needs of parents trying to return to work, and whether specific new initiatives set up by the Corby Sure Start Local Programme to support this were being successful or not

Table 6.1 Simple pro forma layout for recording agency or service used, rating given and any comments

Agency	Score	Reason

- the success of specific government policies intended to encourage mothers back into the workplace, such as family credit and working parents tax credit, could be examined
- the amount of support and childcare provided by the parent's extended family could be investigated and assessed in terms of parents making a return to the workforce.

The semi-structured interview schedule

The Parent-Interviewers used a semi-structured interview schedule to record parents' comments about their families, use of child care in Corby and child care needs and work and employment circumstances. Attempts were made to re-interview all the participants from the 1999 study; however, this was unsuccessful due to reasons such as people moving house and changed telephone numbers. Some of the 1999 cohort who were contacted declined to take part. However, 31 of the original 57 families who took part in the first evaluation were successfully re-interviewed. This allowed analysis of how things had developed for them now that their children were 2 to 3 years of age. This group was designated Cohort 1, and their data was analysed separately from that of Cohort 2, which included parents who were being interviewed about their usage and experiences of services for the first time.

The main findings of this 2001 report follow:

- there was a variety of family types evident in the survey
- generally, family life and employment had to be carefully 'juggled'
- family support and agency support in terms of childcare had to be carefully coordinated to enable mothers to return to work
- the mixed patterns of shiftwork in Corby helped to promote mothers returning to work as long as there was great flexibility in childcare arrangements
- there was some expressed preference for childcare to be undertaken by relatives within the home for children younger than 3 years of age.

Corby Sure Start Local Programme evaluation 2003

This evaluation (McKinnon et al., 2003) was divided into three discrete strands:

- a parents' satisfaction survey, similar to those conducted for the previous two evaluations, which provided a largely summative perspective on the programme
- focus group sessions that were carried out with Sure Start workers, which provided a largely illuminative perspective
- a survey of Sure Start Management Board members, which provided a largely formative perspective.

The Parent-to-Parent User Satisfaction Survey allowed direct evaluations of services by service-users via a number rating regarding the quality of the service they had experienced, plus comments about the services and how they felt improvement could be made. Booklets containing a pro forma single page for every group or service offered by Corby Sure Start Local Programme were used by the Parent-Interviewers to identify and record the parents' responses (see Table 6.2). Parent-Interviewers were also given a list of all the groups and services along with the names of the people who ran them to help parents identify the groups and services they used; it was not uncommon for parents to refer to the group or service in this way as opposed to the title it had on the Corby Sure Start Local Programme database, for example, 'I go to Susan's group on a Tuesday morning'.

This format allowed differentiation of three different ranges of ratings: 8–10, 5–7 and 4 or less. These ranges were then associated with

- a high quality of service and how this could be maintained
- an acceptable quality of service and how it could be improved
- an unacceptable quality of service and how this could be reduced or eliminated.

Table 6.2 Interview Schedule for Users' Satisfaction Survey 2003

SURE START EVALUATION 2003: INTERVIEW FOR USERS OF SERVICES
Name of Service or Group:
Use of Service: Current = C; Previous = P; Not Used=N (circle letter)   C   P   N
Rating based on the value of the service/group for you/your child/family (circle number given)
1   2   3   4   5   6   7   8   9   10
Reasons for Rating: e.g. What differences has this service/group made to you/your child/your family?
Room for Improvement: e.g. How could this service/group be made better for you/your child/your family?

The evaluation also found that some services were particularly significant because of their functions of 'signposting' parents towards other groups and services and/or 'gatekeeping', in the sense that they were instrumental in allowing or promoting access to other groups or services. Two consistently highly rated services, Family Visiting and Transport, exemplified these processes.

Corby Sure Start Local Programme evaluation 2004

This evaluation (McKinnon et al., 2005) was the fourth and final large-scale evaluation to be undertaken by the Corby Sure Start Local Programme. At this point the staff in the Corby Sure Start Local Programme felt that they had developed a deep level of understanding of their programme in terms of its day-to-day operation and its strengths and weaknesses. Many of them had participated in the previous evaluations, had had the findings of each one fed back to them via the evaluation reports and had discussed their implications for practice in team meetings. The 2003 evaluation work had focused on the Corby Sure Start Local Programme's provision at the Pen Green Centre and its outreach locations, primarily the two community houses and seven other smaller venues. However, most of the data in the report reflected the work undertaken at the Pen Green Centre campus. Reasons for this included the following:

- Pen Green has a history of involving parents and their children in groups, consequently people in the community 'knew' the Pen Green Centre and continued to use it as opposed to the services running at other locations.
- The physical scale of the Pen Green Centre meant that it could provide facilities that were not available elsewhere. As a result, a large number of people in the area were attracted to Pen Green and not the other facilities.

The 2003 evaluation had supported workers to learn much about the programme, but most of the data gathered had been about parents' use of Pen Green, even though there was recognition that a significant area of the Corby Sure Start Local Programme's provision was its outreach work taking place in a variety of other locations but mainly at the two community houses and the Kingswood Community Centre. Figures for the use of services in 2003 showed that the outreach locations made up a quarter of the overall attendances at Corby Sure Start's groups and services. (see Table 6.3.)

The decision was taken to evaluate the outreach in its own right so that deeper learning could be gained about this aspect of Corby Sure Start Local Programme's provision. Once again the focus was on the parents' assessment of the quality of the provision as indicated by ratings of, and comments about, the groups and services they had used. As with previous surveys, a team of interviewers was recruited from the local community and trained to carry out semi-structured interviews with the parents. A booklet containing a two-page pro forma per group or service offered was compiled for the Parent-Interviewers to use. This version

Table 6.3 Attendances at the Pen Green Centre and Outreach Provision in 2003

	Pen Green Centre	Outreach Provision
Frequency of Attendances	21,583	7,162
% of Attendances	75.08%	24.91%

asked more detailed questions than the one used in 2003, and it also included at the top of each page the names of the workers co-leading the groups or offering the service. Whilst over 70 interviews with parents were completed, and much high-quality data was gathered and analysed, the Parent-Interviewers felt that the interview schedule I had devised, as the project coordinator, had made the interviews they completed unnecessarily difficult to carry out.

While the Parent-Interviewers were doing the fieldwork, regular support meetings were held so that they could share their experiences and be reassured that they were all, by-and-large, encountering the same problems and difficulties. At the final meeting, in which I asked for a clear and frank debrief of what the interviewing process had been like, the Parent-Interviewers fed back on how awkward the more detailed format had been to use with parents. See Table 6.4 for a proforma of the interview schedule.

At the debriefing meeting the Parent-Interviewers made a number of comments about the interview schedule, saying that it was restrictive for both themselves and the parents they were trying to interview. Their verbatim comments are worth quoting:

- 'by the time that you got around asking "Why did you give it that rating?" they'd say "I've just told you!"'
- 'the ticky things got in the way of parents talking about their experiences'
- 'what we had got in the way of getting the story from people'
- 'last year the page allowed the conversation to flow naturally without all the interruptions that this year's had in it'.

One Parent-Interviewer's comment exemplified the feelings of the parent interviewing team:

- 'Last year we got all the same information but with only three questions'. (McKinnon et al., 2005: 173)

The general lesson learned from this feedback was that sometimes less can indeed be more. The more specific lesson I learned was that any interview schedule should be piloted, at the very least, by those who are being asked to use it. Had I done so, the schedule could have been adjusted and made both more user-friendly for the Parent-Interviewers and parents and more effective as a tool for gathering information. The lesson from this – to keep things as simple as you can

Table 6.4 Outreach Provision User Satisfaction Survey: Sure Start Evaluation 2004

Group/Service Name/Code		No.	Location/Day/Time			
			Leader/Worker			

Use of Service:	Current = C; Previous = P; Not Used = N (circle letter)		C P N

A – Could you tell me how you started to use this service?

B – (1) Did you continue to use this service?

No		Yes	

(2) If you answered No can I ask you why you stopped using it?

(3) If you answered Yes, and continue to use it, can I ask you what your experience of the service has been?

(4) If you answered Yes, continued to use the service for a time and then stopped, can I ask you why?

C – Was the service,

1	Useful?	9	8	7	6	5	4	3	2	1	0	Useless?
2	Helpful?	9	8	7	6	5	4	3	2	1	0	A hindrance?
3	Well-managed?	9	8	7	6	5	4	3	2	1	0	Badly managed
4	Making a difference?	9	8	7	6	5	4	3	2	1	0	Doing nothing?
5	Reliable?	9	8	7	6	5	4	3	2	1	0	Unreliable?
6	Just what you wanted?	9	8	7	6	5	4	3	2	1	0	Not what you wanted?

D – What should definitely be kept about the service?

(Continued)

Table 6.4 (Continued)

E – What should definitely be changed about the service?
F – Would you recommend this service to someone else based on its value for you and your family?
G – (1) Would you like to give an overall rating for the service? Low - 0   1   2   3   4   5   6   7   8   9   10 - High (2) What made you choose that rating?
H – Is there anything else you would like to say about this service?

whilst also achieving what it is you want to do – was used in a more recent piece of research in Corby.

The 'Transforming Early Years' project in Corby

In 2010–11 Corby was one of six locations in England to take part in a national research project funded by the National Endowment for Science, Technology and the Arts and facilitated by the Innovation Unit (see Chapter 8 by Joanne Armstrong and Eddie McKinnon). The Transforming Early Years project invited each location to research and develop an innovative way to change the nature of services in their area for families with pre-school-age children (Innovation Unit, 2012). In Corby, parents, children's centre leaders and practitioners from other agencies in the town, both statutory and from the Private, Voluntary and Independent (PVI) sector, identified parents who were 'disengaged' from and 'disillusioned' about public services as the focus of the research. Parents and children's centre practitioners were trained to use an interview schedule made up of a mixture of closed questions to ascertain specific things about the participating families along with open-ended questions that invited them to talk freely and provide details of their day-to-day lives.

One part of the schedule asked parents to mark up a map of Corby with the places they liked to go to and why, and those that they went to reluctantly or avoided altogether. They also drew onto the maps the daily journeys they made, for example, from home to school and nursery – to shops – to home – to nursery – to Mum's – to school – to home. Several families' stories provided detailed case studies (see Chapter 8).

All of this data, co-analysed by parents and practitioners over three days in June 2011, produced many significant insights into the daily lives of families in Corby who were 'disengaged' and 'disillusioned' with public services. Lessons were learned about the way in which public services needed to change to become truly open and accessible to all of the town's families.

Parents' Voices

The latest version of an interview schedule for use at the Pen Green Centre is called Parents' Voices. It employs a mixture of closed and open-ended questions to gather specific details about families along with parents' more freely expressed responses about, for example, the daily and weekly pressures and 'pinch points' they experience.

This format can be easily adapted so that it can focus on areas of particular concern to both workers and parents at Pen Green to support co-conceptualised research projects.

Understanding the culture, knowing the town

So, why does the Pen Green Centre place such faith in its parent-to-parent interviewing model of assessment and evaluation model? The answer lies in the quality of the data produced by this way of working with parents both as researchers and as participants. We have found that the data is richer because the research projects are co-conceptualised with parents, the interview schedules are co-produced with parents and the data is co-analysed with parents. All of these factors promote the transformation of rich data, through close analysis, to the production of authentic and parent-validated evidence from which deeper understandings of practice can be gleaned that support parent-validated changes in practice to be made.

Training, supporting and rewarding Parent-Interviewers is now an embedded practice at Pen Green. My reflections on one of the earlier examples of parent-to-parent interviewing (McKinnon, 2005; see box below) provide the rationale for why this approach works as successfully as it does and how the thinking that underpins it informs all needs assessment and service evaluation at the Pen Green Centre. They exemplify those factors that Brodie (2003) identifies in relation to the deeper knowledge and understanding that the Parent-Interviewers have about their communities and neighbourhoods.

**ANNUAL EVALUATION OF THE CORBY
SURE START LOCAL PROGRAMME IN 2004**

Parents were recruited from the local community to be trained on Pen
Green's 'Developing the Practice of Parent Researcher' course (Pen Green,
2004). These Parent-Interviewers, applying the interviewing skills and
techniques they had learned, conducted semi-structured interviews with
parents in their own homes in an informal but professional manner. However, this was not the most important reason why this team of interviewers
carried out the fieldwork so well; the main factor here was that they were
all local to the area and had a deep understanding of Corby and its people:

- 'the interviewers' children go to the same schools as those of the interviewees; they use the same shops, pubs, clubs and sporting facilities;
  they go to the same churches. They have a common cultural experience in terms of the unique nature of Corby's development as a town
  and community. Consequently, they are able to strike up and develop
  a rapport and relationship of trust with the interviewees'.
- The use of local parents to carry out this kind of work produces several
  important advantages in terms of the experience for both the interviewer and, crucially, the interviewee. The interview situation is more
  relaxed and informal and the Parent-Interviewers 'know when to
  prompt and follow-up with a supplementary question, how to express
  it and when further prompting might become counter-productive'.
- One of the interviewing team explicitly stated that she found that
  being from Corby and knowing the local culture was a big advantage
  in understanding the things that parents had to say about Sure Start.
  The other Parent-Interviewers at this meeting agreed with the views
  she expressed. She went on to say that 'being a Corby woman' allowed
  her to pursue some of the comments parents made and find out more
  from them.
- 'The parents felt good that they were being asked how they felt about
  things. They felt safe talking to you in their own home. The parent-to-
  parent interviewing really worked because people could see I was just
  like them – they could see that I didn't have a "hidden agenda" which
  they might have thought about a professional interviewer'.

Parent-to-parent, round tables
and socio-spatial mapping

While proving to be a very valuable way of assessing community needs and evaluating services, parent-to-parent interviewing has often been used in conjunction
with two other approaches that Pen Green has found to be methodologically

complementary – Mark Friedman's Outcomes Based Accountability (OBA; 2005) and Socio-Spatial Mapping (Smith, 1999). Outcomes Based Accountability emphasises the need to work at ground level if any significant changes in practice and provision are to take root, grow and become embedded in our public services. Its straightforward, but not simplistic, step-by-step approach supports the authentic involvement of 'stakeholders' who are genuinely interested in making a change to some aspect of their community because the interests of their community will be served. Friedman (2005) argues for the fundamental importance of providers of public services engaging with those in the communities they serve who can act as their 'critical friends'. 'Critical friends' are those who will tell you the things that you may not want to hear, but that you have to hear if there is to be any real shift in professional practice; change rarely comes about if you listen only to those who say the things you like. Inviting the interested stakeholders, including your 'critical friends', to a 'round table meeting' provides the initial step into Friedman's process for the identification of issues in the community where the direction of the trend line needs to be changed. Local stakeholders, sitting at the 'round table' can agree about the most critical issue in their community, the most important matter to 'turn the curve' on, the thing that has to change direction so that it can be taken to a different place.

Socio-Spatial Mapping is a technique that uses the data that settings hold about the families in their community to produce maps showing the locations of families in relation to, for example, the setting itself, areas of deprivation or, in the specific case of children's centres, their reach areas. Families' locations can be linked to data so that they show their demographics, for example, if the family is headed by a lone parent, if anyone in the household is employed, the ethnicity of adults and children, which languages the family speak, and so forth. Family locations can be presented in ways that show which services the family uses and how this has changed over any time period. Practitioners have found this method to be highly valuable:

> We used a socio-spatial map to help us with some of our work. The map used colours to highlight and identify levels of deprivation in Corby . . . The map also pinpointed individual families who were accessing our services, so we could see at a glance whether families in those deprived areas were accessing the services or not . . . The map was really helpful; it's a really good visual aid. You can see information 'at a glance' and quickly share it with people who are unfamiliar with your setting and your community . . . it's a very useful tool and it's something I've gone back to and used many times; I've used it to show things to parents, I've used it with colleagues and I've used it when making bids for funding . . . so, yes I've found it very useful. (Angela Prodger, Pen Green, Corby, 2008).

The Baby and Toddler Nest is Pen Green's Neighbourhood Nursery Initiative provision. Socio-spatial mapping of the Baby and Toddler Nest catchment area in September led to a re-examination of the priorities for and allocation of places. The outcome of this was that all 10 places vacated over the Christmas break in 2007 were allocated to families in the designated catchment area. (Heather Donoyou, Pen Green, Corby, 2008)

Socio-Spatial Mapping helped us to see how widely spread out our families are and how few of them come from the one 10% and two 20% areas of multiple deprivation close by us. Now we know where to do future leafleting and publicity and that we have to develop more effective ways of working with our parents who live in these areas. (Kim Baxter, Wallace Road Nursery School, Northampton, 2008).

Used in combination, parent-to-parent interviewing, Friedman's OBA and Socio-Spatial Mapping form a methodological 'package' flexible enough to be tailored to the research required, depending on whether the issue of concern goes across the community or needs to be focused on a particular part of, or group in, the community. This integrated approach is summarised here:

1. Friedman's 'Turning the Curve' approach requires the involvement of local people and practitioners in jointly identifying a critical issue in their community and the planning of some form of intervention to address it and change the direction of the trend line
2. Parent-to-parent interviewing allows the views of parents to be gathered to form part of the baseline data
3. Socio-Spatial Mapping provides another part of the baseline data and allows all concerned to clearly see where families using services live in relation to the setting and the most disadvantaged neighbourhoods in the community
4. After the intervention has been put in place, and in line with the agreed plan, parent-to-parent interviewing can be used to gather parents' views on how effective they think the intervention has been and whether it has made a difference to them and their families
5. Socio-Spatial mapping can show what the effects of the intervention have been in terms of whether more families in the disadvantaged areas are now using the setting and its services in the ways envisaged by the practitioners, providers and other interested stakeholders
6. Another 'Turning the Curve' round table meeting can then take place so that local people and practitioners can follow up on what the evaluation has revealed and/or agree on the next issue of concern that they want to change.

This cycle of research can be repeated to track the progress of the same intervention over time or applied to other related areas of concern or to different ones. These methodologies, used in combination, can gather both 'hard', quantitative and, so-called, 'soft' qualitative data, allowing settings to combine these in ways that deepen practitioners' understanding of how effective their practice and provision is or, crucially, is not. It is only when you know that something is not working, and why, that you can do something to change it for the better.

This package of complementary methods has been used at Pen Green, and other settings in Corby and Northamptonshire, throughout a number of years to research the effectiveness of practice and provision in communities, for example:

- Corby Sure Start Local Programme annual evaluations in 1999 (Tait et al., 1999), 2001 (Tait et al., 2001), 2003 (McKinnon et al., 2003) and 2004 (McKinnon et al., 2005)
- Specific service evaluations at Pen Green, such as Growing Together, Advanced Childminders (McKinnon, 2006a) and Getting Ahead of Postnatal Depression (GAP) (McKinnon, 2006b)
- Children's Workforce Development Council funded Practitioner Research Projects (McKinnon, 2008)
- Making Children's Learning Visible projects in Northamptonshire's Nursery Schools (McKinnon & Whalley, 2008) and a combined primary school and children's centre study (Hayward & McKinnon, 2011).

Concluding comments

Writing about her work with the national Sure Start programme, Naomi Eisenstadt (2011) comments that the evidence about the effectiveness of public services working in genuinely integrated ways showed that this was only successful where 'it was planned at a local level with both good data on what the population needs were, and extensive consultation to ensure the style of delivery would be appropriate' (Eisenstadt, 2011: 29).

We believe that the methods we use and have developed at Pen Green fulfil Eisenstadt's definition of working effectively with our community and that this has allowed us to provide services that meet the needs of our parents and their families. At the time of writing, in the Spring of 2013, Pen Green had recently been judged as 'Outstanding' in two Ofsted inspections for the Nursery School in November 2012 (Ofsted, 2012) and the Children's Centre in January 2013 (Ofsted, 2013).

While I have argued for the use of parent-to-parent interviewing to be used as part of a package of methods, it is worth emphasising that we see it as invaluable both in identifying needs and evaluating impact. Leaders and practitioners in settings talk to and listen to parents every day, and there is no suggestion here that this information is without value – quite the opposite. However, at Pen Green we believe that parent-to-parent interviewing can ensure that the authentic voices of parents from across the community are heard and influence practice. This can only happen when parents play a full and leading role in the co-construction of the ways in which their needs are assessed, interpreted and in the co-construction of the services that are provided to meet them. As the experience at Pen Green demonstrates, parent-to-parent interviewing is a methodology that can help you to address critical issues in a straightforward and effective way.

References

Baxter, K. (2008) *Socio-Spatial Mapping and Turning the Curve*. Presentation given at an internal seminar for the Head of Children's Services, Pen Green Research, Development and Training Base. Corby, 4 July.

Brodie, I. (2003) *The Involvement of Parents and Carers in Sure Start Local Evaluations*. London: Birkbeck College. National Evaluation of Sure Start.

Donoyou, H. (2008) *Socio-Spatial Mapping and Prioritising the Allocation of Nursery Places*. Presentation given at an internal seminar for the Head of Children's Services, Pen Green Research, Development and Training Base. Corby, 4 July.

Eisenstadt, N. (2011) *Providing a Sure Start: How Government Discovered Early Childhood*. Bristol: The Policy Press.

Freire, P. (1970) *Pedagogy of the Oppressed*. London: Penguin Books.

Friedman, M. (2005) *Trying Hard is Not Enough: How to Produce Measurable Improvements for Customers and Communities*. Crewe, England: Trafford Publishing.

Hayward, K. & McKinnon, E. (2011) *Making Children's Learning Visible in a Combined Primary School and Children's Centre*. Corby: Pen Green Research, Development and Training Base. Unpublished evaluation report.

Innovation Unit (2012) *Transforming Early Years* [online]. Available from: http://www.innovationunit.org/our-projects/projects/transforming-early-years [Accessed 12.03.13]

McKinnon, E. (2005) *Family Life and Family Services: Putting the Jigsaw Together*. Paper presented at the European Early Childhood Education Research Association Annual Conference, Dublin.

McKinnon, E. (2006a) *The Groupwork Programme at Pen Green*. Corby: Pen Green Research, Development and Training Base. England. Unpublished internal evaluation report.

McKinnon, E. (2006b) *Crystallization, Participation and Evaluation*. Symposium paper given at the European Early Childhood Education Research Association Annual Conference, *Democracy and Culture in Early Education*. Reykjavik, September.

McKinnon, E. (2008) *Can an Independent Consortium of Children's Centres Provide an Effective Mutual Support Network for Newly Designated Settings and Enhance the Quality of Service Provision for Children and Families Across the Town of Corby?* Report on the Practitioner Research Projects in Corby 2007–08 for the Children's Workforce Development Council. Summary available at: http://webarchive.nationalarchives.gov.uk/20120119192332/http://cwdcouncil.org.uk/plr-projects-2007–08

McKinnon, E., Fletcher, C. & Whalley, M. (2003) *Pen Green Sure Start Annual Evaluation 2003*. Corby, England: Pen Green Research, Development and Training Base.

McKinnon, E., Fletcher, C. & Whalley, M. (2005) *Outreach Provision: Users' Satisfaction Survey*. Corby, England: Pen Green Research, Development and Training Base.

McKinnon, E. & Whalley, M. (2008) *Achieving Outcomes in Early Childhood Education: Building Practitioner Action Led Research Learning Groups*. Symposium paper given at the European Early Childhood Education Research Association Annual Conference, *Democracy and Culture in Early Education*. Reykjavik, September.

Ofsted (2012) *School Report, Pen Green Centre for Children and their Families*. 13 December 2012.

Ofsted (2013) *Inspection Report for Pen Green Centre for Children and Families*. 8 February, 2013.

Pen Green Research, Development and Training Base (2004) *Developing the Practice of Parent Researcher*. Training pack and materials. Pen Green Centre for Children and Families.

Prodger, A. (2008) *Getting to Know You*. Presentation given at an internal seminar for Northamptonshire's Head of Children's Services, Pen Green Research, Development and Training Base. Corby, 4 July.

Smith, T. (1999) 'Neighbourhood and Preventive Strategies with Children and Families: What Works?' *Children and Society*, Vol. 13, No. 4, 265–277.

Tait, C., Fletcher, C. & Whalley, M. (1999) *Evaluating Services and Defining Local Needs*. Corby, England: Pen Green Research, Development and Training Base.

Tait, C., Fletcher, C. & Whalley, M. (2001) *Parental Employment, Early Years Care and Service Evaluations*. Corby, England: Pen Green Research, Development and Training Base.

Weinberger, J. (2005) 'Listening to Families: A Survey of Parents' Views'. In Weinberger, J., Pickstone, C. & Hannon, P. (Eds), *Learning from Sure Start: Working with Young Children and their Families*. Maidenhead, England: Open University Press.

Whalley, M. (1994) *Learning To Be Strong*. London: Hodder and Stoughton.

Chapter 7

A week in the life of the Pen Green Centre

Mass-Observation comes to Corby

Eddie McKinnon

In 2004 the Research Team at the Pen Green Children's Centre was introduced to the work of the Mass-Observation Project (Madge & Harrisson, 1939). Founders Charles Madge and Tom Harrisson recruited

- Volunteer writers who kept monthly diaries of their day-to-day lives and sent them in to the Project and
- observers who went onto the streets of their towns and neighbourhoods to record what people were doing and saying in the shops, pubs, churches, football grounds and workplaces.

Mass-Observation pioneered a new form of social history based on the experiences and impressions of 'ordinary' people; the recording of contemporary events was now no longer the preserve of the 'great and good' but placed firmly into the hands of a 'mass' of social observers and historians. Mass-Observation continues to collect evidence from diarists and observers; its archive at the University of Sussex is a rich source of material for social historians, researchers and people interested in what life was like for ordinary people in the mid to late 20th century.

However, Mass-Observation's methodological approach was not without its critics, who argued that it was the 'surveillance of the weak by those with power, influence and authority' (Nevin, 2005). Nevin records that, in the eyes of its detractors, Mass-Observation was 'the upper middle classes using the lower middle classes to spy on the working classes' (Nevin, 2005). Furthermore, the critics suggest that the entire approach adopted by Mass-Observation was not systematic enough to make it acceptable as valid social science but only 'A well-intentioned, idealistic attempt at a kind of general sociological study rarely conducted today . . . [which] . . . has been made redundant by more professional sociology, more sophisticated methods of information gathering' (Nevin, 2005).

But Mass-Observation also has its defenders; Hubble (2010) uses it to reconceptualise the relationship between agency, literacy practices and social transformation. He argues in favour of the positive influence of the project on modern social research saying that 'many stalwarts of the Government Social Survey cut their teeth with Mass-Observation' (Hubble, 2005). Furthermore, far from being the dilettantes they have been often portrayed as, they 'were not amateurish but years ahead of their time' (Hubble, 2005).

Inspired by Mass-Observation, the Research Team proposed that the Pen Green Centre for Children and Families should undertake an evaluation project using diaries as the primary method of data-gathering. The other parts of Pen Green were keen to participate, and during one week in November 2004, parents, children and staff were encouraged to keep diaries that recorded their involvement with the Pen Green Centre and the Sure Start Community Houses during that time.

How and why Pen Green adopted the Mass-Observation approach

Why were the researchers and practitioners at Pen Green so taken by the Mass-Observation approach? One answer is that there was an established history of using diaries as a way of developing an understanding of yourself as a parent, a practitioner or a researcher. For example, in 1996 Pen Green ran a five-month research project called Parents Involved in their Children's Learning (PICL) funded by the Teacher Training Agency. The participants included workers at Pen Green and ten parents who had expressed an interest to staff in finding out more about how their children learned (Whalley & the Pen Green Centre Team, 2007: 13). As part of the research the parents were asked to keep diaries of how their children played at home. The parents became keen diarists, especially once they had learned about child development concepts, and they wanted to film their children being 'Involved' (Laevers, 1997) or engaging in schematic play (Athey, 2007). One of the practitioners involved in the PICL project expressed her views about the benefits she experienced when parents kept diaries:

> The families in my group who . . . kept diaries . . . recorded many of their children's interests and this information was invaluable to me when I returned to work after maternity leave. (Whalley & the Pen Green Centre Team, 2007: 30)

She also acknowledged the benefits for the parents and their children:

> I feel most parents who have been involved are able to talk about their child's learning positively and with confidence. I feel that the children have gained and that they are having their needs addressed and catered for. (ibid.)

Parents' diaries significantly deepened their understanding of themselves as parents and of their children as learners. Practitioners experienced a similar effect regarding their understanding of the children *and* the parents. Parents and practitioners gained insights into the complexity of everyday life for families. This complexity has also been consistently confirmed in a range of other ways at Pen Green; for example, Corby Sure Start Local Programme annual evaluations, specific service evaluations, such as drop-in groups (e.g. Growing Together and Messy Play) and also of closed, therapeutic groups (e.g. GAP – Getting Ahead of Postnatal Depression). These research and evaluation projects used a variety of methods to find out about parents' and children's experiences and their feelings about the Pen Green Centre and its provision:

- Parent-to-parent semi-structured interviews (Tait et al., 1999, 2001; McKinnon et al., 2003a, 2005)
- In-depth interviews (McKinnon et al., 2005)
- Focus groups (McKinnon et al., 2003b)
- Case studies (McKinnon et al., 2003a; McKinnon, 2005)

The evidence gathered painted detailed miniatures and vignettes of families using Pen Green in *their own way* and in *their own time* so that the Centre's integrated services fitted into *their family life*, rather than the other way around (McKinnon, 2005). Families' routes into Pen Green were diverse, and their journeys through it were equally varied. The evidence in the evaluations confirmed what practitioners at Pen Green knew from their daily interactions with parents; that parents and families engage with public services that are actually available in terms of types and times of services offered and the ease with which they can be helped to cross the thresholds, both physical and emotional, that lead to them. Workers at Pen Green also knew about this from their own histories: '56 per cent of our 120 staff came in as parents and trained here' (Whalley & Riddell, 2013). Parents' diaries demonstrated that family life in the 21st century does not conform to the rigidities of Core Offers or Core Purposes (DfE, 2012).

At Pen Green we wanted to emulate Mass-Observation, in terms of the advantages of using diaries as a significant way of gathering data and not as a form of surveillance. In line with the established practice at Pen Green, we went to great lengths to ensure that this piece of work was participatory and co-constructed with parents and workers and was not experienced as top-down scrutiny of their lives:

- parents, children and members of staff were invited to participate in keeping diaries
- parents took part voluntarily and were supported in keeping their diaries by members of staff in the area of Pen Green that they used (e.g. the Nursery, the Family Room, Sure Start)
- all the materials used to publicise the exercise made it clear that the parents could write their diaries in any way that suited them, including as much or as little detail as they wished. In addition to the diaries, we also gathered many other materials that recorded the parent's day/week, such as mini-interviews, feedback forms, Dictaphone tapes, photographs and site-diagrams.

These practices were in line with the Pen Green philosophy, which rejects the thinking underpinning 'Us and Them' approaches in favour of a fairer, equal and more productive one that sees the situation as one of 'Us and Us'.

'A week in the life of Pen Green' and the parents' diaries

We knew that we needed to 'enlist' as many parents as possible in diary-writing to make the work successful; the larger the number of diaries gathered, the broader and deeper the picture of how families made use of Pen Green could be. We also knew that in order to achieve this we needed the support and cooperation of our many colleagues across the Pen Green Centre and the Sure Start Community Houses. Training sessions were run for colleagues representing the 11 constituent parts of the Centre who then became our 'Area Leads' in their respective areas:

- Nursery
- Baby and Toddler Nest
- Corby Sure Start Local Programme
- Samuel Lloyd Nursery (private provision in the Pen Green Centre)
- The Corby Home Start Project
- After School Club
- Wider Opportunities (adult education)
- Crèche
- Reception
- Family Room
- The Pen Green Research Base.

All the locations were provided with a box of appropriate materials to facilitate the keeping of diaries in various forms.

The Area Leads and the two project researchers encountered parents who felt that, as 'ordinary' people, they and their lives were not 'interesting enough' to warrant anyone's attention. Dorothy Sheridan argues that the notion of 'ordinary' people contributing to social research clashes with a culture in which there is

> widespread distrust about what might be described as 'non-elite' material; that is, material generated by people who are not chosen by experts but who, on the contrary, choose to elect themselves as spokespersons or social commentators of our times. (Sheridan, 1996, Section 2 The problem of representativeness)

At Pen Green the tradition of involving parents in the work of the Centre coincides with the ethos articulated by Mass-Observation, which 'challenges the idea that there is only one kind of history, or social knowledge, and only certain sorts of people are entitled to create it' (Sheridan, 1996, Section 5 Research relationships: the question of power).

Materials used to publicise and explain the 'diary week' overtly addressed the supposed 'ordinariness' of people and their lives; the significance of parents' experiences and how interesting and important they were to us were emphasised. Posters for the diary week told parents that 'Pen Green Needs You, Yes You!' and encouraged them to 'Be Part Of It', and our newsletter and flyers underlined that we wanted their diaries to record their experiences in their own way and in their own words. We gathered 33 diaries from parents. The diaries ranged from those employing a 'page-per-day' entry to one parent who wrote 48 pages about her week.

Diaries as a significant form of research data

Parents' diaries are potentially a very powerful way of getting access to how people live their day-to-day lives and the thoughts and feelings that their experiences generate. It may be the case that, methodologically, *only* diaries can record, not only the events of the day, but also the results of people's reflections on them and the emotional responses that they experience. As a method, diary-writing places more power into the hands of the parents than other approaches such as interviewing, no matter how flexibly structured and informally conducted. The parent's diary narrates the events of their day or week in a way that reflects that parent's perceptions and concerns as opposed to those of someone else. Furthermore, the diary records the expression of their feelings and reflections in their own words.

Like all research methods, diaries have their advantages and disadvantages, and several of these emerged in the course of our research. On the positive side

- parents were given an opportunity to contribute and participate directly in this piece of research
- the diaries gave us a record of the family's interaction with the Pen Green Centre directly from the point of view of the parent, unmediated by anyone else
- the diary accounts were expressed in the parents' own words and language rather than reconstructed from the notes of an interviewer.

However, some of the problems that arose were as follows:

- as a voluntary exercise it was difficult to get as large a response from parents as we would have liked. However, as one of our aims was to see how the Pen Green Centre 'fitted' into the rest of their busy lives, it is possible that many parents had difficulty finding the time to record this
- keeping a diary was done voluntarily by parents; the diaries we gathered reflect a self-selecting sample, so the data may be valid for our diary-writers but may not necessarily be representative and generaliseable
- as a self-selecting sample some of the parents who did complete diaries may be those who feel a 'debt of gratitude' to Pen Green, and so the information in these diaries may be skewed by this
- what about those parents who did not do diaries?
- what about those parents who feel their needs are not being met and who felt that writing a diary would not change anything for them?

Detail and depth in the parents' diaries

The content of the parents' diaries varied in terms of the level of detail included. Some consisted of a daily 'timetable' of actions and events with little variation from day-to-day. Many were accounts including details of the family's home circumstances, their children's behaviour and family commitments as well as their time at the Pen Green Centre. Some parents wrote diaries that were just as detailed but were also overtly reflective, revealing their thoughts and feelings at the end of a, typically, busy day. Some of the parents revealed feelings of a deeply personal and intimate nature. Consequently, our analysis of the parents' diaries fell broadly into four levels in terms of the detail and depth provided. Table 7.1 summarises how these diaries were differentiated in terms of the depth and detail that parents went into as they wrote them.

The following excerpts from parents' diaries exemplify the criteria for the four levels. Naturally all identities have been anonymised. All of the excerpts included were shown to the parents and discussed with them at some length, with great emphasis being placed on their power to veto any material and control how we used their writing.

Excerpts from parents' diaries that illustrate the four levels of detail and discourse

Level 1: Basic 'timeline' of the day

This excerpt exemplifies those that formed the Level 1 type – a 'timetable' of the events and actions of the day. We have a clear picture of what this parent did, where she went, who she saw and spoke to but little else by way of thoughts, feelings, etc.

Table 7.1 Four discernible levels of information in parents' diaries

Level	Contents
1	Basic daily 'timetable' of actions and events, varying little from day to day in terms of the day's events and/or their presentation.
2	More detailed accounts, including, for example, details of the family's home circumstances, their children's behaviour and family commitments as well as their time at the Pen Green Centre. Many including events 'before and after' time at Pen Green. Some comments reflecting thoughts and feelings.
3	As in Level 2 but more overtly reflective, revealing their thoughts and feelings at the end of a (typically) busy day.
4	As in Level 3 but additional thoughts and reflections of a deeper, more personal and/or intimate nature. Deeply revelatory content.

Monday 08/11/04

6.00 Get up and have a shower
6.15 Do make up
6.30 Blow dry hair
7.00 Wake S (baby) *up and we both have breakfast*
7.30 Get S ready for nursery
8.00 Drop S off at Baby Nest and drive to work
8.30 Start work
12.15 Finish work at Asda, pop in and get dinner for tonight
1.00 Pick S up from nursery
1.15 Have lunch and S goes to sleep
1.30 Ring sister then do ironing
4.00 S up and play for a while whilst watching 'C Beebies'
5.00 S has dinner
5.30 Start mine and B's (partner) *dinner*
6.00 B comes home; have dinner
6.30 Wash and dry up
7.00 S's bath
7.30 S's milk and bed time. Then me and B watch TV until bed time around
*   9.30 ish.*

Level 2: A daily timeline with more detail and some reflection

This excerpt is typical of Level 2 – the parent gives us a clear timeline from the early morning to the late evening of the day with plenty of detail that fleshes out the actions and events of the day. This mother also provides us with comments that show her state of mind, her aspirations and her feelings as the day proceeds:

Monday 08/11/04

* *The crèche course today was very deep and quite emotional and actually I found it quite mentally exhausting . . . Very hard to hear about all the different forms of abuse that children suffer and how to look for the signs of abuse.*
* *. . . looking forward to hopefully passing the course and working with children. I quite fancy studying children and I'm really excited about doing a portfolio on a child that I don't know yet.*
* *I came home for my lunch really wanting to give M a cuddle but he was sleeping and then I was thinking about how I shouted at T the other day for falling and getting his trousers dirty. I felt bad and was wishing for 2.55 to come so I could see him and just love him and talk with him. Me and T have some great conversations, I love sitting chatting with him.*

She also adds a humorous postscript that illustrates the difficulty in recording everything that took place during the day:

• *If I didn't mention earlier, I also did some ironing and sorted out the dried washing and put another load in, to be done tomorrow – it's all go isn't it.*

Level 3: A timeline with greater detail plus more frequent and in-depth reflection

These excerpts typify Level 3; the parent gives us a highly detailed narrative account of each day with comments that encapsulate her emotions and feelings – please note, these are small selections from her entries for each day. This mother does some 'soul-searching' as a result of the day's events and, particularly, her own actions and relationships with her children.

Monday 08/11/04

• *When I left I went to Group B Room for my crèche course which I have been doing for about 7 weeks now and loving every minute of it. Today we talked about child protection. It was very good but upsetting. It made me think about my parenting. For example when P threw herself on the floor I grabbed her arm and pulled her up. This morning I thought nothing of it but now after doing my course I thought to myself 'have I just been physically abusing my child and not realising it'. Thoughts like that keep popping up in my mind . . . M, Ps key worker in the Nursery, came for a home visit. K and B were both very pleased to see her. We talked about P, how she was settling in and if I had any problems with the nursery. I felt a bit guilty as it was all negative stuff about P and her potty training behaviour and stuff. But M said don't feel bad about it, that it is best to be honest.*

Wednesday 10/11/04

• *Potty training is turning out to be a trying time. She is fine at home but at nursery she has no interest in it whatsoever. I am finding this all very stressful. People keep telling me what to do all the time. I know they all mean well, but I feel pressurised myself, so I dread to think what kind of effect this is having on my daughter.*

Friday 12/11/04

• *I am feeling really upset and a failure as a parent. What have I done wrong? Or where? I have decided also to quit my courses, so I can spend more time with P. I feel that I am leaving her too often with crèche and it could be having some kind of effect on her. I am even thinking of quitting my crèche course too. Which I don't want to. But P is far more important. I hope everyone understands (on my course) . . . We played sing songs and danced and read stories before we went and got L from school. L was pleased to see us and greeted me with a big hug and kiss which was lovely after the day I have had. To top it off R finished work early. Just in time to put the kids to bed. They were so excited. Had a few drinks to end a not too good week. Goodbye diary. x*

Level 4: Thoughts and reflections of a deeper, personal, intimate and revelatory nature

The excerpts from this parent's diary clearly demonstrate the criteria for Level 4; she seems to be 'talking' to her diary, 'confiding' in it as she might do with a very close friend. This parent's diary is quoted from extensively in order to demonstrate the intimate nature of what she has to tell us; we are given some vivid insights into what her world is like.

Friday 05/11/04

• *Washing in machine needs hanging out. Clothes mountain in basket needs putting in machine. Pile of dishes in sink needs washing. Muddy kitchen floor. I am a lone parent and as the cleaning fairies don't exist I've only got myself to rely on. It can wait until tomorrow – I can't prise myself off the couch* (NB – this was written after a sleepless night caused by severe toothache).

Saturday 06/11/04

• *I do feel quite sad that I've finished my family but I've been so poor. I'm going to have to knuckle down and get some qualifications a nice car and money for holidays. I hate having to dilute the washing up liquid if I run out. I feel bottom of the food chain.*
• *My children are amazing, I can't believe little me made them! I always tell them how beautiful and clever they are, it's important to boost their confidence. I am so lucky. D's constantly got her head in a book; she spends her money on magazines which is good because they follow the national curriculum.*

Monday 08/11/04

• *Got to nursery at 10.30 instead of the usual 9.00 am. Couldn't motivate myself all day. I feel so grateful to be able to use the services of Pen Green. I feel like the staff are family, I see them more than my own family.*
• *B picked us up at 1 pm when C finished nursery. He is an absolute gem, he's been the father I never had these past few years. I've always felt scared of older*

men but he's never once made me feel uncomfortable. He is a major part of my support network (this comment refers to the driver of the minibus that transported families between the several sites offering the Corby Sure Start Local Programme services).

- *I feel so lonely at home. I never get any visitors so Pen Green is the only adult company I get. I have it all at Pen Green, friends, a place where I feel incredibly comfortable and the best pre-school education in the world.*
- *Pen Green hasn't taught me to be a parent, it's taught me to be a great parent.*
- *As an abused child I've never felt I belonged anywhere, but at Pen Green I feel totally relaxed and safe. Being a parent is an amazing roller coaster ride and at Pen Green you really get the encouragement to mould your children into wonderful, clever individuals.*

Tuesday 09/11/04

- *Picked D up at 1.00 then went to Kingswood. D and P* (Sure Start worker) *have formed a special bond from D's time in respite earlier this year. The staff really do much more than their job entails. I've never felt so understood in all my life. They are friends, not staff.*

Wednesday 10/11/04

- *After breakfast I cleaned the house from top to bottom. D and F wound each other up all day. D is just whingeing constantly, she's fine as soon as we are out at Kingswood but when we go home she starts. I try to make home as fun as possible.*
- *Maybe I'm a bit more sensitive than usual. It's been a year since he died. I miss him so much, I feel sad that my kids won't get to know what an amazing man he was.*
- *Today we made families with D's Barbies. I put 2 men with a baby, a single mum family, a single dad family and a family with 2 women. I want my girls to know that there are different types of families. Just because they only have a mum doesn't mean our family isn't normal.*
- *I am so proud of my kids and what I have achieved as a parent. My kids are amazing.*

Thursday 11/11/04

My hopes for my children are:

- *To be well balanced, considerate and confident individuals*
- *To respect other people's views and opinions and never judge others*
- *To have pride in whatever they achieve whether it's scrubbing toilets or Prime Minister*
- *To know wherever they are and whatever they become mummy loves them with her heart and soul and every breath in her body.*

As a mum I am a

- *Confidence builder*
- *Children's bather*
- *Teeth brusher*
- *Hair brusher*
- *Dresser*
- *Cleaner*
- *Cook (normally burnt)*
- *Toilet scrubber*
- *Hooverer*
- *Wet bed changer*
- *Love giver*
- *Disciplinarian*

- *Fun and enjoyment giver*
- *Shopper*
- *Chauffeur*
- *Advice giver*
- *Bum wiper*
- *Shitty nappy disposer*
- *Decorator*
- *Referee of arguments*
- *Window washer*
- *Nurse*
- *General provider of everything*

Yet I still don't get paid. I am so good at multi-tasking I should have been an octopus!

The power of some of the entries in this parent's Level 4 diary lies, not only in their revelatory nature, but also in terms of the diary as a methodological tool. The level of personal detail given, and the expressed depth of feelings displayed, would, we feel, be very unlikely to emerge in any methodological form other than a personal diary.

The ethics of parents' diaries

The use of diaries raises methodological questions relating to the different roles played by researchers and participants and the ethical considerations that arise. Hatch and Wisniewski put the questions like this:

> Who speaks for whom and with what kind of authority? Whose story is it? Who owns the product of the work? Who is the author? What does the researcher gain from the research? The subject? (Hatch & Wisniewski, 1995: 119)

These important questions have to be considered in all social research work. In this piece of research we attempted to address them in the following ways:

- there were no 'hidden agendas'. We were completely open with parents as to the nature of the research aims for the 'diary week'; publicity materials for the diary week explained the rationale behind the exercise and Lead People were able to explain these matters to parents
- ensuring that parents understood that they provided us with diaries on a voluntary basis
- all identities were kept confidential by substituting names with capital letters that did not coincide with anyone's actual initials

- any use of diary material was discussed with parents beforehand, and their consent was given for this to happen
- while our newsletter and flyers clearly delineated what we wanted parents to write about, we had no power as such to make that happen; this was reflected in the diaries being classifiable into four different layers based on depth and detail
- we hoped that parents would enjoy the opportunity to become involved in a research project where they had a large measure of control over what they recorded
- we hoped to 'gain' a deeper understanding of families in the community, their relationships with the Pen Green Centre and its impacts on their lives.

Those diaries that fell into Levels 3 and 4 raise the issue of researchers' access to information of a personal nature and, in the case of Level 4 diaries, to parents sometimes revealing matters of an intimate nature. Michel Foucault refers to 'technologies of power' such as 'examination', like social research, and 'confession' as forms of 'discipline' in society. Foucault argues that the propensity of people to 'confess' renders them amenable to increased social and political control (Foucault, 1981: 174). In this respect Foucault's concerns echo Nevin's comments about Mass-Observation being the surveillance of the weak by the powerful. In the case of the 'Week in the life of Pen Green' research, we would certainly question these points. We feel we have demonstrated that our research practices veer away from the route of surveillance and control, following instead a path towards greater involvement by parents in the research process.

Purposeful and self-selecting samples

The 'Week in the life of Pen Green' exercise was necessarily dependent on a self-selecting sample of parents who were willing to participate and keep diaries. In terms of representativeness, self-selecting samples are often seen as suspect; for example, what about those parents who were too busy to keep a diary? Even our Level 2 diarist makes a specific reference to the difficulty in recording everything. What about all those parents who did not keep a diary at all, irrespective of the reasons? Looked at in these terms, our sample was not representative; however, this does not invalidate the data because 'even if the sample . . . proved highly skewed, it might provide useful information about this particular population' (Stanley: 1981: 149). Sheridan goes on to argue, 'statistical "representativeness" becomes less important as a factor than the capacity of the data to reveal a more in-depth understanding of social processes and social meanings'.

This view is also taken by Michael Quinn Patton who talks about 'purposeful samples' and 'information-rich cases'. While we did not actively select our sample of parents, they did form a 'purposeful sample' in that they fulfilled Patton's definition of 'information-rich cases' from which it is possible to learn 'a great deal about issues of central importance to the purpose of the inquiry . . . Studying information-rich cases yields insights and in-depth understanding rather than empirical generalization' (Patton, 2002: 30).

The diaries provided significant information about the day-to-day lives of families, and the role that Pen Green played in them, in ways that other methods were unable to reach. From these sources we have produced 'a "thickness" of data precisely because it is not confined by the normal narrowness of the printed questionnaire' (Stanley, 1981: 149).

At Pen Green we do have an interest in the 'who', 'when' and 'where' questions, but we want to develop a much deeper understanding of the 'how' and the 'why' questions as they relate to the complex lives of modern families.

Methodological considerations

Parents' diaries can potentially tell us much more than interviews or even case studies. Material from a semi-structured interview can allow the 'creation' of a viable backstory about a parent. However, this will inevitably be mediated and interpreted by the researcher in ways that may not concur with the diary-writer's own words or intentions. Diaries, as private and confidential documents, are not often shared with others, even anonymously. Like Mass-Observation, we overtly departed from this position with our 'Week in the life of Pen Green' project. Parents who submitted diaries allowed us a privileged access to their worlds: Level 3 and, particularly, Level 4 diaries revealed parents' innermost thoughts, feelings and personal experiences. Parents 'confided' in their diaries things that other methods would be highly unlikely to reveal. This is because they chronicle

> the immediately contemporaneous flow of public and private events what are significant to the diarist . . . for each diary entry . . . is sedimented into a particular moment in time; they do not emerge 'all at once' as reflections on the past, but day by day . . . to record an ever-changing present. (Plummer, 2001: 48)

Like Sheridan we want to challenge views in academic circles and the wider community where 'there seems to be a common popular belief about what constitutes "proper" or scientific social research' (Stanley, 1981: 149).

Past, present and future

At Pen Green we want to develop interesting and effective ways of revealing the part played by the Centre in the lives of the families in our community. Approaches such as Parent Led Needs Assessments (Tait et al., 1999, 2001; McKinnon et al., 2003, 2005) ascertained parent's feelings about the quality of the groups and services and played a necessary part in the development of provision and practice.

However, the data we gathered through the parents' diaries gave us some significant insights into the complicated lives of the families who use the Centre's services. This convinced us that, in spite of the methodological strengths of using semi-structured interviewing, the relationships that families have with Pen Green are too complex to be effectively captured by interviewing alone.

Outcomes and implications for practice: A critique

The two project researchers fed back the findings to the parents and workers at Pen Green in the form of a report (McKinnon et al., 2006). However, it has to be pointed out that the impacts and outcomes for practice in the Pen Green Centre were minimal. This was largely because the researchers did not come from early years practitioner backgrounds; before working at the Pen Green Research Base, one had had a social science research career and the other a teaching career. Consequently, in the project, and in its writing up, they adopted an observational and analytic stance as opposed to one that would have enabled them to really engage with the parents and workers at Pen Green in a meaningful way. For example, neither of the researchers understood the necessity to work with the leaders and workers at Pen Green *after* the report was written in order to see if the report's findings and recommendations were being considered, worked with and put into operation in any part of the Centre's practice and provision. For example, the researchers could have led on setting up meetings with parents and workers to review the report and agree on an action plan of how the learning gained could be put into effect. This lack of 'following up' shows that, while Pen Green can demonstrate a genuine track record of nurturing practitioner-researchers, some who work with the Centre in these ways need to develop themselves as 'researcher-practitioners' and develop a deeper understanding of how an integrated provision like Pen Green works with the families who use it and the inherent complexities that this engagement produces.

The 'Us and Us' culture that prevails at Pen Green is fundamental in challenging and breaking down the barriers between 'researchers' and 'subjects' that can lead to the objectification of those people who willingly take part in social research. We believe that everyone – parents, workers and researchers – has something that they can bring to the research 'table'. In its evaluation research Pen Green has always attempted to shrug off the strictures of methodological orthodoxy while conducting work that has revealed the part played by Pen Green in the lives of families in Corby. By involving the parents and workers as co-constructors of the research, we hope to produce evaluation data that is deeper and richer in nature.

This thinking has been put into operation more recently in the 'localised ethnography' that was at the heart of the Transforming Early Years project in Corby in 2010–11 (see Chapter 8). Having identified parents who were 'disengaged' and 'disillusioned' with public services, parents and practitioners from the town's four children's centres co-interviewed parents whose use of services was minimal in order to find out why and to see how the town's services could redress this. The interviewing included asking parents to tell their stories in terms of their daily routines. They were asked to show on maps of Corby where they went, who they saw, what they did and why. Some parents completed pro forma journals that captured a week in their lives. Case studies of particular families were produced. The data gathered provided practitioners and professionals across Corby with some key insights into the ways in which local services were not engaging with families who were in great need of their support.

At Pen Green, philosophically and methodologically, we align ourselves with Sheridan, originally Harrisson's research assistant and now a trustee of the Mass-Observation Project and its archive. Talking optimistically of changing fashions in social research, Sheridan observed that

> What was considered trivial and pointlessly detailed about Mass-Observation's interest in minutiae is now valued as commitment to the study of everyday life. What was once regarded as 'unscientific', biased and unrepresentative can now be appreciated in our postmodern world as nuanced, qualitatively rich and ethnographically pioneering. (Sheridan, in Nevin, 2005)

In the same way, the parents' diaries provided the Pen Green Centre with richer insights and deeper understanding about the intricacies and complexities of family life in our community and where engagement with Pen Green 'fitted' in.

References

Athey, C. (2007) *Extending Thought in Young Children: A Parent-Teacher Partnership* (2nd Edition). London: Paul Chapman.

DfE (2012) *Core purpose of Sure Start Children's Centres* [online]. Department for Education. Available from: http://www.education.gov.uk/childrenandyoungpeople/early learningandchildcare/a00191780/core-purpose-of-sure-start-childrens-centres [Accessed: 14.03.13]

Foucault, M. (1981) *History of Sexuality Volume 1*. London: Harmondsworth-Penguin.

Hatch, J.A. & Wisniewski, R. (1995) *Life History and Narrative*. London: Routledge.

Hubble, N. (2005) 'Over to you'. *Guardian Weekend*, 26.03.2005.

Hubble, N. (2010) *Mass-Observation and Everyday Life: Culture, History, Theory* (2nd Edition). Basingstoke, England: Palgrave-Macmillan.

Laevers, F. (1997) *A Process Oriented Child Follow Up System for Young Children*. Leuven: Leuven Centre for Experiential Education.

Madge, C. & Harrisson, T.H. (1939) *Britain by Mass-Observation*. Harmondsworth, England: Penguin.

McKinnon, E. (2005) *Family Life and Family Services – Putting the Jigsaw Together*. Symposium paper presented at the European Early Childhood Education Research Association Annual Conference, *Young Children as Citizens: Identity, Belonging and Participation*. Dublin.

McKinnon, E., Fletcher, C. & Whalley, M. (2003a) *Parent to Parent User Satisfaction Survey 2003 Corby Sure Start.* Corby: Pen Green Research, Development and Training Base.

McKinnon, E., Fletcher, C. & Whalley, M. (2003b) *Evaluations from Staff Focus Groups and a Survey of Management Board Members.* Corby: Pen Green Research, Development and Training Base.

McKinnon, E., Fletcher, C. and Whalley, M. (2005) *Outreach Provision Users' Satisfaction Survey.* Corby: Pen Green Research, Development and Training Base.

McKinnon, E., Leisten, R. & Pearson, H. (2006) A *Week in the Life of the Pen Green Centre. A Research Project inspired by the Mass-Observation Project.* Unpublished internal report.

Nevin, C. (2005) 'Just looking'. *Guardian Weekend*, 19.03.2005.

Patton, M.Q. (2002) *Qualitative Evaluation and Research Methods* (3rd Edition). Thousand Oaks, CA: Sage.

Plummer, K. (2001) *Documents of Life 2: An Invitation to Critical Humanism.* London: Sage Publications.

Sheridan, D. (1996) *Damned Anecdotes and Dangerous Confabulations; Mass-Observation as Life History.* Mass-Observation Archive Occasional Paper No 7, University of Sussex Library.

Tait, C., Fletcher, C. & Whalley, M. (1999) *Evaluating Services and Defining Local Needs.* Corby: Pen Green Research and Training Base. Unpublished internal report.

Tait, C., Fletcher, C. & Whalley, M. (2001) *Parental Employment, Early Years Care and Service Evaluations.* Corby: Pen Green Research and Training Base. Unpublished internal report.

Whalley, M. & the Pen Green Centre Team (2007) *Involving Parents in Their Children's Learning* (2nd Edition). London: Paul Chapman.

Whalley, M. & Riddell, B. (2013) 'Pen Green Children's Centre – Standing the Test of Time'. *Nursery World*, 25 February–10 March, 34–35.

Chapter 8

Localised ethnography, local advocacy and community development

Touching, and being touched by, your community

Joanne Armstrong and Eddie McKinnon

Introduction

This chapter gives an account of how a project, intended to improve the lives of young families in Corby, was initiated, took form and produced some significant outcomes. The work in Corby took place within a national project funded by the National Endowment for Science, Technology and the Arts (NESTA) and facilitated by the Innovation Unit (IU), called 'Transforming the Early Years' (TEY). The TEY project had a planned focus on exploring how services for families with children aged five and under could be reorganised so that they were more responsive to families' expressed needs as opposed to a universal offer. One of the key findings of the Corby TEY project was that, while families did indeed want different and improved services for their pre-school children, they also wanted additional services for their older children and for themselves. The project gave rise to the emergence of a group of parents who wanted to become more engaged in shaping services in Corby through existing political structures. These parents wanted to actively encourage and involve other parents in this process.

The 'Transforming Early Years' project in Corby

In early 2010 leaders and practitioners working in the four children's centres in Corby, Northamptonshire, were invited to become involved in the NESTA project. The national project's aim was 'to find innovative ways of delivering radically better and more affordable services' for families with children under five who most needed them (Innovation Unit [IU], 2012a). The Innovation Unit argued that the way to achieve this was to think in terms of 'radical efficiency'; that is 'not tweaking existing services' but 'generating new perspectives on old problems to ensure a genuine shift in the nature and efficiency of the services on offer' producing 'better public outcomes at much lower cost' (Gillinson et al., 2010: 2). The IU's own research had found that 'Although most of the children's centres . . . are well-regarded by the parents who access them . . . only 1 in 10 of the families most in need of support actually use them' (IU, 2012a). Consequently, rethinking how services for families with young children were planned and offered to them was 'crucial to ensure families do not miss out on vital support that can help them' (ibid.).

Responding to an invitation from the Innovation Unit, a team represented Corby at a meeting of staff from the IU and NESTA, along with teams from more than 20 other localities in England. Corby's team was made up of

- a local authority officer
- a head of a nursery school and children's centre
- a local authority early years advisor (who soon after became a deputy head teacher of a Corby primary school and manager of its children's centre)
- a head of research in the early years field and
- a parent who used two of the town's four children's centres.

The inclusion of a parent on the panel from Corby is significant here; Corby was the only locality group that included service users. It demonstrates the commitment among many service providers in the town to ensure that the 'voice of the parent' is not only heard, but that parents are involved, from the outset, in the co-construction of the services that they want to use. This thinking was based on our shared experience as Corby parents and practitioners in relation to a plethora of initiatives that had been introduced across the previous three decades but had not produced the outcomes that were expected or promised. As one Corby Children's Centre director reflected,

> The poorest communities in England throughout the 1980s and 1990s began to feel like guinea pigs for government strategies, and government interventions began to sound like viruses; we had the Community Programme (CP), the Community Enterprise Programme (CEP), the Volunteer Project Programme (VPP), MSC, ESF, Urban Aid and the rest. Then in the 1990s we had 'the zones', the Health Action Zone, the Healthy Living Zone, the Education Action Zone, and the workers began to talk about zone fatigue. (Whalley, 2006: 2)

This experience was aptly captured in the comments of a local wag who said 'Corby's had more visions than Mother Teresa and more pilots than British Airways'. These examples of top-down service delivery inevitably failed to engage the local community, failed to take root and, once the funding ended or the people leading them had moved on to another project elsewhere, were unsuccessful in making the intended differences for people in those communities (Friedman, 2005).

Having learned the lessons of the past, parents, leaders and practitioners in Corby were determined not to repeat them. We applied successfully to be funded as one of the six localities in the UK to run its own Transforming Early Years project, with support from the Innovation Unit.

Practitioners were keen to engage with parents in collaborative ways so that, as well as being the users of services, they could also co-construct new and innovative ways of designing, providing and running more relevant and responsive services for themselves and their families. The underpinning principles for this way of working with parents are as follows (Armstrong et al., 2011):

- services need to engage with families in ways that meet their needs – not vice versa
- families know if services are working well – or not
- stories of lived experiences are essential to effective service development
- parents are active and equal partners in driving service development.

Those actively involved in the project work in Corby wanted to 'move from the existing model of a predominantly centre-based and professionally-led service (which involves parents variably) to one with "parents being the agents of change and the drivers of transformation" (Innovation Unit, 2012b: 1).

Corby Locality Workshop Day, 20th of April 2010

To these ends, the first event that was set up in conjunction with the Innovation Unit, our Locality Workshop (20 April 2010) ran for a whole day and was attended by 52 people, including

- parents who used children's centres and the range of services and provisions offered by the local authority, borough council and health services in the town
- parent governors and parent representatives on children's centres' Boards of Trustees and Partnership Boards
- representatives from Corby HomeStart
- representatives from service providers in Corby
- representatives from the Corby Borough Council
- representatives from Northamptonshire County Council and
- representatives from the Primary Care Trust.

The Locality Workshop started with local parents presenting their experiences of services in Corby to the professionals and practitioners who provided many of them. Parents were also able to share their ideas about how services could be improved as they took part in small group activities and in presenting the feedback from group discussions to all those present.

Understanding the fine grain of the community

One of the objectives of the Locality Workshop was that the participants would share their understanding of the 'fine grain' of the community via an exercise that involved 'segmenting' the families who used public services. The Innovation Unit's notion of 'segmentation' involves the creation of groupings focusing on behaviours and attitudes as opposed to demographics or stereotypes. This exercise produced a range of 'types' of users, including, for example, 'multi-service users', 'restricted engagers' and 'culturally alienated' groups. Whilst this new typology was useful and raised critical and recognisable issues for all participants, it was understood, and articulated in the room, that we all needed to be wary of potentially stereotyping individuals, families and whole communities; the 'segments' were still not flexible enough to capture the lived complexity of families and their lives. We did not want to label users, and these 'types' were not homogeneous, nor were they 'fixed states'; families' lives can change and develop slowly over time, but they can also experience rapid, even instantaneous, changes when an unexpected event occurs like the sudden death of a family member.

Participants felt that thinking in terms of 'personalising' children, parents and families, rather than 'segmenting' them would be more useful if we were to understand the 'fine grain' of the community. For example, no two lone parent families are the same; the needs of a financially insecure lone mother, with three children under the age of six, one of whom has a medical condition and consequent additional needs, will not be the same as a lone mother with one child with a childcare/nursery place, able to resume her own education and with plenty of family support. This thinking allowed for a clearer understanding of the complexity of family life and families' actual needs as opposed to the assumptions that underlie any kind of labelling, however well-intentioned. Thinking and working in this way, it was felt, could promote more effective work with families; for example, 'restricted engagers' could be supported to use a range of other services if practitioners developed a deeper understanding of precisely why individuals did not engage with children's centres. Working with these new insights the professionals would have to change *their* practice and develop *new* strategies. They would have to collaborate with parents who were 'restricted engagers' to discover how actual and perceived barriers could be surmounted, circumvented or removed altogether.

The most significant development arising from the 'segmenting' activity was agreement within the group that the most important families who practitioners needed to redouble their efforts to engage with were those who had become 'disengaged and disillusioned' with public services. 'Disengaged and disillusioned' families then became the focus for the next stage of the Corby TEY Project. In preparation practitioners were asked to think about who they felt their 'disengaged and disillusioned' parents were. Why did they think parents had become 'disengaged and disillusioned'? Were these parents contactable? If not, how might they make contact with 'disengaged and disillusioned' parents in order to meet with them and ask them how services could be made more attractive, more accessible and more useful to them? Answers to these questions and other systems-based thinking (Seddon, 2008) were brought to the Corby Localised Ethnography Workshop, which took place on June 11, 2010, some three weeks after the Locality Workshop day.

Localised ethnography in Corby

The engagement of parents continued to be an important dimension of the second stage of the Corby TEY Project, the 'localised ethnography'. This initially entailed a training workshop at a local children's centre for parents and practitioners. In the session participants were introduced to the model of interviewing parents that was to be used across all six localities taking part in the National TEY project. At this event it was decided that the interviewing of 'disengaged and disillusioned' parents would be carried out by parents and practitioners 'paired' from each of the four children's centres in the town. Each of the pairs in each of the children's centres would work with local parents and other contacts they had in the community to identify and contact 'disengaged and disillusioned' parents so that they could interview them about their experiences and see what could be learned about how and why these parents were reluctant to engage with their local children's centre.

The interviews themselves were based around an interview schedule designed by the Innovation Unit based on the principles and practices of parent-to-parent interviewing, which had been established over many years at the Pen Green Centre. The interviews were to be as informal as possible with one of the interviewing 'researchers' engaging the parent in conversation and putting the questions to them, while the other 'researcher' concentrated on capturing the parent's responses as accurately as possible. Some parents did not want to meet and talk with two people but were happy to be interviewed by one person. When this occurred the participant met with the parent from their local children's centre. Research carried out previously by the Pen Green Research Base had demonstrated that parent-to-parent interviewing produced rich and authentic information that parents may not have shared with a professional or practitioner. This view was expressed by a Parent-Interviewer who had carried out interviews with parents as part of the annual evaluation of services offered by the Corby Sure Start Local Programme, which ran from 1998 to 2006:

> The parents felt good that they were being asked how they felt about things. They felt safe talking to you in their own home. The parent-to-parent interviewing really worked because people could see that I was just like them – they could see that I didn't have a 'hidden agenda' which they might have thought about a professional interviewer. (McKinnon et al., 2005: 28)

The advantages of parents asking other parents what they think about the quality, availability and effectiveness of public services in their area lie in the fact that

> the interviewers' children go to the same schools as those of the interviewees; they use the same shops, pubs, clubs and sporting facilities; they go to the same churches. They have a common cultural experience in terms of the unique nature of Corby's development as a town and community.

Consequently, they are able to quickly strike up and develop a rapport and relationship of trust with the interviewees. (McKinnon et al., 2005: 28)

Being themselves embedded in the local culture, its history and lore, means that Parent-Interviewers 'know when to prompt and follow-up with a supplementary question, how to express it and when further prompting might become counter-productive' (McKinnon et al., 2005: 29). This approach is in line with Pen Green principles for working with parents; it produces deeper and richer data as it is drawn from authentic stories told by real people that can then be used to inform changes in practice and provision that meets the expressed needs of the community.

For a variety of reasons some parents preferred not to be interviewed but did want to participate and contribute to the Corby TEY Project. These parents completed a journal of a week in their lives and that of their family. The format of the 'Parent One Week Journal' booklet supported parents in its completion by having each of its seven days laid out over two pages with six columns; the three columns on the 'Parent' page were headed 'What I did today', 'Where I was' and 'Who was with me' while those on the 'Children' page said 'What they did', 'Where they did it' and 'Who were they with'. The final two pages were laid out under the heading 'In a perfect world . . .' with areas to complete the sentences 'My child would have more . . .', 'My child would have less . . .', 'I would have more . . .' and 'I would have less . . .'.

The interviewing fieldwork was carried out in Corby in May and June of 2010 and produced some very high-quality data, including some in-depth case studies that parent–practitioner interviewing pairs had elicited with the full cooperation and consent of the parents involved. Several of the journals captured the intricacies of what might otherwise have appeared to be lives of simplicity and routine, showing in fact that all families are complex in their own ways. A week of co-analysing the completed interview schedules and journals was arranged and took place at the Pen Green Research Base in July 2010. Parents and practitioners who had been involved as interviewers worked together on the analysis of the data they had collected by applying an open coding method to the comments of parents and their entries in their journals (Strauss & Corbin, 1998). Working in pairs, and sometimes threes, parents and practitioners jointly 'made sense' of the material gathered. The key findings from the localised ethnography were that 'disengaged and disillusioned' families in Corby

- had typically experienced negative responses from public services in the town and tended to avoid further engagement with them whenever possible
- looked primarily to their families, both nuclear and extended, for emotional and practical support in times of need
- sought professional support in the areas of family health and their children's education
- had low material aspirations – e.g. to live in a house with a garden – but high educational aspirations for their children – parents wanted their

children to have chances and opportunities that they had not themselves enjoyed

- had relatively 'restricted' patterns of day-to-day movements and interactions – e.g. many mothers spoke about daily routines typified by a 'home-school-shops-home-school-home' pattern
- were 'good citizens', looking out for others in their communities and especially the vulnerable in their neighbourhood – cutting their elderly neighbours' grass and hedges and taking their bins out was common
- appreciated the early childhood education and care available to them, along with family support, but wanted more of both that were more accessible to them when needed as opposed to when professionals and practitioners offered it.

Interviews with some of the parents had produced responses that allowed more in-depth interviewing to be done, which then allowed the development of case studies about some of the parents and their particular circumstances. The key themes from four of the case studies are as follows:

1. **A young mother of two children trying to remain drug-free: Theme 1 "We can set people up to fail"**

   - On a community drugs detoxification programme
   - On probation for drug-related offences, which requires her to attend 'self esteem and confidence building' sessions in three different towns; her home town, one that is eight miles away and another that is 16 miles away. Transport is sometimes provided by probation officers but more often she relies on public transport
   - She also has to travel the eight miles to the neighbouring town by public transport to see her drugs support worker and to review her medication
   - When she makes these journeys and attends her sessions and appointments she has to organise the care of her two children
   - She is not working and is living on benefits, as does her partner; both she and her partner receive incapacity benefit, and he has recently come out of a three-week residential drugs rehabilitation programme run in a town 180 miles away; he is struggling to remain 'clean' being back in the community
   - The local drug dealers know their routines so when she goes to her bank to withdraw some money, they are often waiting and put great pressure on her to buy from them; they also phone and turn up at the family home.

2. **A young mother of three children experiencing conflicting requirements from different agencies: Theme 1 "We can set people up to fail"**

- This mother has mental health issues and was given one week's notice that she was required to go an a 13-week course involving 20 hours of voluntary work a week and another five hours of self-esteem and confidence building
- As her partner was also expected to look for work, they had to find childcare by the following week for their three children (aged 4, 3 and 2), and for the further 12 weeks of the course, which included six weeks of school holidays
- If she did not do this then their benefits would have been affected
- The 13-week course is run in a neighbouring town and, having no car, the mother has to leave the family home before 8.00 a.m. to use public transport and gets home after 4.00 p.m.

3. **Young mum with two sons experiencing unresolved trauma: Theme 2 "We may need to home visit intensively before families engage with centres"**

- Her own mother left the family home when she was very young so she felt abandoned
- She lost one baby who was stillborn
- Her brother suffered mental illness and committed suicide; she feels that she has "lost him twice" (HomeStart Worker)
- Her youngest son is presenting challenging behaviours at home and at nursery, and she fears that "he is going to end up like my brother" (HomeStart Worker)
- She frequently takes her sons to the local cemetery, at least three times a week, to visit her dead baby and brother
- She is dealing with her unresolved trauma by visiting the baby and the brother she has lost – "to her and her beliefs, her alive family and dead family are equally important to her so that's where she kind of goes in return" (HomeStart Worker).

4. **Young mother with three children aged, 6, 4 and 3, one of whom has special rights: Theme 3 "Physical access to children's centres can be problematic"**

This parent felt strongly that the design of children's centres creates barriers for families who want to access them compared to other more family-friendly spaces:

- 'Children's centres are built the wrong way round. When you put the coffee rooms in the middle of buildings you have to get through a door to get to them, whereas at the Boating Lake, you actually walk into the area, the playground is there and you go to the café'

- 'People take their children to playgrounds and don't fear their children playing there, so why when they're in a children's centre do we start fearing that people are going to worry about their children playing in an outside space?'
- 'Maybe we should think about taking down the boundaries; have the fence removed or put gates in it so that families can go into the playspace first and then into the coffee area'
- 'It is difficult, it would be quite radical and would mean quite a bit of money spent on doing that kind of thing, taking down fences and putting in gates instead, but it would break down a boundary where people feel that there is one. There is a physical boundary, there is a gate, then another gate and then a door and then there is a person to get past. It doesn't have to be unsafe, obviously playgrounds can be unsafe, but you know, it's just a different way of looking at it, a different way of thinking about how people can access that building'
- 'It's a different of way of managing it. You've got to think "outside of the box" and not just think "Oh my God, it won't work", you've got to think "This will work" and "How are we going to make it work" and that's what part of this innovation project is about, it's not about saying "No"'.

The desire to have parents included and involved in the work of the TEY project at every point permeated the thinking of the children's centres' teams, and this became increasingly important as the project progressed through its various stages. Parents were actively involved in meetings about the TEY project scheduled by the Innovation Unit and held in Corby, and they were supported to take part in the events in London hosted by the Innovation Unit or NESTA. In addition, each of the four children's centres in Corby held their own meetings with parents to support the work of the project.

These meetings produced a variety of ideas as to what the solutions could be in terms of engaging more effectively (or at all) with those parents who were 'disengaged and/or disillusioned'. At the Clarifying the Challenge workshop held in Corby in September 2010, the practitioners and parents came up with the following ideas:

- Recruit and train local parents to provide whole family activities in places where 'disengaged and disillusioned' families already hang out
- Children's centres to provide rigorous accredited training for parents in their communities so that these parents can identify and engage with 'disengaged and disillusioned' parents in their street or neighbourhood
- Identify and map language skills in Corby to provide multi-lingual support
- Identify and map where families already go then run support activities in these places and locations
- Use these local, parent-run activities to start conversations with families about existing services they could access and about other services they want

- Identify and map what the borough council provides and which of their workers could play a role in training and support, e.g. Park Wardens
- Support and develop Community Activists and Parent Champions.

A Parent Focus Group meeting was held in Corby in December 2010 and was attended by 13 parents from the town's children's centres, two senior local authority officers and one facilitator from the Innovation Unit. The group agreed that the most feasible thing to do at that time was to support the creation and development of some kind of parent body that would meet the criteria of promoting parents as Community Activists and Parent Champions. This body was conceptualised as being more than a parent forum in which discussion could take place and concerns and issues could be aired. Instead, the idea was to support the creation of an organisation that would have real power and would become a genuine force in Corby, reshaping existing services for families by ultimately having a key role in the creation and provision of new ones. Several names for this new parent organisation were considered, and the One Corby Parent Coalition (OCPC) was agreed upon. It was envisaged that the OCPC would be involved in

- Clarifying the focus of all services
- Eliminating duplication
- Creating a local network of people across the borough
- Making public services more accountable to families
- Seeking and accessing both public and other funding so that the OCPC would be a service-commissioning entity in its own right, bringing into being the kinds of service provision identified by authentic consultation with parents in Corby
- Ensuring that avenues were created so that parents as users of services could provide critical feedback on all services, old and new, for example, by setting up an online parent forum specifically for this purpose.

Parents who had been involved throughout the TEY project were asked to become the nucleus of the OCPC and to think of ways in which parents from across Corby could be made aware of this new organisation and become engaged with it. It was the view of parents and practitioners involved in the TEY work that parents needed to be authentically involved in running the OCPC and that the nucleus would become a 'critical mass' of parents shaping its aims and objectives, as outlined previously, and bringing them to fruition.

Children's centres and the borough council offered rooms in which the OCPC could meet and go about its work; however, these proved not to be successful as venues for this kind of community action. Meetings held in the children's centres attracted parents who were familiar as users of those settings but not other parents; similarly, a space offered in the local council headquarters seemed unattractive to parents and difficult to access. In the end a 'nucleus' of parents met in a café-restaurant in the main shopping centre in Corby, and this proved to be a better place for parents to meet and express their views.

The One Corby Parent Coalition and the politics of local activism

The nascent OCPC, supported by children's centre workers, researched their local borough council so that they could engage with the councillors who represented them. The councillors could be informed about the OCPC, and their support could be confirmed. County councillors were also contacted for the same reasons and to see if some of the small amounts of funding that they had at their disposal to support initiatives and events in their wards could be secured and pooled. These monies could then be used as 'seed corn' money for attracting matched funding from charities and trusts. Parents looked to see which councillors' wards they themselves were in and which wards were, as yet, not represented by a parent in the OCPC who lived in the ward. They then used their own networks of contacts to locate and recruit parents who lived in the 'unrepresented' wards. As they went about these activities, the OCPC identified issues of concern to themselves and other parents so that they could lobby borough and county councillors and other agencies about them. Examples included

- Provision of a pedestrian-controlled crossing to a much-used local park and children's playground near three busy road junctions
- The local bus services allowed only a limited number of prams or buggies on board, schedules did not match up with the beginnings and endings of children's school days and weekly passes were only available to adults and not to children. Several mums reported being left at a bus-stop in the rain with a baby and a toddler because there were already two prams/buggies on board – and the same thing happening with the next one
- Housing Benefit was not being regularly updated, which meant that some families were getting into debt.

The underlying aim of the OCPC was to provide a route so that parents could make a journey from being interested in local services for children and families to becoming engaged with other parents as part of the coalition and then to become 'community activists' and change-agents as shown in the model in Figure 8.1.

This model is not as linear as it may at first appear in that 'The steps imply a rigid hierarchy but the reality is that the sequence is more fluid and individual' (Whalley, 2013). For example, a parent may become involved in work in their community as a parent governor in their child's school and then, having become more aware of other opportunities to engage in community work, could train as a Home-Start volunteer. A parent of a child with special rights might start as a single issue activist and then formalise his or her engagement through a volunteer programme at a local children's centre.

During the period of time covered by the TEY project in Corby, an opportunity for community activism presented itself in late 2010 and early 2011. Proposals

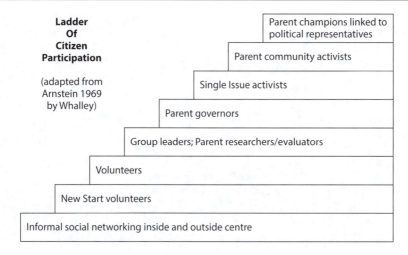

Figure 8.1 The Ladder of Citizen Participation (adapted from Arnstein, 1969, by Whalley, 2013) shows the various entry points that parents may have in terms of their actual, and potential, participation and engagement.

Figure 8.2 Parents, practitioners and governors from Pen Green protest against the proposed cuts and lobby a full County council meeting at County Hall, Northampton, Thursday, 24 February 2011.

Figure 8.3 Parents, children, practitioners, governors and people from across Corby hold a protest meeting and march around the Pen Green Centre, Friday, 28 January 2011.

to cut funding to the Pen Green Centre for Children and Families by 56% in one year were met with stiff opposition from parents in Corby. Within a few hours of this news becoming public, several hundred parents offered support to the Centre and its workers. Mobile phones and social networking sites were used by parents to communicate with each other and mobilise a community protest against the proposals. Parents met to plan the logistics of transporting parents, children and workers to Northampton to lobby and speak at full County Council meetings.

Two meetings of the Northamptonshire Schools Forum, the body with responsibility for deciding on the funding for schools and nursery schools in the county, were also lobbied by parents. Unusually, Pen Green parents and workers were given permission to address the Forum and put their cases to the assembled head teachers. A protest and march of some 1,500 around the streets encompassing the Pen Green Centre took place and was supported by local tradespeople, public sector workers and the local press.

Parents also lobbied the local MP and, with her support, delivered petitions to 10 Downing Street.

Parents at the centre of services

The ultimate aim of the One Corby Parent Coalition is to establish parents as the co-producers of public services for the families of Corby. As Boyle and Harris (2009: 16) express it, 'co-production occurs in the critical middle ground when

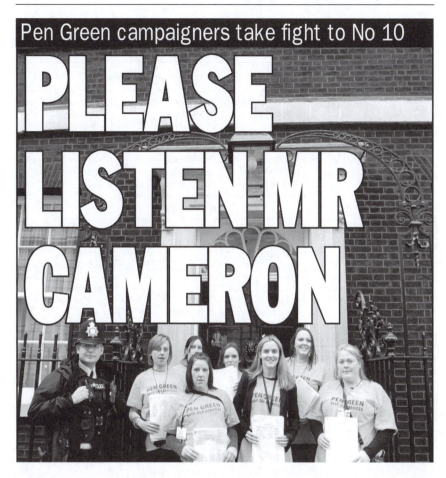

Pen Green campaigners take fight to No 10

PLEASE LISTEN MR CAMERON

Figure 8.4 Parents from the Pen Green Centre and Corby's Member of Parliament deliver a petition, with more than 8,000 signatures against the proposed funding cuts, to the Prime Minister, Tuesday, 8 February 2011 (photograph with kind permission of Northamptonshire Newspapers Ltd., Johnston Press).

user and professional knowledge is combined to design and deliver services' as illustrated in Figure 8.5.

Boyle and Harris argue that our public services have become 'constrained by the New Public Management of centralized targets, deliverables, standards and customer relationship management software which has narrowed the focus of many services and often undermined the relationships' (2009: 5) between providers of those services and the very people that they are intended to support. They go on to locate the reason why 'our current services are so badly equipped to respond' to the needs of local communities and the families who live in them:

One Corby Parent Coalition
User and professional roles in the design and
delivery of services for children and families in Corby.

		Responsibility for design of services		
		Professionals as sole service planners	Professionals and service users/ community as planners	No professional input into service planning
Responsibility for delivery of services or commissioning of these services	Professionals as sole service deliverers	Traditional professional service provision	Professional service provision but users/community involved in planning and design	Professionals as sole service deliverers
	Professionals and service user/ community as co-delivers	User co-delivery of professionally designed services	One Corby Parent Coalition	User/community delivery of services with little/no professional
	Users/communities as sole deliverers	User/communities delivery of professionally-planned services	User/communities delivery of co-planned or co-designed services	Self-organised community provision

Figure 8.5 A model for the authentic co-production of services for children and families.

Source: Adapted from Carnegie Trust (2006), 'Commission for Rural Community Development – Beyond Engagement and participation, user and community co-production of service'. By Tony Bovaird, Carnegie Trust. Further amended by One Corby Parent Coalition, 2011.

'they have largely overlooked the underlying operating system they depend on: the social economy of family and neighbourhood' (ibid.).

The way in which the TEY project was run in Corby shows that, with vision, forethought and good will, things can at least begin to be different:

- parents, practitioners, professionals and local authority officers and workers at Pen Green Research co-conceptualised the national TEY project with the Innovation Unit
- the input of all the interested stakeholders in the community shifted the focus of the project from seeing parents, however inadvertently, as 'objects' of research to being co-constructors, co-analysts and co-authors of research
- a 'done to', 'othering' approach to people, with a subtext of assumptions about them, was replaced by a 'being with', non-judgemental approach that authentically engaged the stakeholders involved
- the thinking underpinning the 'segmentation' of users of public services implies homogeneity – e.g. that 'dads', 'lone parents', the 'disabled' or 'non-English speakers' are 'hermitically sealed' groups whose members are

essentially the same, all having the same unchanging needs. The Corby TEY project challenged these assumptions, arguing for a more open-minded 'personalisation' of users that foregrounds the wide diversity of families within any segment and that their personal usage can cut across segments. Each and every family has its own unique set of needs and only a unique combination of responses can meet those needs.

Only a setting which is *at* the heart of its community, and *in* the hearts of its community, can be sustained, nourished and strengthened by the parents, children and families who use it in the present and sustain these engagements across the generations. This solidarity, this groundswell of fellowship and unanimity of purpose – which can be called upon, for example, to defend a key part of the community's resource when it is threatened – comes from the consistent involvement of parents and families in the life of the Pen Green Centre at all levels and in myriad undocumented but remarkable ways. It has been said that friendship is not a big thing, it is a million tiny things. The everyday interactions of Pen Green with its families, and theirs with it, reflect this axiom about friendship not only at the level of individual children, parents and practitioners, but also at the level of a whole community: it is about touching people.

References

Arnstein, S. (1969) 'A Ladder of Citizen Participation', *Journal of the American Institute of Planners*, Vol. 35, No. 4, 216–224.

Armstrong, J., McKinnon, E. & Whalley, M. (2011) *Total Place Corby – One Corby Parent Coalition: Parents and Practitioners Co-Researching and Co-Producing Services for Children and Families*. Presentation at the European Early Childhood Education Research Association Annual Conference, *Education from Birth: research, practices and educational policies*. University of Geneva, September.

Boyle, D. & Harris, M. (2009) *The Challenge of Co-Production: How Equal Partnerships Between Professionals and the Public Are Crucial to Improving Public Services*. London: National Endowment for the Sciences, Technology and the Arts.

Friedman, M. (2005) *Trying Hard is Not Enough: How to Produce Measurable Improvements for Customers and Communities*. Crewe, England: Trafford Publishing.

Gillinson, S., Horne, M. & Baeck, P. (2010) *Radical Efficiency: Different, Better, Lower Cost Public Services*. London: National Endowment for the Sciences, Technology and the Arts.

Innovation Unit (2012a) *Transforming Early Years* [online]. Available from: http://www.innovationunit.org/our-projects/projects/transforming-early-years [Accessed 12.03.13]

Innovation Unit (2012b) Radical Efficiency in Early Years Settings: Parents as Agents of Change in Corby. Available from: http://www.innovationunit.org/sites/default/files/Transforming%20early%20years%20-%20Corby%20case%20study.pdfs [Accessed 12.03.13]

McKinnon, E., Fletcher, C. & Whalley, M. (2005) *Outreach Provision Users' Satisfaction Survey*. Corby: Pen Green Research, Development and Training Base.

Seddon, J. (2008) *Systems Thinking in the Public Sector: The Failure of the Reform Regime . . . and a Manifesto for a Better Way.* Axminster, England: Triarchy Press.

Strauss, A. & Corbin, J. (1998) 'Basics of Qualitative Research: Techniques and Procedures for Developing Grounded Theory'. In Robson, C. (Ed.), *Real World Research* (2nd Edition). Oxford: Blackwell Publishing.

Whalley, M. (2006) *Leadership in Integrated Centres and Services for Children and Families: A Community Development Approach: Engaging with the struggle.* Paper presented at the National Early Years Seminar. Wellington, NZ, June.

Whalley, M. (2013) 'Engaging with Families: From Community Development to Co-Production'. In Whalley, M., Arnold, C. & Orr, R.(Eds), *Working with Families in Children's Centres and Early Years Settings.* London: Hodder Education.

Chapter 9

Narrative enquiry

The Architecture of Access

Kate Hayward

The focus on improving outcomes for vulnerable families is a key component of the newly revised Ofsted Framework for Children's Centre inspections (Ofsted, 2012) and central to the core purpose of children's centres (DfE, 2011). At Pen Green we have always maintained the importance of offering high-quality universal services within which more targeted support is available. There is a paradox in the recent Government emphasis on targeted services (ibid.) as such services run the risk of stigmatisation and disengagement from the community, resulting in less uptake rather than improved access by those who may be the most vulnerable.

Workers at Pen Green have challenged the terminology used to describe the access of services by 'vulnerable groups'. 'Hard to reach families' suggests that these families are to blame. We were interested in turning this concept on its head and challenging ourselves with the notion of 'hard to reach services'. We wanted to know what it was about the way services are offered that makes it difficult for some families to engage and participate.

In order to explore the experiences of families who have traditionally found access to public services difficult, we decided as a Centre Leadership Team (CLT) to carry out a research project. The policy of supporting professional development among staff at Pen Green meant that all but two of the senior staff on the CLT involved in the project had experience conducting research projects, either as Masters students within the organisation or through engagement in accredited courses off site. Of the eight CLT members involved:

- two were tutors and two were former students on the MA in Integrated Provision for Children and Families in Early Years taught at Pen Green;
- one had recently completed an MA in Child Protection and Complex Child Care; and
- one was studying for a certificate in counselling.

[NB – the research outlined in this chapter was published in the *European Early Childhood Education Research Journal*, Volume 21 Number 1 March 2013]

The investment of time in a research project by senior leaders within such a large organisation had several potential benefits:

- increased awareness by leaders of current children's centre issues through first hand experience
- an opportunity as a leadership team to engage in research and reflection
- an opportunity for leaders to work alongside families in throwing light on access issues enabling the parents' voices to be *directly heard* by the CLT
- as members of the CLT came from different professional backgrounds – social services, education, community development, community education and voluntary work – we all had a different perspective to offer.

A senior Pen Green Researcher also joined the eight members of the CLT to form the research team.

Previous research at the Centre

Research on the Pen Green approach to working with families between 1997 and 2000 showed the vital importance of community involvement in the development of services (Whalley & the Pen Green Centre Team, 2007). The approach is co-educational in that parents and workers share knowledge about the child and work together to support the child's learning both at home and in the setting. It is called 'Parents Involvement in Children's Learning' (PICL) and is underpinned by a set of principles that respect parents' knowledge of their children and seek to engage parents in an equal dialogue (Easen et al., 1992). The research illustrated the importance of a flexible and responsive development of different models of engagement that took into account parents' specific needs and circumstances (Tait, 2007: 42). This is supported by the work of Bekerman and Tartar who also observe that multiple contextual issues need to be taken into consideration before parental choice or parental involvement can produce the desired outcomes (Bekerman & Tartar, 2009: 183).

Previous experiences of engaging with professionals will have an effect on parents' ability and willingness to engage in services. Parents at Pen Green had previously articulated how their early childhood experiences influenced their engagement (Arnold, 2007: 99). The Pen Green team were aware of the possible organisational barriers that may be an issue. For example, in order to ensure children's safety, the entrance to the Centre is via a path that has gates at either end. One parent has commented that negotiating their way in to the Centre can feel like 'walking the plank'. In addition there is always a possibility of staff 'othering' parents who appear to have different family contexts to themselves (Levinas, 1987; Muhr, 2008). As Michel Vandenbroeck (2009: 168) suggests, the actions of workers in early childhood centres will 'inevitably remain micro-political and disputable decisions', and he challenges workers to question taken-for-granted assumptions about 'the Other, the one we do not know'.

The research focus

The central question we were seeking to address was 'are those who may benefit most from our services able to access them?' We decided to approach parents who had succeeded in accessing Pen Green services. We wanted to gain a perspective on how parents may overcome some of the potential barriers to access by engaging specific parents in the research.

The critical questions were:

- What enabled some parents to overcome potential barriers (e.g. gender, ethnicity, language, additional needs) and to access services for their children at the Pen Green Centre?
- What was it about them personally? What was it about the Centre?
- And what was it about the relationship between them and the Centre?

Developing theories of knowledge through practice

We have developed a research approach that uses qualitative methods within an interpretive framework. Our methodological approach is formulated to optimise our understanding of processes in our practice (Fletcher, 2008). We are interested in the knowledge and understanding that is generated through practice that will enable us to improve practice as posited by Cohen and Manion, who say that

> interpretive researchers . . . begin with individuals and set out to understand their interpretations of the world around them. Theory is emergent and must arise from particular situations; it should be 'grounded' on data generated by the research act. Theory should not precede research but follow it. (1994: 37).

Our intention was to build our theory with parents from their accounts of their experience of accessing services and our collaborative understanding of the issues involved. We have been influenced by the thinking of Geertz, who aligns himself with Max Weber in asserting that 'man is an animal suspended in webs of significance he himself has spun' (Geertz, 1973: 5). By describing and reflecting on the process of accessing services, parents and researchers raise important issues 'whose investigation may lead to generalisations of perspective relevance and actionability' (Schon, 1995: 31). Schon links his ideas about a new way of knowing through reflection-in-action to what Kurt Lewin (1946) meant by 'action research':

> In Lewin's work we find the idea that a practitioner's reflection on knowing and reflection-in-action give rise to actionable theory. Such verbally explicit theory, derived from and invented in particular situations of practice, can be generalised to other situations, not as covering laws but through what I call 'reflective transfer' that is, by carrying them over into new situations where they may be put to work and tested, and found to be valid and interesting, but where they may also be reinvented. (Schon, 1995)

We intended to use this notion of 'reflective transfer' to enable staff and parents to draw from the knowledge and understanding we achieved through this study and to forge new and improved processes to support access to services.

A collaborative process, researching with parents as partners

This was a collaborative research project. The rationale for our method was 'to go for depth, to explore and see through the eyes of a knowledgeable participant' (Fletcher, 2008: 4). The philosophy that underpins our way of working at Pen Green, including our methodological approach to research, has been strongly influenced by an awareness of the power dynamics between workers and parents, drawing particularly on the work of Paulo Freire (1970). Whalley and the Pen Green Centre Team (2007: 12) set out our shared code of ethics, which states that research at Pen Green should always

- be positive to all participants;
- provide data that are open to, accountable to and interpreted by all the participants;
- focus on questions that the participants themselves (parents, children and staff) are asking;
- be based on a relationship of trust where people's answer's are believed; and
- produce results that are about improving practice . . . or at least sustaining it.

Given that in this project we were seeking the views and insights of parents from groups who, typically, may have found services hard to access, the issues around power needed serious consideration. In addition, the research team were all senior staff who were in obvious positions of power within the organisation. We did not seek to measure the impact of engaging CLT members as researchers, but there was an awareness throughout the project of the probable influence of this imbalance of power. We were mindful of the work of Bob Holman (1987), who promotes what he terms 'Research from the Underside' and advocates for research by and with those who are typically marginalised, where

- ideas are initiated by the research population
- participants have a strong influence on the form and means of the study

- participants are involved in the data analysis and dissemination
- participants use the findings to pursue their own interests.

Although the idea for the research came from an organisational quest to understand how some parents were able to access the Centre, the parents who engaged in the research process were involved as much as possible in the analysis of the data through a collaborative coding exercise whereby key themes and processes were described. Parents were able to use the process and the findings of the research in various ways, and we endeavoured to document some of the parents' reflections on what they got out of the study. To fulfil our obligations regarding anonymity and confidentiality, all real names have been replaced with pseudonyms.

Technique for gathering the data

The research team decided on the technique of semi-structured interview. We discussed a set of prompts, rearranged the order of the prompts to make more sense and agreed that the prompts would be used to open up the discussion with parents. The interviews were recorded on a digital sound recorder, in accordance with the informed consent of participants, and transcribed. Parents were asked where they wanted the interview to take place, and five of the nine parents who collaborated in the research requested to be interviewed in their own homes. Parents were given a written copy of the interview prompts at least a day before the interview.

Sample selection

Within the parameters of this study, we were interested in finding out about a range of parents' views in different family contexts typically associated with low access to services. We decided to use a purposeful sample of families using the Nursery or the Baby Nest. These families were not intended to be representative of any group. As Michael Quinn Patton explains, 'What would be "bias" in statistical sampling, and therefore a weakness, becomes intended focus in qualitative sampling, and therefore a strength' (2002: 230). The intention was that working with these families would provide 'information rich cases' or 'exemplars'

> from which one learns a great deal about issues of central importance to the purpose of the inquiry . . . studying information rich cases yields insights and in-depth understanding rather than empirical generalisations. (Patton, 2002: 230)

In order to gain as much insight as possible, we also ensured that the children in the families that would be approached for interview were located in different parts of the Centre. There are three clearly designated but interconnecting areas

Table 9.1 Parent's identifying context and child's area within the Pen Green Centre

Parent	Context	Area of Centre
Tendai	Zimbabwe culture	Den
Benti	Polish culture	Snug
Amy	Traveller community[1]	Den
Margaret	Adult with learning disabilities	Snug
Simon	Dad not in family home	Baby Nest
Jacob	Turkish culture	Snug
Lisa	Child in Nurture group[2] complex family	Den
Sarah	Child with special rights[2] complex family	Baby Nest
Billy	Dad in family home, reconstituted family	Dads' groups

1. Traveller community – a community of people who have a nomadic habit of life and/or live in a caravan or vehicle.
2. Complex family – a family who has more than one characteristic relating to disadvantage (for characteristics of disadvantage see Social Exclusion Task Force, 2007).

of the Nursery – the Snug, the Den and the Baby Nest. Table 9.1 gives the 'identifying context' of the parents together with the area of the Centre in which each child was located.

Analysis of the data

The analysis of the data was initially approached in pairs. Research team members worked on their own interview transcript and studied that of their research partner's. They then discussed the key themes that emerged from the data from both interviews. Parents were invited to a shared session where they took part in the analysis of the transcripts, and emerging themes were identified. This was a mixture of small group work and work in pairs.

The parent's own words provided the illustration of the theme that had been identified. The parent's words were key in the development of a grounded theory on access. In addition, a narrative of the parent's story was either written by the parent, or written by the researcher and edited by the parent, to represent their story. One of the parents' stories follows.

Amy's story

Amy described herself as 'a member of the travelling community'. She lived with her partner S, her 9-year-old twins B and J, and 4-year-old Ji, who was attending nursery at the time of the interview. Her oldest son R, 17, was living on a different site at that time.

Amy described how she 'had had no experience with nurseries, due to not many travellers had their children in nursery when my eldest was young, so it was a whole new experience for me'. The traveller education worker who was working with her eldest son realised that the twins were only six months off starting school and helped Amy to find a nursery place by ringing Pen Green. The Head of Nursery came out to see Amy the next day, and Amy remembers, 'my twins were in nursery within three days, which I was completely amazed with as normally getting R in school . . . took longer . . . and that was if the school would take traveller children!'

Amy said, 'I was made to feel very welcome by all of the staff and was overwhelmed by the facilities that were at the Centre. I had never experienced an Education Authority that had been this welcoming. Usually, going to school with my eldest son was actually a very daunting and horrible experience, for example, standing in the playground at the end of the school with parents telling their children not to come near or even holding their noses . . . very narrow minded people who would push their views onto their children which would then mean our children (travelling community) would never fit in'.

Amy and her family have moved in the 20-mile radius around Corby in the previous 12 years. As her family grew her beliefs changed about children accessing state education. Amy felt her way of life offered her children many rich learning experiences alongside people she had chosen to live with, but she also wanted her children to have the opportunity to 'integrate with people who live in different environments'. As R had struggled with a late diagnosis with dyslexia, she also wanted continuity for her other children and said, 'Pen Green basically changed my life and views towards education, I no longer felt daunted to take my children'.

Amy found the settling-in period very important for the twins. She said 'they just wouldn't let go of my leg'. She enjoyed playing with the other nursery children during the settling in time: 'I was in the sandpit building dragons and everything'. After two or three weeks they were fine. After the twins had left nursery, Amy and her family moved sites, and she lost touch with the Centre. She happened to meet the Head of Nursery in a local supermarket, and she told her where she was now living and they swapped current mobile phone numbers. Nursery staff had also kept in touch with other traveller families who had helped staff to 'hold' members of their community 'in mind'. Staff went to visit Amy, S and Ji on the new site before he started nursery.

Amy remembers how settling into nursery was easier for Ji. 'He'd seen all the things there and that was it, he was gone . . . he is more independent . . . Ji is the boss'. Amy appreciates the documentation on the children: 'It's just something to keep isn't it – it's a keepsake . . . I think that is brilliant just to do that and to give them something like that to keep after is amazing'. The family have shared many photographs of the site and their life experiences, which have featured in the children's files and in handmade books at nursery. As well as the learning environment at Pen Green, Amy liked the way the staff listen to the children. She talked about Ji being asked about where he lives and how to get to his home. He drew his Family Worker a map and accompanied her on the way back from nursery so that she could find the site.

Amy had poor experiences of her own schooling, and she felt she was never given a chance due to the reputation of her older brothers and sisters. She felt she had also experienced prejudice against her lifestyle when admitted to hospital following a car crash with a ruptured spleen that went undiagnosed for 27 hours. Engaging with services was therefore difficult for her, and engaging in learning experiences for herself at the Centre was a challenge.

Amy said the opportunities for adults at Pen Green were very important but the thought of joining a group, possibly being judged or discriminated against, was daunting. When the twins were at nursery she started an NVQ in childcare at the Centre, but because she was pregnant with Ji, she was only able to attend for six weeks. Amy offered some helpful challenges to the CLT. She passed a first aid course during this time but has never been awarded the certificate. In addition, her CRB check did not come through, and as this was not followed up prior to the interview, Amy was not then able to volunteer in the Centre.

Although Amy was aware of other facilities at Pen Green, such as the use of the washing machine, she had not used it because she said, 'I don't really like taking liberties'. She has used the local launderette but was banned at one time from there because her washing was said to be 'too dirty'. Since the interview she has used the Pen Green washing machine.

On a recent home visit, Amy asked Ji's Family Worker if another traveller on the same site could access a nursery place for her 4-year-old son. She was told that the nursery was full. However, she persisted with the request and brought the issue up during the interview. The boy has since been offered a priority nursery place.

Analysis of the nine cases

Through analysing each transcript from parents and the research team, two areas of interest in relation to access became significant: factors within the parent and factors within the Centre.

We have related these two areas of significance to what we are describing as the 'Architecture of Access'. (See Table 9.2.)

Foundations: Factors within the parent

Parents' confidence, their ability to trust and their strong motivation to support their children were all important factors within the parents themselves that

Table 9.2 Architecture of Access

STRUCTURE	Factors within the Centre
FOUNDATIONS	Factors within the parents

enabled them to gain access. Previous positive experience of accessing services was also important. In each case study, the parents' disposition to access services for their children was clearly evident (Katz, 1993). Their personal resilience enabled each parent to persist despite difficulties (Rutter, 2007). Parents were able to be reflective, to question and to begin to trust. They were motivated by *their desire to support their children's learning,* and they had an *awareness of their own needs* as shown in the following comments:

LISA 'The kids enjoyed it, so I gave it a couple of weeks to try it and some of the people that were here I wasn't too sure, being the way I was myself but gradually . . . I've been here nearly two and a half years now. I used to be terrified to walk out the front door – world was too big for me and I couldn't cope with it. Now I am getting myself back together on my own, trying to take steps'.

BILLY 'It is not worth my while not to come. My misses kept saying, "It's Pen Green, it's Pen Green" the kids would bounce on the bed, pull my hair and yank my ears! "Dad, dad Pen Green!"'

More than half the parents interviewed *trusted workers to be honest and were seeking a trusting relationship with staff where they did not feel judged.*

SARAH 'Like you see your child as this lovely little bundle of joy and you bring them into nursery and they don't want to go. Or they are having a particularly bad day and they box the home visitor. That was quite hard because it is really embarrassing. Or you think "What have I done?" and [that] they will judge you. But they didn't at the time. It was good that they didn't judge me, and I thought they would have done because my kids hit'.

Many parents wanted to know about their children's progress and gained a lot from *sharing knowledge about their child through shared video reflection and dialogue in Pen Green Parents Involved in their Children's Learning (PICL) groups.*

MARGARET 'Well I was at the PICL group on a Wednesday, the involvement group with your child and they had videos of what G was getting on with in crèche and it was shown in the video what she was doing and the things she was getting into. [When] she came here we didn't really understand what she was saying and what she wanted'.

SARAH 'My Lily watches Luke's 18-month-old video all the time and she knows [it] word for word. His first word was taxi and when he points, his grasp, his feel, his touch – she'd rather watch that than Dora [TV programme]. She'll say "Mum, mum come and have a look what Luke is doing" and I am running up the stairs thinking Luke's doing something and it's the video again. Lily watches that and she is really into it, I'm thinking what is she thinking when they are doing that – how do I explain that to her?'

One parent was particularly reflective about the difficulties she experienced in sharing some knowledge about her family:

TENDAI 'But you know sometimes people are just being polite! It is something about the British that I have noticed, they might say that it is OK but thinking "Oh my God!" so when I am from a different background sometimes you . . . maybe you nod sideways or upwards and I'm thinking you are saying that it's not . . . because the educated people back home in Zimbabwe they speak English so in most cases back home if you are English speaking, you are speaking English very well, your children, our children are speaking in English very well, it shows that you are living comfortably and that you are well off. Amongst the Zimbabweans speaking in English is sort of like, "We don't want it, but it's there", speaking in English gives you an idea of where you are – status thing. When M first came to my house and she was asking me "so how many languages do you speak?" . . . I said "just English" . . . but then when I thought about it now, giving what I am learning from school, I actually notice that it is wrong for me to want to push away my own language'.

Structure: Factors within the Centre

The structure of what was offered to parents through the Centre was extremely important. Parents wanted different things at different times. The settling in period over the first two weeks of a child's time at the Centre was significant. Parents deepened their relationship with staff, came to know the Centre environment and gained reassurance in terms of seeing staff working with children, knowing their child was safe. Staff attitudes and how staff interacted with parents was also seen to be significant, and these themes have been included as factors within the Centre. *Being reflective and flexible and the warmth and openness with which staff engaged with parents seemed to play a large part in enabling parents to actively maintain access.* In their study on the narratives of immigrant mothers using child care, Vandenbroeck et al. (2009: 213) also describe the importance of the 'welcoming ability' of the staff in creating the context in which parents' agency can take form.

JACOB 'What we saw and when she came here as well it was, she made us feel, um, we felt good, we felt good and comfortable knowing that, like I said, you know, when we got there'.

BENTI 'At the beginning when I started to come with M we were with him for one and half hours every day and the staff in the nursery started to tell him, they didn't understand what he said and he didn't understand what the staff said to him but it was . . . It was good that many of the staff come to me with the paper and write Polish words and translate this word in English'.

SIMON 'We then came in for his settling in, this was good as she got to watch us with C and saw what he liked and how we were with him. Like when he gets upset he likes to be cuddled, held up, I demonstrated how C likes to be held, with his blanket and his dummy. K could see us doing that so she knew if he got upset she knew what to do. How to hold him, how to cuddle him. He needs a cuddle if he is upset. Then he's okay'.

Parents *appreciated the different roles adopted by staff* (e.g. as a Family Worker/ key worker and also a group leader), which *enabled parents to develop staff-parent relationships in a variety of contexts.* A particular person who was able to act as a 'cultural broker' (Chrispeels & Rivero, 2001) between the Centre and the community or from another agency was in some cases *key to 'a way in'* to the Centre.

SARAH 'I was referred to the Centre by the Health Visitor when I had my second child. You came out to visit and then through that I got speaking to members of staff and then I got asked to do a bit more because I got a bit more familiar with the staff in the Centre. I did a few groups with the staff like CLAIT and stuff'.

BILLY 'C was like a support worker for us and she tried for ages and ages to get me to come to Dad's club because I was confined to the house, I couldn't get out of the house. Eventually she talked me into coming, I walked up one day and couldn't get into the place and I thought I am not coming back, do you know what I mean, I tried, gave it up and she pestered me again and pestered me again and I came back again. I came and I met . . . L'.

LISA 'I was pregnant and I was really ill and C was my midwife at the time and at that time we were struggling, we were in my mum's house, still living there, she mentioned a family support worker. Well I was a bit scared and I did say no at first because of me being me I was so possessive at the time because I didn't know much about anything, if it had been someone else, I don't think I would have, it would have depended on who told me really'.

TENDAI 'At some point there needs to be a reference point for people like me . . . Somebody like me has to be a reference point'.

BILLY 'I came because of C, she said "just try it, that's all I'm asking, if you don't like it you don't have to come back"'.

All nine parents mentioned *access to courses* and highlighted *the importance of being able to engage in something for themselves.* The affordance of the environment in terms of *staff attitudes and responsiveness* was also highlighted.

TENDAI 'So there was of course the problem that I noticed there was only one black child but I wanted to see whether Pen Green is racist or its just that there are no black families around for them to take children. It was one of the things that my antennae switch was up for. My child is very free. If she likes someone, if she knows you she'll run to you and hug you and she does that a lot with K, with M so that answers a lot of questions for me, I know that she is happy here'.

SIMON 'They never rush and they are always dead friendly, all of them. The older one has a chat and tells me what he has been doing. The singing one she told me about the Dads' club'.

Parents did not feel under pressure to do specific activities or join specific groups.

LISA 'You do what you want there is no pressure . . . she talks to us with respect as well, she doesn't push us into doing nothing and she just tells us our choices . . . It's just meeting new people I don't do all that stuff . . . we don't really speak to anyone, we just go in and pick them up and then bring them home'.

The provision of home language speakers and access to additional support was valued.

BENTI 'It is very important that K [language worker] is working here because we can understand much more. We know much more about the learning of our child in the nursery because she is speaking in our language'.

However, there were *some structural difficulties and uncertainties* that raised several questions for the CLT:

TENDAI 'I don't know or I am not sure if I can just bring my other daughter with me one afternoon and just spend some time around. But I have noticed sometimes when I could I came with my youngest and we hung around the nursery with R and M didn't seem to mind but I always thought to myself "is it OK?" or "am I now going over the boundaries?"'

Was it acceptable to bring younger siblings into nursery?

BENTI 'Many time I didn't understand what people said to me, I understand that everything was fine . . . but lately it wasn't enough; I'd like to know much more what is my son. I know that he started to say in English, he has started to play with . . . and talk to him and I like to know what he is doing in the nursery – how he learns and what he is doing everyday.'

Could the documentation have been translated?

SIMON 'That would be good to see his file and talk about what he has been doing. I would like to take his file, to take it home and look through it'.

Did all parents, mothers and fathers have open access to their children's files?

LISA 'We get told how they are getting on but not what they enjoy doing'.

Why were all parents not asked about their children's learning at home and within the Centre?

SARAH 'The thing with the Centre is it's always going to have a stigma no matter what you say and no matter how you do it. Families that are on social security benefits, families that are under social services, child protection, problem families, but haven't all families got problems?'

Despite universal services being offered by the Centre, is there a stigma around accessing a centre for children and families? Amy completed a first aid course at the Centre but was never awarded with her certificate. Additionally, her CRB check did not come through, and this was not followed up, so she was not able to volunteer at the Centre. Could Centre staff put more checks in place to ensure that the opportunities for families and important communications about their own involvement and learning are followed through? Amy also found that she had to advocate for her friend's child to be considered for a place at nursery as she had been told that there were no places available. How are equal opportunities for children from vulnerable groups supported in the allocation of nursery places, and do all staff have the knowledge and power to offer places to such families?

Critiquing the methodology

This study enabled Centre leaders to grapple first hand with some of the issues faced by parents around access to services. There was an honest attempt to hear and value parents' voices in the analysis and presentation of the data. Their words tell this story.

On reflection however, the research team thought that the semi-structured interview was too restrictive a method. Debriefing after the completion of the study, researchers said that if we were going to embark on this study again, we would look into other techniques such as narrative interview (Sarantakos, 1998) or life histories (Robson, 2002). We might begin the engagement with parents with the simple phrase 'Tell me about . . .', for example, 'Tell me about how you came to Pen Green and what it was like for you'.

Other aspects of the method were discussed:

- the importance of *where* the dialogue with parents took place. Having the time to talk with parents in their own home, with support for their children as required, seemed more productive and respectful. When the interviewer physically located themselves in the parent's own space, they were more likely to be able to 'enter their world'.
- the importance of *how* the interview was conducted and the sensitivity with which the follow-up questions were employed. Some researchers were extremely skilled at following up on what the parents said with further questions, assurances and acknowledgements that supported the telling of the stories.

- the *transcription* of the narrative. Writing down what was said, and allowing each party to analyse it and then discuss what was significant to them, offered the possibility for parents and workers to engage as *equals in the analysis.*
- using *parents' quotes* to voice their own issues and to form the basis of a deeper theoretical understanding about access to services. Selecting quotes has enabled parents' voices to provide the grounded theory that was developed through this study.

As centre leaders, engaging in a research project of this kind was a risk. The allocation of time to the study was always a struggle with so many competing demands on their time. Once the parents were engaged, the time element was important. The momentum needed to be maintained so that everyone was engaged in a respectful way. This project took many months longer than was at first planned, risking disengagement by the very people we were seeking to understand.

Despite this, some of the parents identified positive outcomes from the study. Jimmy attended a Computer Literacy and Information Technology (CLAIT) computer and public speaking course at Pen Green and has presented his story at conferences and at a national 'Think Fathers' event, at which he said that his involvement in the project had given him the confidence to come into the Centre and to have some 'space' for himself and his own needs. Amy was able to display her photographs in the Centre and received acknowledgement for her work as a photographer. She said the project had made her 'more positive with doing something with my life'. Benti was able to work with a Polish worker to translate Pen Green materials into Polish, which she enjoyed. Liz was thinking about going to college the following September and said she had gained confidence through being involved with the Centre and was experiencing being with people in more positive ways.

The Architecture of Access metaphor has given the CLT and parents involved in the study the means to analyse access to the Centre. The experience of working on the project together has provided a focus for our reflections on research methodology and design at Pen Green. This study has also illuminated some of the structural and organisational challenges that must be faced if access to the Centre is to be maintained and promoted as a truly open and living reality.

References

Arnold, C. (2007) 'Persistence Pays Off: Working with Parents Who Find Our Services "Hard to Reach"'. In Whalley, M. & the Pen Green Centre Team, *Involving Parents in their Children's Learning.* London: Paul Chapman.

Bekerman, Z. & Tartar, M. (2009) 'Parental Choice of Schools and Parent's Perceptions of Multicultural and Co-Existence Education: The Case of the Israeli Palestinian-Jewish Bilingual Primary Schools'. *European Early Childhood Education Research Journal,* Vol. 17, No. 2, 171–185.

Chrispeels, J. & Rivero, E. (2001) 'Engaging Latino Families for Student Success: How Parent Education Can Reshape Parents' Sense of Place in the Education of their Children'. *Peabody Journal of Education,* Vol. 76, No. 2: 119–169.

Cohen, L. & Manion, L. (1994) *Research Methods in Education* (4th Edition). London: Routledge.

DfE (2011) *The Core Purpose of Sure Start Children's Centres.* London: Department for Education.

Easen, P., Kendall, P. & Shaw, J. (1992) 'Parents and Educators: Dialogue and Developing Through Partnership'. *Children and Society,* Vol. 6, No. 4, 282–296.

Fletcher, C. (2008) *Pen Green Research: A Review of Progress.* Corby, England: Pen Green Research Base. Unpublished internal working paper.

Freire, P. (1970) *Pedagogy of the Oppressed.* Harmondsworth, England: Penguin Books.

Geertz, C. (1973) *The Interpretation of Culture.* New York: Basic Books.

Holman, B. (1987) 'Research from the Underside'. *British Journal of Social Work,* Vol. 17, 669–683.

Katz, L. (1993) 'Dispositions as educational goals'. *Eric Digest.* http://www.ericdigests.org/1994/goals.htm

Levinas, E. (1987) *Time and Other.* Pittsburgh: Duquesne University Press.

Lewin, K. (1946) 'Action Research and Minority Problems'. *Journal of Social Issues,* Vol. 2, No. 4, 34–46.

Muhr, S. L. (2008) 'Othering Diversity – A Levinasian Analysis of Diversity Management'. *International Journal of Management Concepts and Philosophy,* Vol. 3, No. 2, 176–189.

Ofsted (2012) *Inspection of Sure Start Children's Centres Consultation Document.* Manchester: Office for Standards in Education, Children's Services and Skills.

Patton, M. Q. (2002) *Qualitative Evaluation and Research Methods* (3rd Edition). Thousand Oaks, CA: Sage.

Robson, C. (2002) *Real World Research* (2nd Edition). Oxford: Blackwell Publishing.

Rutter, M. (2007). 'Resilience, Competence, and Coping'. *Child Abuse & Neglect,* Vol. 31: 205–209.

Sarantakos, S. (1998) *Social Research* (2nd Edition). London: Macmillan Press.

Schon, D.A. (1995) 'Knowing-In-Action: The New Scholarship Requires a New Epistemology'. *Change,* Vol. 27, No. 6, November/December, 27–34.

Social Exclusion Task Force (2007) *Reaching Out: Think Family.* London: Cabinet Office.

Tait, C. (2007) 'Getting to Know Families'. In Whalley, M. & the Pen Green Centre Team, *Involving Parents in Their Children's Learning.* London: Paul Chapman.

Vandenbroeck, M. (2009) 'Editorial'. *European Early Childhood Education Research Journal,* Vol. 17, No. 2, 165–170.

Vandenbroeck, M., Roets, G. & Snoeck, A. (2009) 'Immigrant Mothers Crossing Borders: Nomadic Identities and Multiple Belongings in Early Education'. *European Early Childhood Education Research Journal,* Vol. 17, No. 2: 203–216.

Whalley, M. & the Pen Green Centre Team (2007) *Involving Parents in Their Children's Learning* (2nd Edition). London: Paul Chapman.

Chapter 10

The voices of their childhoods

Families and early years practitioners developing emancipatory methodologies through a tracer study

Margy Whalley, Cath Arnold, Penny Lawrence and Sally Peerless

Background: Why undertake a tracer study?

The Pen Green Tracer Study questions the difference we may or may not have made to the lives of children and families who have used our services. An initial cohort of young people, now aged between 8–21, revisited their nursery in 2010. Their stories prompted discussion on parental involvement and advocacy within the education system, key worker attachment, and children's sense of self. Our second cohort was composed of young people whose experiences of the education system were characterised by difficulties and challenge. Using video within a groundbreaking new research methodology, our findings gave us new insight into the child's voice, transforming our understanding of a child's world. Through the tracer study we are questioning our own practice:

- Did our commitment to encouraging agency and autonomy work for every child?
- Did children experience disequilibrium on transition to school that inhibited their development?
- Did we engage effectively with all their parents?

Like Weikart, we would argue that tracer studies ask the 'difficult questions regarding effectiveness of services that the broader field of research and evaluation often overlooks' (Weikart, 2002: 17).

Introduction to the Centre

Pen Green opened in 1983 as a fully integrated centre for children and their families, funded through Education, Social Services and Health at a local authority level. Pen Green developed from the outset as an organisation where practice was informed by research. Research projects emerged out of the daily challenges experienced by nursery staff, parents and children. From day one all staff were encouraged to see themselves as practitioner researchers with dedicated time for practitioner enquiry (Whalley & the Pen Green Centre Team, 2007). This ethos was formalised in 1996 when a dedicated Research Base emerged out of the

Table 10.1 Previous research projects at Pen Green

Research Projects	Research & Dissemination	Shifts in practice at Pen Green
Parents Involved in their Children's Learning (Esmée Fairbairn Foundation) 1997 – 2000	Publications and dissemination materials: Whalley, M. & the Pen Green Centre Team (2001) *Involving Parents in their Children's Learning.* London, Paul Chapman. Whalley, M. & the Pen Green Centre Team (2007) *Involving Parents in their Children's Learning* (2nd Edition). London: Paul Chapman. PICL materials for ECEs Early Learning Partnership (ELP) project materials (2007) Institute for Public Policy Research (IPPR) evaluation (2011) Parent self-assessment tool developed. PICL Approach and evaluation measures C4EO validated (2012) Dissemination through Early Years Teaching Centres (DfE/Pen Green, 2011–2013)	PICL study groups and models of engagement PICL approach embedded across Centre and in other children's centres and schools across the town PICL parent packs National Open College accredited
Emotional Well-being Project 2001–2004	Internal Pen Green publications & series of conferences Arnold, C. (2009) 'A Case Study Showing How One Young Child Represented Issues Concerned with Attachment and Separation in Her Spontaneous Explorations', *European Early Childhood Education Research Journal*, Vol. 17, No. 1, March 2009, 147–162. Arnold, C. (2009) '"Understanding Together and Apart": A Case Study of Edward's Explorations at Nursery'. *Early Years*, Vol. 29, No. 2, July 2009, 119–130.	Development of key concepts to support parents of children under 3 – attachment, holding, containment, companionship Growing Together – adult child companionship groups, established locally, regionally and nationally

(Continued)

Table 10.1 (Continued)

Research Projects	Research & Dissemination		Shifts in practice at Pen Green
	Arnold, C. (2010) *Young Children's Representations of Emotions and Attachment in their Spontaneous Patterns of Behaviour: An Exploration of a Researcher's Understanding*. Ph.D. Coventry University.		
Adult Attachment Project – Pen Green/ University College London 2002–2004	Charlwood, N. & Steele, H. (2004) 'Using Attachment Theory to Inform Practice in an Integrated Centre for Children and Families'. *European Early Childhood Education Research Journal*, Vol. 12, No. 2, 59–68.	➤	GAP groups established for parents experiencing postnatal depression Comprehensive infant adult mental health service developed
Tracer Study 2010–	Whalley, M. & Arnold, C. (2010) *Finding Out About Change Over Time: Developing Methods to Trace the Long Term Impact of Early Education and Family Involvement*. Symposium presentation given at the 20th Annual Conference of the European Early Childhood Education Research Association, University of Birmingham, England. Arnold, C., Whalley, M. & McKinnon, E. (2011) *Parents, Families, Practitioners and Researchers: Collaboratively developing emancipatory research methodologies*. Symposium presentation given at the 21st Annual Conference of the European Early Childhood Education Research Association, University of Geneva, Switzerland. Arnold, C., Lawrence, P., Peerless, S. & Whalley, M. (2012) *How Did We Make a Difference? A Tracer Study Engaging with Children and Families Who Used the Centre Years Ago*. Symposium presentation given at the 2nd British Early Childhood Education Research Association, Midlands Arts Centre, Birmingham, England.	➤	Development of comprehensive parent support and parents sharing knowledge approach

Table 10.1 (Continued)

Research Projects	Research & Dissemination	Shifts in practice at Pen Green
	Whalley, M., Arnold, C., Lawrence, P. & Peerless, S. (2012) 'The voices of their childhood: families and early years' practitioners developing emancipator methodologies through a tracer study'. *European Early Childhood Education Research Journal*, Vol. 20, No. 4, December 2012, 519–535. Whalley, M., Arnold, C. & Orr, R. (Eds) (2013) *Working with Families in Children's Centres and Early Years Settings.* London: Hodder Education.	

Centre for Children and Families, allowing both facets of the organisation to evolve as two halves of one whole.

The Pen Green Research, Development and Training Base has practitioner enquiry at its heart; Pen Green's Continuous Professional Development (CPD) training materials develop out of our research projects, which are co-constructed with staff and parents in the Centre. Research proposals and research questions are generated by users, staff and parents, and by our practitioner research team.

This tracer study has developed out of a series of research studies undertaken by the Research Base. Pen Green's first research study focused on 'Involving Parents in their Children's Learning' and ran from 1997–2000 (Whalley & the Pen Green Centre Team, 2007). Subsequently, we developed a study of children's well-being and resilience from 2001–2004 (Arnold, 2010).

As a centre for children and families, Pen Green's primary objective has always been to support children to become strong, decisive and powerful learners, and for their parents to be powerful advocates on their behalf. Corby has a poor record for young people's engagement in further or higher education. At Pen Green we are committed to reversing this trend.

The children involved in this tracer study formerly attended the nursery and are now aged between 8 and 21 years old. Many of the families still live in the area and some are still engaged with the Centre. We were curious about whether Pen Green's very specific offer to these children – our pedagogical commitment to developing strong, independent challenging children – resulted in the hoped-for outcomes. Were these children now strong, independent reflective young adults who had survived and succeeded in the education system? (see Table 10.1.)

We also wanted to question our engagement with their parents. Some of the parents' engagement with the Centre had led to a development in their social capital. Parents reported increasing confidence and capability and strong networks of relationships. Other parents had engaged specifically with the Parents Involved in their Children's Learning (PICL) programme, which was designed to increase parents' cultural capital by

- encouraging them to be aspirational
- facilitating their engagement with the school system and
- helping them to become effective advocates on behalf of their children.

Tracer study research questions

The tracer study began in 2010. We developed a set of research questions to inform our study:

- What were the things that we did that were significant to children and their families?
- What was significant about our engagement with the children and their families?

- What continues to be significant to those young people and their families?
- How are the nursery's shared beliefs and ways of working manifested in our dialogue with parents and children now?

Purposive samples

The aims of our study clearly led us towards a strongly qualitative and participative research design. We knew that our means of sampling would impact upon the degree to which we could generalise from our study:

> Every instance of a case or process bears the stamp of the general class of phenomena to which it belongs. However, any given instance is likely to be particular and unique. Thus, for example, any given classroom is like all classrooms, but no classrooms are the same.
>
> (Denzin & Lincoln, 2000: 370)

When looking at a small group, through an in-depth, narrative research approach, there needs to be an awareness, as Denzin and Lincoln state, that 'any given classroom is like all classrooms, but no classrooms are the same' – that any given family will have experienced Pen Green like all other families, but that simultaneously no two families, no two children, will have had the same experience. Although trends in the data generated may inform our perception of the experiences of different groups, a study that investigates every previous Pen Green child and family would be the only way to allow us to generalise trends within our data. What we are able to do, however, is use the continued, close links between Pen Green and many of the families who used our services to allow an informed perspective when developing our sampling method. Denzin and Lincoln (2000) describe the purposive sampling model:

> Many postpositive, constructionist, and critical theory qualitative researchers employ theoretical or purposive, and not random, sampling models. They seek out groups, settings, and individuals where and for whom the processes being studied are most likely to occur. At the same time, a process of constant comparison – of groups, concepts, and observations – is necessary, as the researcher seeks to develop an understanding that encompasses all instances of the process or case under investigation.
>
> (Denzin & Lincoln, 2000: 370)

Through a process of constant comparison between the diverse and purposively chosen case studies, we are able to gain a broad perspective of the different experiences that may have occurred in different families. These groupings are based on our in-depth knowledge of families and children, often spanning twenty years or more, but are in a state of constant change, revision and flux, open to surprise, and often defying our expectations.

The young people and their parents who participated in our research project formed a 'purposeful' sample selected because they provided us with 'information-rich cases', cases from which we could learn. 'Studying information-rich cases yields insights and in-depth understanding rather than empirical generalisations' (Patton, 2002: 230).

Our first purposive sample of children and parents consisted of families with whom we had a strong, connected relationship, where children had attended nursery for at least two years, and where parents were actively engaged in their children's learning at home and in the nursery. Most of the parents in this cohort had not attended further or higher education establishments and had gone from school to work at age 16 or 18. The parents of these children had enthusiastically attended knowledge-sharing sessions at the Centre. They had shared data with their children's key workers, participated in research projects, and attended PICL study groups. With this first sample, our research focus centred on methodology, as we explored whether we could use a tracer study to gather data on both children's and parents' experiences of Pen Green. Our findings showed a group of fairly academically successful children with strong parental advocacy and a family-wide commitment to learning and to supporting their children's engagement within the education system.

Our second purposive sample was drawn from families where children had attended nursery for at least two years and where parents had been involved in the Centre using family support services and had been engaged in activities designed to promote parents' mental health and/or to access 'second chance adult education' for themselves. We were aware that these were children who had faced

Figure 10.1 Alice: 'This is what it used to be like'.

Figure 10.2 Beccy:'Remember you had a photo-frame?'

Figure 10.3 Scott:'It brought back memories'.

Figure 10.4 Curtis: 'I looked like a smart kid'.

Figure 10.5 Hayley: 'I felt like a grown-up girl'.

considerable difficulties on transition into the school system and, in some cases, had been regularly excluded from school.

Our working theory has developed throughout the two years of the project. Children who experienced consistently authoritative parenting (Whalley, 1996),

Figure 10.6 William: 'I just liked the feeling of being able to control everything that was happening'.

with appropriate boundaries at home, developed optimally when this home experience was matched with a nursery curriculum and pedagogy that emphasised freedom of choice and encouraged decision making. In most cases, the parents of these children were engaged with the PICL approach while their children attended nursery, which may have strengthened their commitment to their children's education. Children from the second cohort had engaged in the same nursery experience and had family lives that were more challenging. Their parents had been deeply involved in using services in the setting but had not engaged systematically in our parent involvement approach (PICL). These children may have experienced a greater disequilibration on transition to school. Their parents seemed less well equipped to act as advocates, which may have made it more difficult for them to engage effectively with the education system.

Methodology

Our concept of a tracer study has developed from the work of the Bernard Van Leer foundation, which launched a programme of tracer studies in 1988, carried out in majority world countries, aiming to find the 'story behind the story' (Smale, 2002). Jim Smale describes the common characteristics of Van Leer tracer studies in this way:

- they follow up the progress of the children, their families, programme staff, the communities or the organisations, five or more years after they participated, to find out how they are faring

- they are generally small in scale (tens rather than hundreds of respondents) and short in duration (months rather than years)
- they are qualitative rather than quantitative in nature
- each is designed locally and overall control is in the hands of the programmes, even when the study is undertaken by independent outside researchers
- the emphasis on qualitative methods and the use of quotations means that reports help readers to get to the 'story behind the story'
- the methods used are understandable for virtually all those involved in the study and
- the studies are manageable in a wide variety of circumstances. (Smale, 2002: 3)

We placed a particular emphasis on 'holding onto the importance of what people said about what happened to them and how it changed them, while trying to synthesise meaningful lessons that can feed into practice' (Cohen, 2002: 9). In Pen Green terms, we interpreted this as a commitment to ensuring that critical questions about the nature of services are generated by users, and staff believe in parents' capacity to generate ideas and solutions.

The 'fundamentally democratic' (Cohen, 2002: 9) nature of a Van Leer tracer study complemented our research ethics and commitment to involving participants in emancipatory research experiences. The views of the participant were of paramount importance throughout the study. The use of video was handled with care throughout, ensuring that each participant was first happy to be filmed, and then given the edited film to view and make any changes they'd like. Editing was handled sensitively; care was taken that the context of comments was preserved and that participants felt that they were represented accurately. Parents of children younger than eighteen were involved in both the initial contact with the family and also in the filming and editing process. When participants were older than eighteen, we reacted sensitively to their family circumstances to involve their parents and families in appropriate ways. We took care to ensure that each participant's visit to Pen Green was a positive experience.

Within our first research cohort, we began to test our methods designed to elicit information. With the parents, we tried out audio- and video-taped interviews, using a set of prompts. With the children, we used various methods, including a walk around the nursery with a camera or video camera, interviewing at home, and using their own Celebration of Achievement Portfolios from nursery to reflect on their experiences. We experimented with different age groups, different gender balance and with different combinations of children: friendship groups from their nursery days, current friendship groups, individual children, dyads, trios, children attending with their parents, and parents attending individually, as couples and in small groups.

Using a video camera for recording purposes led us to consider the impact of this technology on our participants. Shrum and colleagues make a clear distinction between using a camera as an impartial observer, or as new research technology (Shrum et al., 2005: 2). We used cameras as a recording tool in a formal interview setting, where the participant speaks following a series of prompts. We also adopted a 'guerrilla style' approach, where the camera is an actor in the research process, and behaviour and observations occur in both directions. Shrum et al. describes the situation as a 'fluid wall' between researcher and subject (2005: 19), so the camera moves with the participant, trying to anticipate where he or she is going to next. The children were also filmed while using cameras themselves, so we have access to what they chose to film as well as what we chose to film.

Since several members of our research team taught or worked with these children when they were in the nursery, we were concerned about our influence on them. We have memories of their time with us but were concerned with eliciting *their* memories. The team engaged two interviewers: The first, Sally, is in her early 20s and did not attend our nursery, but she is from Corby and is close in age to the young people we were studying and genuinely curious about their experiences. She has a music/theatre background, and this experience was useful during the research and interview process. The second researcher is an early years educator/researcher with extensive experience as a camera person and interviewer of young children. According to Shrum et al., 'The status of observer arises because of *differences* between investigator and subjects. The status of participant arises because of *sameness*' (2005: 10). We have attempted to enter their worlds of memory.

Sally describes her engagement in the research process:

> I first became involved in the research project because of the methodology we wished to pursue. The emphasis has always been on hearing the participants' stories *in their own words*, so I saw myself as a researcher who was neutral, friendly, reachable, and very involved – someone who is close to them in age, who doesn't remember them as a child, doesn't have a huge contextual knowledge of the nursery – but who participants can talk to and tell their memories to without fear of being wrong.

This role requires the researcher to be adaptive to every participant and their styles of engagement. Sally continues,

> I have shepherded three 11-year-old boys around the Centre, laughed with teenagers when they showed me video of themselves playing on the slide in the garden, and jumped into the ball pool after another participant to give them a 'way out' after they had jumped in there alone! We want the participant to gain from their experience as much as the researcher, so it has been important to adapt my behaviour to synchronise with theirs – without ever overshadowing their style, or their 'groove'.

Groove is a musical term that seemed appropriate to apply to the research process:

> 'Being in the groove' . . . is a sense of musical dialogue happening between all the players. People are open to each other . . . the music is spontaneous and authentic . . . People talk of losing their self-awareness and of being at one with the group and the music. (Forrester & Bailey, 1999: 3).

As Sally reflects,

'Really, that's just the way I wanted to be able to engage as a researcher'.

The main aim in using video was to encourage participation. We want to hear their voices and to 'access their views without "frightening off" participants through intrusive personal questioning' (Haw & Hadfield, 2011: 100). We want to know what the children and parents remember and think about their experiences. We want to access their different ways of knowing, through feelings and through their bodies; feelings of being together as well as actual memories of being together. We did not want to force participants to reflect on what we think they might remember. We are 'open to the unexpected and surprises' (Cohen, 2002: 9).

Some children and parents were filmed while looking at photographs of themselves or their children at nursery. Harper (2002: 15) suggests that 'photo elicitation can be regarded as a postmodern dialogue based on the authority of the subject rather than the researcher'. Importantly, he points out that less may be more: 'the sharper and more isolated the stimulus memory receives, the more it remembers' (Harper, 2002: 14). Seeing a photograph that reminds the young people of that time may stimulate their memory more than seeing a photo of themselves that depicts a specific moment.

Initially, we thought we might 'surprise the unconscious' during their first visit after a number of years' absence and that subsequent visits might be less exciting and revealing. However, we found that the process was more like unpeeling layers of memory and that the participants' reflections between visits deepened the dialogue and narrative account.

We developed a series of engagements that we aimed to incorporate into our involvement with each participant:

- A visit to the Children's Centre, using video cameras for both participant and researcher; the visit involves a friend of the participant who also attended nursery
- Engaging the participant in at least two visits/methods of engagement
- Meeting with the child's key worker; the important adult who would have home visited the family, contained the child's anxiety in nursery, extended and supported the child's learning in nursery, and collaborated with the important adults in their lives
- Viewing of archive video, photographs, and Celebration of Achievement Portfolios documenting the child's time at nursery
- Interview with parent or groups of parents.

There were certain questions we also tried to work into each visit when it seemed appropriate, such as:

- If you could take home one thing from nursery, what would it be?
- Which three words would you use to describe the nursery at Pen Green?
- Who got to choose what you did at nursery? Was this important?

Table 10.2 Observed characteristics of participants

	Cohort 1	Cohort 2
	26 participants	31 participants (research in progress)
Children (while in nursery)	Feeling able to challenge and make good choices	Feisty and challenging, boundary pushing
	Mastery oriented	Sometimes experienced by others as a 'bully' or a challenge
	Engaging positively in school from the start	Have difficulty with transitions
	Able to critique self and others	Respond negatively to critique
	Persistence in face of obstacles and seeking out challenging tasks	Avoids challenges, underestimates own capability
	Good understanding of boundaries in difference places	Boundary surfers, boundary pushers
	Cohort 1	Cohort 2
Parents	Parents actively engaged in their children's learning and development through study groups, sharing information about learning at home, knowledge sharing sessions	Parents use Centre as a base for themselves, using family room many hours a week. Child's quotation: "the Family Room – my mum's den"
	Parents take on role of mediator/ broker/advocate, especially during transitions	Parents slowly reclaim second chance to adult education
	Parents become involved in the school system as parent helpers, train as Learning Support Assistants, school administrators, etc.	Parents volunteer to become paid support workers, e.g. crèche, after school club, etc.

With the second cohort, we began to question more deeply their transition from nursery to school:

• How is a Family Worker (at nursery) different from a teacher (at school)?
• Did anything come as a surprise when you went to school?
• Is there anything you wish you could have learnt/you think we should have taught you at nursery that might have helped you on transition to school?

How we regard the participants in this research process

The participants need time. We are in a process of generating memory and meaningful evaluation, which is fundamentally different from journalism or from a positivist approach, where a researcher extracts or mines data (Kvale, 2007) from participants and regards this data as a truth that can be taken from the participant and viewed in isolation. We are in an on-going relationship; a continuing dialogue with the participants that makes our day-to-day personal reactive attitudes meaningful (Strawson, 1962).

We experienced the research as a kind of 'holding' of the experience of rediscovery, an experience that can be delicate as it emerges. It is suspended in trust and can be weighed down by self-consciousness.

Although we are not 'mining', we are dealing with depth. There are layers of understanding that start with reconnection, perhaps through a first visit or conversation, and then the resulting renaissance: a birth of re-knowing nursery experience. Other reconnections come through photo or video elicitation and, importantly, through meeting the significant people from nursery. Some participants have had the opportunity to construct, revisit and revise and 'own' an autobiography of their childhood because of how they discuss experiences and memories at home (Van Abbema & Bauer, 2005). For others, the tracer study is an opportunity to begin to construct this autobiography. We need to facilitate the co-construction of this auto-biography if we are to access the range of experience that we are reaching out for in this phase of the research. There is a difference between hearing others speak and speaking about an experience for themselves, which is the participant voice we hope to reach.

As well as concurrent and subsequent discussion, memories may have persisted because of their distinctiveness, personal salience, or emotional valence – so the participants may remember building with blocks daily, a car wash experience, or going on a trip to a key worker's home. They can be memories of internal states triggered by the encounters with the environment, objects (such as the rocking horse), or the important people.

Modes of knowing

People have different approaches. Some immediately verbalise their thoughts and feelings as they walk around. This is actually two levels of encounter happening at once: the experiential and the recounting. Others may encounter, perhaps becoming very responsive and tactile, and then reflect verbally later. Video can help to do this. Video can 'hold' the narrative responsibility for an event as a 'tool of the mind', leaving the viewer's mind freer to access and recount the meaning of the content (Forman, 1999). Video is also multi-modal (Flewitt, 2006) and can help connect the research to other forms of knowing, allowing us to note the physical contacts: the touches of the rocking horse, the wooden blocks caressed, the facial expressions, the ranging or at ease energies, and so on. Our video methodology is entwined with how we are generating knowledge – our epistemology.

Reflective functioning

We are interested in the concept of 'reflective functioning': the parents' and children's capacity to reflect on experiences of and with others, and to integrate and use these experiences in understanding themselves.

> Reflective function enables children to conceive of others' beliefs, feelings, attitudes, desires, hopes, knowledge, imagination, pretence, plans and so on. At the same time as making others' behaviour meaningful and predictable, they are also able flexibly to activate from multiple sets of self-other representations the one most appropriate in a particular interpersonal context.
>
> (Fonagy, 2001: 165)

Children need to be able to make sense of, and take responsibility for their interactions with other people.

> Exploring the meaning of actions of others is crucially linked to the child's ability to label and find meaningful his or her own experience. This ability may make a crucial contribution to affect regulation, impulse control, self-monitoring, and the experience of self-agency.
>
> (Fonagy & Target, 1997)

This ability to use learning from other relationships seems critically important to children and young people who find themselves in a formal, highly structured school environment where they are unsure or insecure about what is expected of them and why.

What we have discovered about our methodology over time: Learning from the 'How'?

At Pen Green we have a particular view of the nature of the knowledge we are trying to access. It is the knowledge of the community who learn in our Centre. For this reason we decided to document their experiences together using video as a process. It is not an expert 'icy picture' (Wittgenstein, 1958) determined by external experts but a representation of experience generated together in a slower travelling participatory mode (Kvale, 2007; Haw & Hadfield, 2011).

After working with the two cohorts of children, the methodology has been reviewed and reversioned and can be summed up as follows:

1. Sequenced – memory and evaluation may not happen in the first encounter; layers of reconsideration add depth to the reflection, generate knowledge, build trust and participation

2.   Participatory – to find out what difference the nursery made we need the children and families who experienced it to generate the knowledge; they co-construct it with their Family Workers and researchers

3.   Phenomenological and multi-modal – knowledge of their nursery experience may be in many forms, or modes.

What we have discovered about the children over time

A number of themes have emerged across both cohorts as participants have shared what was important and meaningful to them about their time at nursery:

*   **Relationships including 'attachment for security' and 'attachment for companionship'** (Trevarthen, 1996). Most children interviewed remembered their own 'key person', other important adults and sometimes friends with whom they had lost touch. For example, a 12-year-old boy from our first research cohort explained, '[My key worker] was one of the most important people in my life at the time'. From the second cohort, participants expressed their wish to see their key workers again and remembered specific details about things they had done together. Jonathan named adults who have long since left the Centre, as well as people who are still working there. He recognised the voice of a worker, who 'used to be my helper in school' and who now works at the Centre.

*   **Emotional and embodied learning using all senses.** Most children interviewed mentioned the rocking horse even before seeing it, and when they saw it, many re-experienced the sensation of rocking on it and/or had specific memories connected to using the rocking horse on a regular basis. The soft room and snoezelen elicited similar actions and memories. In the nursery children can choose to go to the snoezelen, a soothing multi-sensory relaxation and therapy space, which is placed close to the water therapy room, and a soft-play room for bouncing and romping around in. A participant in the second cohort particularly mentioned the 'smell' of the wooden blocks and stated that if he could take one thing home, it would be a block. Fourteen years previously, when in the nursery, he had built giant towers in the block area. Jonathan remembered the soft room, snoezelen, gym and rocking horse, showing how important embodied learning was to him. He seemed to enjoy 're-experiencing' the same equipment on his visit. All of the children mentioned the different experience of being much bigger in relation to the equipment they had experienced as young children.

*   **Self-worth and self-efficacy.** One participant spontaneously commented how at nursery, 'Everybody liked me'. Another, a 17-year-old excluded from school and living outside the family home, saw himself at nursery as a 'smart kid' and mentioned that he 'learned how to do important things' at nursery. Jonathan remembered using a real hammer and nails at the workbench and tried this again during his visit, 18 years later. Other participants

remembered being shown how to do things, while one made the distinction between 'choosing [at nursery] . . . not like school'. This links with 'autonomy' and fostering a 'mastery-oriented' approach to learning (Dweck & Leggett, 1988). At nursery, children felt that they were listened to.

- **Following each child's interests.** This featured strongly in children's memories, especially in relation to special outings or provision. One participant remembered going to Peterborough Cathedral as part of a small group when she was interested in the story *The Hunchback of Notre Dame*.

Participants also remembered

- 'conveyor belts' set up to match their interest in transporting and envelopment
- going to 'the carwash' with their key worker
- 'the trip to the sleeping farm'
- 'sellotaping' two doors together (connecting) that are no longer there
- 'going to McDonald's for lunch and setting up, with other children, a McDonald's in the block area' for role play; and 'playing babies'
- *Regrets* were few, but one participant from the second cohort reflected that he wished he had 'learned what to do back then so we don't keep getting told now'. Another remembered 'taking things from other children because I wanted them'.

Some themes related specifically to each cohort group: the first cohort of highly engaged and academically successful children whose families were very engaged with their children's learning and development, and the second cohort, where parents had struggled with their social and psychological circumstances and children had faced more difficulties and challenges in sustaining their engagement in the education system. (see Table 10.3.)

Findings: Emergent themes in each cohort

Jonathan's case study

Jonathan came to Pen Green at 14 months. He was born prematurely and developed retinopathy of prematurity (incubator blindness). During his infancy there were serious concerns over many aspects of his development. Despite challenges from various agencies who believed that he should be at a more specialised, structured setting, Molly, his mum, elected that Jonathan should continue to attend nursery at Pen Green.

Molly was highly involved in the Centre, using the nursery, parents' groups, family room and going on trips abroad with Centre staff. She was a passionate advocate on Jonathan's behalf. We realised that the family was still in the area after a local newspaper published a story about Jonathan – now a talented musician – and we decided to get in contact. We were interested in Jonathan's experience

Table 10.3 Emergent themes

Cohort 1	Cohort 2
Importance of the Family Worker to parent and to child	Child needed the Family Worker hugely for emotional containment
Children with a strong voice/able to advocate for others	Children's perception that they needed to have understood boundaries better on transition to school
Belonging and connectedness to nursery as a site for community engagement	Strong sense of belonging and connectedness; many families still involved with the Centre ten plus years later
Strong sense of self-worth and self-efficacy	Memory of being liked by staff at nursery but not any longer
Following own interests, valuing freedom to choose	Memory of being seen as 'smart' at nursery but not any longer
Responding to highly personalised curriculum content when learning at nursery reflecting home learning	Responding to highly personalised curriculum content when learning at nursery reflecting home learning
Emotional and embodied learning using all senses	Emotional and embodied learning using all senses
Parents strong as advocates/brokers/mediators with high aspirations for their children	Parents committed to supporting their children

of education after Pen Green and both his and Molly's memories and thoughts about his time at the nursery.

Jonathan is now 21, so contact was made by our young researcher, Sally, who also has an interest in music and is close to Jonathan in age. He was keen to participate in the study, and when given a choice of different methods of engagement, chose to be initially interviewed in his home.

Engaging with Jonathan and eliciting his memories required a new approach. We decided to play archive footage of him at nursery so that he could hear both his own and his workers' voices. We brought photographs to show Molly, which might trigger her memory and lead to discussion with Jonathan. A Family Worker who Jonathan might remember from his time at Pen Green, Margaret, also attended. Sally describes her own engagement with Jonathan in the following way:

'I thought it was important that Jonathan and I are similar in age and have interests in common, and I wanted to use this connection to make the interview an enjoyable experience. I felt at ease talking with him, and the breadth and range of his responses to questioning suggest that he felt the same. Before I left, Jonathan invited me to hear him play [his keyboard], which was an important part of building a relationship between interviewer and participant.'

Jonathan's memories focused on

- people and relationships – the names and characteristics of a range of workers who were important to him at nursery (more than 18 years ago)
- the soft room – the soft play area and ball pool at Pen Green
- story time, and those who read him stories
- his interests – market stalls, pianos, the soft room.

Our archive footage shows Jonathan mimicking the accents of people he heard at Corby market and of his nursery worker, Katey, whose Irish accent interested him – particularly the words 'pound' and 'bananas'. During the interview, he again often mimicked voices – such as his own as a child – and used different accents to signify a joke or a certain reference.

In line with our research plan, we invited Jonathan to engage with the study for a second time. We suggested that he might like to visit the nursery, to which he responded enthusiastically. For continuity, Sally maintained her role as researcher, while Cath, Jonathan's key worker from his nursery days and a researcher in this study, accompanied him on his journey around the nursery.

The parts of the nursery that Jonathan remembered most were

- the soft room
- pots and pans in the Home Corner
- the workbench: hammers and nails
- wooden blocks
- stories being read to him by Cath and other workers
- workers, specifically who would have been with him in different areas of the nursery.

These memories built upon and added to what he had remembered during the initial interview in his home.

Jonathan fully immersed himself in the experience of visiting the nursery. He recreated experiences he had had as a child: banging pots and pans together, hammering a nail into a piece of wood, sitting on the small chairs, jumping into the ball pool and bouncing on the trampoline.

As well as sharing his memories of nursery, he let us get to know him now, as he played and sang at the piano in the gym and engaged workers in conversation about their musical tastes. He was enthusiastic about visiting each area and absorbed and unselfconscious in recreating his memories.

Jonathan and Molly responded positively to our interview prompts. After joining in with him as he played on the trampoline and in the ball pool, Sally asked him about choice, and who chose which activities he engaged in at nursery. He described his worker giving him options and allowing him to choose and also explained that he would almost always pick the soft room. However, his worker would sometimes suggest somewhere different, and he would then agree to this and go on to have 'a whale of a time' there, too.

Figure 10.7 Jonathan: 'We're in synch!'

When asked if there was anything that nursery could have done to help him with the transition to school, Jonathan replied,

> I can't think of anything . . . Because when I went to school I still had someone with me the whole time . . . The only thing that, obviously, no nursery can really change is that you sometimes get told off at school, but that's – that's nothing . . . as frightening as it is at the time, you know, it's part of growing up.

Sally explored the question of whether nursery could have prepared him for this by limiting his freedom of choice. Jonathan disagreed:

JONATHAN: No, I think school, I think that's the right place to learn that. I didn't get that at nursery, I didn't get told off at any time at nursery which was good.
SALLY: You think that's good, that you didn't get told not to do things? I suppose it's like a progression as you get older, maybe?
JONATHAN: I got told *not to do things*, but not *told off* . . . there's a difference.

When asked to pick a word to describe Pen Green, Jonathan replied:

> Idyllic or . . . magical, 'cause, let's face it, nursery is a time of magic, it's brilliant, in terms of . . . that whole kind of, anything you want to do you can

do, it's all there, and there's no 'No you can't do this, no you can't do that.' Everything I wanted to do I could do. Go wherever I pleased . . . It was great. Then, obviously, you don't realise that 'cause you're three . . . that's what growing up's about, this happy, idealistic time.

Jonathan not only enjoyed his memories of Pen Green, but also the experience of revisiting the nursery:

> I used to love this place. I still think it's a great place, isn't it? . . . You haven't lost your magic . . . whatever it is . . . And I'm not just saying that to make you feel better. You haven't lost your magic . . . whatever it is.

Discussion: The way ahead

The pedagogical priorities when these young people were in nursery were to support the children's natural disposition to learn, to encourage the children to make decisions and to challenge, to develop their capacity to make good choices and take personal responsibility. We have challenged ourselves throughout the project as to whether we could have done more to equip some of the children to function more effectively and successfully within the statutory school system. Whilst we share the view that some schools need to fundamentally review their approach to the youngest children, we also know that we must support children's transitions and encourage their parents to develop advocacy skills; we know that they will need them.

As a research team we are exploring the literature on 'self-regulation' and 'emotion-regulation'. We are concerned with the problems and insecurities some of the children experienced on transition into school. Could this be connected to their capacity '*to be in relation to others*?' (Vassu Reddy, personal communication with the Pen Green team, December 2012). We noticed that in the first cohort, the children's parents were somehow better able to help their children integrate their different experiences. These children had benefitted from their constructivist nursery education and Pen Green's pedagogical approach based on responding to what each individual child brings to the learning situation (Athey, 1990). They had been supported by their parents on transition and at many other critical points in their schooling. They had a clearly developed narrative. Stern makes it clear that every child should be given the opportunity to co-construct their own life story:

> In childhood most autobiographical narratives are co-constructed with others, usually the parents or siblings . . . the parent and child work together to gather the pieces of the story, order them sequentially, give them a coherence as a story, and then evaluate the story by establishing its emotional highpoints and values . . . A new body of research views the co-construction between parent and child as a form of regulation having much in common with other forms of regulation. (Stern, 1998: xxiv)

Questions we want to ask the young people in future encounters

- How is a Family Worker in nursery different to a teacher in school?
- What does 'being strong' mean to you? (We run an Assertiveness Programme for nursery children, called 'Learning to be Strong', which has evolved over 26 years.)
- What weren't you allowed to do? At nursery? At home? At school?
- Do you feel you are still getting told (how to behave)?
- What hobbies have you pursued?
- How was the way we worked helpful to you? (Did it help you lead your own learning?)
- What did you struggle with on transition to school?

Our aim is to develop the powerful video interviews that we have captured as provocations for a wider discussion with the early childhood community. Hopefully we can help early years educators and leaders re-engage with their passion for making a difference for children.

Activities

You many want to invite former nursery children back to elicit their stories. Perhaps you could contact these children through Facebook. Alternatively your former nursery students may already be young parents bringing their children to the setting.

Arrange to discuss the young person's thoughts in as many layers as possible.

1. Invite them to visit the setting and see what experiences of being in that place arise in conversation. There may be corners, stairs, resources, smells, and textures that bring back memories. "What did it feel like arriving at this place as a young child?", "Where did you spend time?" and "Who decided what you did?".
2. If possible, arrange for them to meet a member of staff from the time your participant was at nursery. Preferably this would be the Family Worker or a person with whom they had formed a particular relationship. You could ask each, "What do you remember about being with each other?" You could ask the participant, "What have your relationships been like with other adults in different schools?"
3. Make a video of their first visit back to nursery; review it with the participant, and consider what has surprised them.
4. Review any video together dating from the nursery period. Video record the watching so that you can follow up on any reactions or particular moments. "What kind of person did you seem to be when you were at nursery?"

5. Review the 'special book'/portfolio containing photographs and graphic work from nursery. Participants sometimes read the written observations in great detail, so allow time for those reviews, too. Concentrate on what is elicited by these prompts, prioritize the strongest strands of thought that emerge, and find connections with what they value now.
6. Review all the memories that have emerged and decide which are the most important with the participant.
7. Reflect as a group of early childhood educators on what you have learnt from engaging with former nursery students and what you want to do about it?

References

Arnold, C. (2009) 'A Case Study Showing How One Young Child Represented Issues Concerned with Attachment and Separation in Her Spontaneous Explorations', *European Early Childhood Education Research Journal*, Vol. 17, No. 1, March 2009, 147–162.

Arnold, C. (2009) "Understanding Together and Apart": A Case Study of Edward's Explorations at Nursery'. *Early Years*, Vol. 29, No. 2, July 2009, 119–130.

Arnold, C. (2010) *Young Children's Representations of Emotions and Attachment in their Spontaneous Patterns of Behaviour: An Exploration of a Researcher's Understanding.* Ph.D. Coventry University.

Arnold, C., Lawrence, P., Peerless, S. & Whalley, M. (2012) *How Did We Make a Difference?' A Tracer Study Engaging with Children and Families Who Used the Centre Years Ago.* Symposium presentation given at the 2nd British Early Childhood Education Research Association, Midlands Arts Centre, Birmingham, England.

Arnold, C., Whalley, M. & McKinnon, E. (2011) *Parents, Families, Practitioners and Researchers: Collaboratively Developing Emancipatory Research Methodologies.* Symposium presentation given at the 21st Annual Conference of the European Early Childhood Education Research Association, University of Geneva, Switzerland.

Athey, C. (1990) *Extending Thought in Young Children: A Parent-Teacher Partnership.* London: Paul Chapman Publishing Ltd.

Charlwood, N. & Steele, H. (2004) 'Using Attachment Theory to Inform Practice in an Integrated Centre for Children and Families'. *European Early Childhood Education Research Journal*, Vol. 12, No. 2, 59–68.

Cohen, R. (2002) 'Following Footsteps: Why, How and Where To?' *Early Childhood Matters, The Bulletin of the Bernard Van Leer Foundation*, December, No. 100, 8–15.

Denzin, N.K. & Lincoln, Y.S. (Eds) (2000) *Handbook of Qualitative Research* (2nd Edition). Thousand Oaks, CA: Sage.

Dweck, C.S. & Leggett, E.L. (1988) 'A Social-Cognitive Approach to Motivation and Personality'. *Psychological Review*, Vol. 95, 256–273.

Flewitt, R. (2006) 'Using Video to Investigate Preschool Classroom Interaction: Education Research Assumptions and Methodological Practices'. *Visual Communication*, Vol. 5, No. 1, 25–50.

Fonagy, P. (2001) *Attachment Theory and Psychoanalysis.* New York: Other Press.

Fonagy, P. & Target. M. (1997) 'Attachment and Reflective Function'. *Development and Psychopathology*, Vol. 9, 679–700.

Forman, G. (1999) 'Instant Video Revisiting: The Video Camera as a "Tool of the Mind" for Young Children'. *Early Childhood Research and Practice*, Vol. 1, No. 2. Available at http://ecrp.uiuc.edu/v1n2/forman.html

Forrester, P. & Bailey, J. (1999) 'The Improvisational Music Group – A Human System Simulation'. In *The System Dynamics Society*, proceedings of the 17th International Conference of the System Dynamics Society and 5th Australian New Zealand Systems Conference. New York: The System Dynamics Society.

Harper, D. (2002) 'Talking About Pictures: A Case for Photo Elicitation'. *Visual Studies*, Vol. 17, No. 1, 13–26.

Haw, K. & Hadfield, M. (2011) *Video in Social Science Research*. Abingdon: Routledge.

Kvale, S. (2007) *Doing Interviews*. Thousand Oaks, CA: Sage.

Patton, M. Q. (2002) *Qualitative evaluation and research methods* (3rd ed.). Newbury Park, CA: Sage.

Shrum, W., Duque, R. & Brown, T. (2005) 'Digital Video as Research Practice: Methodology for the Millennium'. *Journal of Research Practice*, Vol. 1, No. 1, M4.

Smale, J. (2002) 'Following Footsteps: ECD Tracer Studies'. *Early Childhood Matters, The Bulletin of the Bernard Van Leer Foundation*, December, No. 100, 3–7.

Stern, D. (1998) *The Interpersonal World of The Infant*. London: Karnac.

Strawson, P. (1962) 'Freedom and Resentment'. In *Proceedings of the British Academy*, Vol. 48, 1–25.

Trevarthen, C. (1996) 'Mother-Child Communication as a Paradigm: Mental Basics for Effective and Just Policies in Child Care. In S. Pantelakis and S. Nakou (Eds), *The Child in the World of Tomorrow: The Next Generation* (57–69). Amsterdam: Elsevier Science (Pergamon).

Van Abbema, D. & Bauer, P. (2005) 'Autobiographical Memory in Middle Childhood: Recollections of the Recent and Distant Past'. *MEMORY*, Vol. 13, No. 8, 829–845.

Weikart, D.P. (2002) 'Tracer studies: An opportunity and a challenge'. Following Footsteps: ECD tracer studies. *Early Childhood Matters*, December 2002, No. 100.

Whalley, M. (1996) *Confident Parents, Confident Children*. Milton Keynes, England: Open University Press.

Whalley, M. & Arnold, C. (2010) *Finding Out About Change Over Time: Developing Methods to Trace the Long Term Impact of Early Education and Family Involvement*. Symposium presentation given at the 20th Annual Conference of the European Early Childhood Education Research Association, University of Birmingham, England.

Whalley, M., Arnold, C., Lawrence, P. & Peerless, S. (2012) 'The Voices of Their Childhood: Families and Early Years' Practitioners Developing Emancipator Methodologies Through a Tracer Study'. *European Early Childhood Education Research Journal* Vol. 20, No. 4, 519–535.

Whalley, M., Arnold, C. & Orr, R. (Eds) (2013) *Working with Families in Children's Centres and Early Years Settings*. London. Hodder Education.

Whalley, M. & the Pen Green Centre Team (2001) *Involving Parents in their Children's Learning*. London: Paul Chapman.

Whalley, M. & the Pen Green Centre Team (2007) *Involving Parents in their Children's Learning* (2nd Edition). London: Paul Chapman.

Wittgenstein, L. (1958) *Philosophical Investigations* (2nd Edition). Oxford: Basil Blackwell.

Index

Page numbers followed by a 't' in italics refer to tables